WHAT T[...]
WITH T[...]
REST OF YOUR
LIFE

To Ken and Dottie

With gratitude that
we are brethren and sistin
in Christ:

Love in Him

[signature]

2/19/09

Also by J. Keith Miller

The Taste of New Wine

A Second Touch

Habitation of Dragons

The Becomers

The Edge of Adventure (with Bruce Larson)

Living the Adventure (with Bruce Larson)

The Passionate People (with Bruce Larson)

Please Love Me

The Single Experience (with Andrea Wells Miller)

The Scent of Love

The Dream

Hope in the Fast Lane (formerly titled *Sin: Overcoming the Ultimate Deadly Addiction*)

A Hunger for Healing: The 12 Steps as a Classical Model for Christian Spiritual Growth

A Hunger for Healing Workbook

Facing Codependence by Pia Mellody, with Andrea Wells Miller and J. Keith Miller

Facing Love Addiction by Pia Mellody, with Andrea Wells Miller and J. Keith Miller

Highway Home Through Texas

Ten Minute Magic

Compelled to Control

The Secret Life of the Soul

With No Fear of Failure by Tom Fatjo and Keith Miller

Power Money by Tom Fatjo and Keith Miller

Reality and the Vision

WHAT TO DO
WITH THE
REST OF YOUR
LIFE

Awakening and Achieving
Your Unspoken Dreams

J. KEITH MILLER

A Crossroad Book
The Crossroad Publishing Company
New York

The Crossroad Publishing Company
16 Penn Plaza, 481 Eighth Avenue
New York, NY 10001

Printed in the United States of America

This text of this book is set in 10/12 Cheltenham.
The display face is Torino.

Library of Congress Cataloging-in-Publication Data

Miller, Keith.
  What to do with the rest of your life : awakening and achieving your unspoken dreams / J. Keith Miller.
      p.   cm.
  Includes bibliographical references (p.   ).
  ISBN 0-8245-2320-2 (alk. paper)
  1. Self-actualization (Psychology)   I. Title.
BF637.S4M5483 2005
158.1 – dc22

                                                    2004027799

1   2   3   4   5   6   7   8   9   10   10   09   08   07   06   05

Contents

Acknowledgments

It is not possible for me to adequately express thanks to all the people whose thoughts and lives have slipped into this book as it has unfolded. I first attempted to present some of these ideas in a more primitive form in smaller books entitled *Ten-Minute Magic* and *What to Do with the Rest of Your Life.*

Regarding this book, I am particularly indebted to four men, two of whom, I believe, are among the most capable and innovative business-men in America: Tom J. Fatjo Jr. and Roy H. Williams. Tom changed the approach to building very large companies by the time he was forty years old. He did this using the original combination of the creative dreaming and action planning processes on which this book is based. With these methods he developed Browning Ferris Industries (sold to Allied Waste Industries for $7.3 billion), Republic Services ($1.2 billion in sales in 2000), Trans-America Waste Industries (sold in 1998 for $100 million in stock), and his present venture, Waste Corporation of America (which in its fourth year, 2002, had sales of $80 million).[1] Studying Tom's business building methods as we wrote two books together on the entrepreneurial process gave me the idea of mining one's unconscious mind for personal life goals. These processes were first described in a book we co-authored, *With No Fear of Failure.*[2]

Roy Williams, another of the most original thinkers I know, has been creatively chipping away at changing the face of advertising and marketing, and helping a host of people see the possibilities for transfor-mational change in the United States and beyond. His approach resulted in the development of "Wizard Academy" (a division of Roy H. Williams Marketing, Inc.) and books like *Secret Formulas of the Wizard of Ads* (number one *Wall Street Journal* and *New York Times* business best sell-ers).[3] Roy, like Tom, is interested in helping individuals tap and use their latent creative wisdom.

The third person whose life and work prompted me to write this book was my mentor and friend, the late Paul Tournier of Geneva, Switzer-land, who mentored me during the last twenty years of his life. He wrote almost three dozen books, more than twenty of which were translated into English (e.g., *The Meaning of Persons, Guilt and Grace*, and *The Heal-ing of Persons*).[4] When his books began to be translated, the response led Dr. Tournier to found *Group Médecine de la Personne,* a worldwide network of physicians demonstrating the healing power of a particular kind of personal interaction between physician and patient.

Finally, my friend and editor Roy M. Carlisle saw a more primitive presentation of the technique set out here and invited me to let him publish the book in his line of books at The Crossroad Publishing Company. I am very grateful to Roy for his confidence in me, and for his vision in recognizing the power of intuitive thinking in business as well as life.

Many other people have counseled and helped me over the years. Where possible, I have given credit to those and others I can identify. Some of these are John Bradshaw, Howard Butt Jr., Paul Franklin, T. George Harris, Frances Heatherly, Chuck and Carolyn Huffman, Vester Hughes, the Rt. Rev. Everett H. Jones, Earl Koile, Bruce and Hazel Larson, Pia Mellody, Henri Nouwen, M. Scott Peck, Bob Slocum, and the late Elton Trueblood. Other authors appear in the endnotes, and I am grateful to them all.

The following friends have taken time to read all or part of the present book in manuscript form. Some of them helped with typing or editing or have made suggestions regarding clarity and, as it turned out, all kinds of other helpful things for which I'm most grateful. They are Joe Brown, Linda Carswell, John Castle, Jan Cronk, Beverly Horne, Chuck and Carolyn Huffman, Emily Kaye, Bob Lively, Glenda Monroe, Janice Reinkin, Phebe Spiller, Adrien Van Zelfden, Janice Watson, Martha Webb, and Tom Wells. Our secretary/administrative Assistant, Jane Buergner, has held the project together and guided it and the author through the final storms of creation to publication. Since I didn't take all of their suggestions, I can't blame them for any mistakes or omissions that may have reached these printed pages. But I am deeply grateful for the help and support of these friends.

Our friends at Wizard Academy Press, especially Monica Ballard, Anthony Garcia, Dave Nevland, Corinne Taylor, Juan Guillermo Tornoe, Tom Walters, and Roy and Pennie Williams have been lifesavers in the process of editing, structuring, designing, and encouraging while meeting our deadlines.

My wife, Andrea, should be in all the categories of people listed here on terms of sources of help I've received and any wisdom that may appear in the characters' lives. But most of all she has lived many of the experiences and exercises described in this book. We are in the process of accomplishing the dreams we have discovered. Writing this book is one those dreams.

J. KEITH MILLER
Austin, Texas

A Brand New Day!

For centuries there have been wise men and women who seem to be in touch with who they are and where they are going. They are able to access a certain practical inner wisdom that allows them to see their dreams and life goals in specific and concrete terms. They can recognize and deal with the essential elements in almost any situation that might fulfill or block their dreams. With a minimum of stress, they often solve — in a short time — complex problems that leave the rest of us gasping.

Wondering to myself, "How do they do it?" I have traveled all over America and to several European countries for the last forty years to talk with men and women who have this fundamental contact with their own deep inner wisdom. Though on different paths, these individuals have all found ways to tap the usable wisdom of their unconscious minds. They have learned to listen and pay attention to what they discover. They exhibit unusual hope and sensitivity. They act in realistic ways to achieve an underlying sense of fulfillment. Their lives and wisdom are wonderful to behold — if one has the eyes to see.

As I began to use their methods in my own work as a writer, a management consultant, and a counselor, for a long time I didn't connect the fact that the methods I was using in several different areas of my life all involved facets of the same simple process that often spins off seemingly specific tailor-made "tools" or approaches to transform the inevitable obstacles toward achievement into wisdom and creativity. In this book, I present a practical approach to this process and some tools that emerged on a journey toward simplicity.

Four objectives for the awakening of your unspoken dreams and the transformational journey toward achieving them are:

1. to discover and define clearly some of your specific options and dreams that awaken your passion to achieve them

2. to explore the feasibility of these dreams to see if accomplishing them is realistic for you in the real world

3. to commit to accomplish the dream no matter what

4. to address personal and relationship problems and questions of meaning that arise as you begin to live your dreams

I have embedded a description of this process into a fictional story about the work of a physician, Dr. Charles Magie (Mah'jhee) and his protégés, John and Carol Martin and their son, Wil. What happens to them in this book is true in the sense that the situations come from real people's experiences, although the identities of the real people have been changed and their experiences merged into these few characters. By embedding the process in a narrative, I hope to immerse you in the dramatic experiences of people who find the courage actually to commit and step into the threatening process of change necessary to reach significant life goals — whether these goals be large or small.*

In an earlier, more instructional manuscript describing the process for awakening and achieving life dreams and goals, I had hung the processes on the clothesline of a simple story. Roy M. Carlisle suggested that I expand the story to include some of the stark and painful real-life situations and questions that can blindside practical dreamers as they get in touch with their unspoken dreams and actually move forward to make them come true.

At first I thought writing this book would be an interesting, simple undertaking, but I was in for a huge surprise. As the story began to unfold, the characters took on a life of their own as they each uncovered their life dreams and made commitments to achieve them in their real worlds. All hell broke out in their relationships with each other and with their lifelong problems and fears. I tried to calm them down, but they wouldn't have it. So I had to follow them and counsel them through relationship difficulties and conflict I hadn't planned. I was advised by some of my more literary friends to "cut out the story. It sounds melodramatic and simplistic." But since I could still see the haunted, surprised looks on the faces of *real dreamers* who were confronted with these painful disappointments, relationship changes, and fears of failing, I decided to tell the truth about what can happen, since personal problems can — and do — jump up and defeat people in devastating ways on the journey toward their dreams if the problems are not faced.

Looking back now that the book is finished, I can almost *see* the powerful creative energy and wisdom that was released in the characters' lives by a serious decision and commitment to achieve their dreams. I watched as the characters used this energy to do battle with character defects and dramatic situations and obstacles that threatened to sabotage their progress or destroy their family. I wrestled for several months with whether the story might be distracting for readers who are looking for practical help to accomplish concrete goals.

---

*The student of the history of graduate business education and literature will note that the processes described here are descended from the empirical-inductive modes of thinking characteristic of the practical American approach to education rather than the theoretical-deductive mode of the Europeans. See James Bryant Conant, *Two Modes of Thought* (New York: Pocket Books, 1965).

I decided to risk including in this book the usually undealt with personal challenges when I recalled that using the intuitive processes described here has led a number of people beyond the successful achieving of their material goals to ask questions like: "How much success is enough?" and "What does it all mean?" The questions about God in this story arose out of the characters' experience of powerlessness and were not premeditated in the book's plan. Regardless of whatever else you may learn by means of this fictional story, my point in writing the book is to illustrate life-changing processes, and what it takes, to *actually create new vocations or build significant businesses or professions — and satisfying lives, in real time.*

To this end, embedded in the story are exercises that set out specific steps to reach goals and also ways to relate to one's family and associates on the journey. Step-by-step instructions follow each chapter that describes such an exercise. The appendix (p. 248) provides a ready reference list of the locations of all the exercises.

I am against quick fixes to complex problems because they seldom get at the real issues and because they don't work. The processes in this book are not intended to be quick fixes to serious psychological or emotional symptoms, but are rather practical, usable material that has helped many people reach beyond their confused thinking to find and move toward achieving their unspoken dreams.

After discovering one's dreams, paying the price to accomplish them takes a great deal of commitment, discipline, and hard work. Although there are no guarantees that the methods described will work for everyone, these pages contain some realistic and tested approaches to focusing on your dreams and your life.

My hope in writing this book is that those of you who choose to go on the dream-seeking adventure will have the best possible chance of awakening some dreams with your name on them and actually achieving them. Welcome to the journey!

1

The End of the Runway

—␣␣␣—␣␣␣—

"Listen. I'm sick of arguing with you, Carol. I know you think under all that shouting your father does is a teddy bear, but at the office he's a mean, self-centered son of a...behind his back, they even call him Saddam! Doesn't that tell you anything?"

"John, honey, I don't want to argue, either. I know you're upset, but you're just not being yourself lately. Are you feeling okay? Isn't it time for your checkup? Did you make your appointment?"

John just stared at his wife. Then he said evenly in a slightly slurred voice. "There is nothing wrong with me!"

"Well, for one thing, you've had too much Scotch." Carol's voice had changed into her mother's crystalline, ascetic tone, slicing the air as she closed their bedroom door, leaving him standing alone in the dark hall. John started to force the door open, snorting like an injured bull near the end of a bullfight, but then he stopped and slowly leaned forward, head down, quietly nudging the solidly closed door instead. After a moment he backed away.

John Martin was exhausted, and somewhere in a foggy back corner of his mind, he knew Carol was right. He had drunk too much. He pulled himself upright, turned, and promptly stumbled over a care package he now recalled that Carol had gotten together to send their son, Wil. "Damn!" he swore, "that boy can get to me from fifteen hundred miles away." John struggled to recover his balance and walked unsteadily down the black hall toward his walnut-lined study, sliding one hand along the wall, feeling for the doorjamb.

"What's the matter with you, Killer?" John grunted out loud, and continued to study his image in the bathroom mirror. As he brushed his teeth, his strange, plastic face gazed back at him with a hurt expression. The man in the mirror still looked good at forty-three, his six-foot-one cornerback body intact, with a fifteen-pound outer layer, for warmth — no, more like five pounds, he thought, sucking in his stomach. He shook his head and said to the mirror, "How the hell could you be miserable? You've got it all." He tried to recall the list he'd gone over so often lately. Senior vice-president of a $30 million company, top-dollar income, beautiful wife I love — loved — who was an honor student in accounting and English literature at Colorado University, who helps abused women, volunteers at the church soup kitchen, and takes good care of our college sophomore son at Stanford. And who, John stopped his inner recital and then added sarcastically, although inordinately jealous of any woman I speak to twice, used to take good care of her handsome, intelligent, hardworking husband, that All-Conference cornerback, "Killer John Martin."

John sat abruptly on the toilet and tried to clear his head by shaking it. "Maybe you just ought to leave," he said to himself sadly. "Everyone has gone sour on you."

mm

Between John and Carol, something had changed drastically. They hardly spoke anymore, except when necessary to keep the household running.

John worked like a demon in his father-in-law's building supply business. Robert Latner had founded Latner Builder's Supply thirty years before, and now there were stores in six cities. But over the years the old man had nearly bankrupted the company, taking money out to invest unsuccessfully in the stock market. After John came to the business fifteen years ago, with an incredible effort he managed to turn the business around virtually by himself. John had never told Carol about her father's disastrous investing. He was respectful to Mr. Latner, who was no doubt secretly very relieved that John had saved the business, but never mentioned John's contribution. The day before the old man had said to John, "I've about got the company turned around, and I'm getting tired of working my butt off for you all. I'm about ready to hang it up and give you the keys." John just sat nodding his head — but his teeth were clenched and his stomach was on fire. Mr. Latner had said the same thing five years before, and the old man hadn't made a move since to turn the business loose. Never a patient person, by now John was at his wits' end and his whole body was tense with unexpressed feelings.

The anger he felt had popped out in the open with Carol at last, and John was really seething. He had been taking his frustration out on everyone at the office, but he was harder on himself than anyone else. By most people's standards, John was a financial and personal success, but now, just as he seemed to have the brass ring in his hand, he felt miserable, his life energy draining away. His body felt as if it were prematurely aging. He was losing interest in the business and his family, and it all irritated and bored him. Lately he had begun to calm his anger with a few drinks on the way home after work.

Until tonight with Carol, he hadn't told anyone how he felt. In fact, he could only get fleeting glimpses of these feelings himself. Yet from the flashes of rage he felt, he feared that speaking the feelings out loud, especially to Robert Latner, might destroy everything for which he had worked so hard. But he felt horrible all over. As he fell asleep at four that morning, John told himself he would make an appointment to get a physical exam the next day.

John had a splitting headache when he sat up and mashed the alarm off at 6:30 a.m. Always able to drive himself through pain to get back in the game, he once again dragged himself out of the hideaway bed in his study and walked gingerly, trying not to jar his head.

By eight o'clock, he knew in his gut that something was desperately wrong, and by the time he got to the office he felt gray-sick all over, somehow trapped in his aching body. John could usually make fast and good business decisions, so he couldn't understand why it was hard to act on almost anything now, even like sitting down and calling the doctor.

—*wm*—

SAMUEL MOSES, M.D.
INTERNAL MEDICINE

John looked at the plaque on the door of the hospital office.

"Hello, Killer, how've you been? Haven't seen you in a while." Sam had played tackle on the same defensive team with John when they were in college.

"Hello, Doc."

Sam said, "You look like a fly that's just been drunk by a spider. How do you feel?" When John hesitated, Sam added, "And don't get slippery with me."

"I don't know, Sam, but I've managed to spit in the eye of just about everyone I care anything about. I feel mean as a turpentined cat. I'd like to kill a certain old man, and dying doesn't look like a bad career move. Other than that, things are good."

Sam looked at his best friend, "A little depressed? Go in that room; change out of those clothes — you know the drill — and I'll check you out. Then you can fast all night and we'll run some cardio and other tests tomorrow."

—*wm*—

The next morning, ten minutes into a treadmill exam, John began to feel some heart irregularities, and then suddenly searing pain shot through his chest and an incredible tightness clutched what he assumed was his heart. Without changing his expression, John Martin felt panic. Sam glanced at John's face and stopped the treadmill.

He gripped John's arm to guide him. John started to shake off Sam's hand, but was frozen. "Killer, put your sorry hide down on that gurney." Sam was a big man, six-foot-four, 240 pounds. John did not trust many men, but he did trust this one. After studying the treadmill printout,

Sam brushed his hair off his forehead and said deliberately, "John, you could be in big trouble here. I want you to have a group of tests to check out the condition of your ticker."

Three days later, after a Holter monitor and several other tests, John sat in Sam's office. The doctor looked John in the eyes and raised his eyebrows.

"John, you're like an acrobatic pilot who can do astounding tricks in the air — but you don't seem to know how to land, or even where you're flying to. There's nothing wrong that we can operate for, but, old friend, if you don't change your life soon, chances are you're going to die — a little prematurely."

"Die?" John repeated. "What the hell do you mean?" And he added sardonically, "If there's 'nothing wrong' with me, then exactly what can I do to keep from dying?"

"Listen, bonehead, I didn't mean there's nothing wrong with you. I said there's nothing we can cure with surgery. It's not 'plumbing.' If it were, we could operate, and you'd no doubt be fine. Your heart's problem is 'electrical,' and frankly, John, we don't know that much about 'electrical' — except that some life problems are often buried under your sort of symptoms."

John felt like the scared first grader he'd been when the teacher asked him to let the school nurse give him the first smallpox shot in front of the class so the other kids wouldn't be afraid. He'd been terrified of needles and had felt like he was going to start crying and run out of the door, but he had instead calmly rolled up his sleeve and stuck out his arm.

Sam's voice brought him back to the present. "I can give you medication so you can get some rest, and an exercise and diet program to help you get back in shape. But, John, if I were you, I'd take some time off by myself and rest, do nothing — maybe for a month. Try to get in touch with what you want to do. You're bored and depressed, a walking advertisement for an affair or a substance abuse treatment center. What's happening to you is not just about your physical symptoms now. The whole time I've known you, you've never told me anything about what you really want to do with your life — in the way of a career. But from the way your body's screaming, it sure ain't voting for what you're doin' now — especially where you're doin' it.

"Buddy, you seem to have stumbled into everything you've done: football, baseball, golf, your marriage, your job. And the wonder is, you made touchdowns or hit the ball out of the park in most all of them. But in the twenty-five years I've known you, you never seem to have . . . *chosen* anything." John started to object, but Sam shook his head, took a deep breath, and exhaled as he said, "John, it's really important for you to take a look at your life. Your heart is mainlining you a message, and I don't want it to be a termination notice. Hear me?"

A knot of fear twisted in John's stomach as he stared out the window behind the doctor's desk. Sam was the best friend he had in the world, and Sam wasn't given to being dramatic. "Die!" he thought, "You're going to die if you don't change your life and find out what you want out of it." Out loud he said, "Sam, you may be right, but I seem to be paralyzed. I can't take off for a month. I can't even seem to get far enough away from the telephone to take a weekend off."

Sam pulled on his chin, and for a few seconds he looked out the window at the mountains on the other side of Denver. "John, I know a little family hotel in Glion, Switzerland, in the Swiss Alps, just above Lake Geneva. An old French couple owns it. It's private and beautiful, and you can take some therapeutic baths there. I can prescribe the trip for you as treatment, so you can take sick leave. That way even the old man will give you time off from the company. You can rest and read and relax in the spa. Take some long walks. Write what comes to you in a journal. When you get back, you may want to go to a therapist to talk it all over, or you may be feeling fine. I sense your body knows what you need to find out, but you just haven't taken the time to listen."

John shook his head. "I can't do that by myself," he said. "I'd feel guilty about not taking Carol. And she'd be sure I was meeting a girl-friend. You know how jealous she's always been — even when we were first dating." Sam nodded, remembering a time in college when Carol was about to break up with John for taking Sam's visiting cousin out to dinner as a last-minute favor to Sam, who had a lab final. Carol had gone ballistic when a friend reported John's "disloyalty." "But she's worn out with my thrashing around too. I feel stupid about spending that much time and money just to think things over. Besides, her old man would never let me forget wimping out to get my life adjusted."

"John, you don't seem to get what I'm saying. Talk it over with Carol. At this stage in your marriage I don't think she'll have any problem once she understands how important it is. Your life may be at stake here, old friend. You're wound as tight as Shaq's taped ankle before a basketball game. Besides," Sam continued, "you fly all the time. Use some of your frequent flyer miles. But go — while you still can."

"Hello, Daddy?" Carol greeted her father, as he answered the phone. "I'm sorry to bother you at work, but I'm really worried about Wil."

"Wil? What's the matter with my grandson, honey?" Mr. Latner asked, concerned.

"He and his dad are *not* getting along. When Wil came home for Easter vacation last week, they passed each other in the hall like two enemy battleships' guns tracking each other. John is so hard on him, tries to give Wil advice about everything, and Wil just waits till John's finished and leaves the room."

The old man laughed. "Well, Wil *is* just out of adolescence, Carol, and besides, as I recall the bad blood started when Wil got picked up for drug possession his freshman year in high school. But if you're asking me, I think the problem is with John instead of Wil," her father said with a suggestive tone. "He's just not normal lately, Carol."

"What do you mean, *not normal!* He is very normal!"

"I'm not talking sex here. John's just spoiled rotten about life. I've trusted him like my own son — given him everything a man could want, and I tried to help him learn the business, but he's just stubborn. Wants to do everything his own way. And his work ethic sometimes stinks. Frankly, I don't know how long I can carry him."

Carol's stomach knotted. She felt an uneasy tightness in her stomach when someone was not telling her the truth, and now she was totally tense. Someone was lying about the way things were going at work: John or her father. She knew John had always worked hard. He'd brought work home, and he used to talk to her enthusiastically about new expansion deals he was working on. In fact, his continual talking about the business bored her, until finally a year ago she'd told him she didn't want to hear "quite as much" as he was telling her. After that he quit talking about the business, but he still kept bringing work home and being enthusiastic about the company with everyone they knew. Nothing in his behavior or attitude indicated that he was anything but a very conscientious worker.

On the other hand, why would her father discredit John to her? But now she remembered John's face the night before and his angry words about people at the office calling her father Saddam behind his back!

After a few seconds of Carol's silence, her father said gruffly, "You still there?"

"Yes, I'm still here. What do you *mean* you don't know how long you can carry John? He's worked his tail off for you, ever since he's been there. He's been a very loyal and a dedicated worker."

"Oh? Well, he just left my office and wants to take time off in the midst of our busiest season to take a month long sightseeing trip to Switzerland — *by himself.*" Carol started to tell him that she knew he might be having some heart problems, but her father interrupted her.

"I hate to ask this honey, but has John been acting unusual? I mean, making phone calls and hanging up when you come in the room? Drinking more than usual?"

"What are you trying to *say?"* Carol felt her anger and fear rise into her face. John had told her about Sam's insistence that he take some time off, that he was going to Switzerland. He'd also told her his physical had revealed some heart irregularities.

"Nothing, honey. Except that John is going into midlife. And men sometimes — but I'm sure John would never be disloyal to you...in any way."

———

John opened his eyes and looked around the stately but timeworn hotel room with its high ceiling and heavy, ornate molding. The only light came from a shaft of bright morning sun knifing through the crack between the tall interior wooden shutters covering the huge east window. As he lay there watching the tiny dust particles riding the light beam into the darkened room, John remembered the evening cab ride from the Geneva airport to Montreux, and the cog railway train — the only public transportation — chugging straight up the mountainside through the forest to the little village of Glion. It was after 10:00 p.m. by the time the old train clanked to a stop. The station was deserted, except for an attractive athletic-looking young woman in a quilt jacket. In one hand she held a cardboard sign with John's name written on it in big, black letters, and she looked up when John got off the train with his bag. Smiling, she rose to greet him. *"Bon soir."* She was from the hotel, and at first John thought she did not speak English. But then with a French accent she said, "I'm Celeste."

John smiled to think how he had dropped off to sleep that night in the incredibly soft feather bed, sleep coming easily for the first time in months. Now, feeling quiet and relaxed, he said out loud, "I could stay in bed all day or I could go see what Switzerland is all about." He yawned, searching for his slippers with his feet and enjoying the smell of strong coffee brewing somewhere below his room. John then took the vitamins and other pills Sam had prescribed for him with a glass of cold water.

After fresh croissants, orange marmalade, and coffee on his private balcony, John sat in the warm morning sunlight and absorbed the incredible view over the tops of the giant pine and silver-tipped firs below him. As the sun burned the fog off the bottomless blue lake far below, the pine smell of a campfire coming from the forest brought to mind memories of his childhood summer vacations camping in the Colorado Rockies with his father and his brother, Larry.

After lunch, John decided to start on a not-too-strenuous walking program, slowly at first and only down the village's single street of shops and back. His heart wasn't exactly damaged, but Sam had said, "Take it easy on the exercise till you get accustomed to the altitude."

Because few of the visitors at the small hotel spoke English, John had a lot of time by himself to think. The hotel manager assigned him to a table in front of a ten-foot plate glass window with an astounding view of the Swiss Alps to his left and the bottomless blue water of Lake Geneva below. His dinner companions were an elderly German couple named Bruner, who spoke German and a little French. He was relieved that he wouldn't have to make conversation. As he sat waiting for dinner to be served that first evening, John realized he really didn't know what to do with his future. For years he'd just been putting out fires that flared in his overcommitted life. As he looked out into the darkening sky, he saw his reflection and the candlelit dining room behind him. In his mind were scenes of himself making mad dashes to the airport and running to the gate to catch a plane. He sighed and savored the aroma of dinner as a steaming plate of soup arrived, brought by Celeste, the girl who'd met his train.

During the next week, the whirring motor of thoughts and memories in John's head shifted into a quieter gear. He wrote in his journal and then read a few pages of a book about stress Sam had given him. Walking around the charming little village he looked in the shop windows at the Swiss clocks, woodcarvings, and clothes and found himself thinking about Carol and wishing she were with him. Impulsively he bought her a beautiful cashmere scarf — and laughed as he said to himself, "Well, you must not be too angry with her for taking sides with her father about taking time off." He remembered their silence when Carol drove him to the airport. They had argued the night before about whether Sam had really insisted that John needed to go on this trip and about whether John knew anyone in Switzerland he hadn't told her about. John had gotten angry, picked up the phone, speed-dialed Sam at home and handed the receiver to Carol. Since she trusted Sam, that conversation ended the argument, but also their plan to make love that night. And John recalled that for the first time he could remember, he didn't care that she turned her back on him sexually.

At the end of a week, John got up late one morning, skipped lunch and took the old cog train up past several stops, clear to the top of the mountain, to the tiny village of Caux with its breathtaking view of snow-capped mountain peaks and deep blue-black crevices below. He walked around the extensive grounds of a large old hotel for a long time and watched a movie for guests about that area of the Swiss Mountains. Afterward, John saw a trail leading up, first thinking it was probably too long and strenuous a climb at this altitude. But after gazing up the trail as far as the first turn, he finally thought, "Aw, to heck with it," and began to hike. Early in the evening, he made it to a lookout point near the top of the mountain, and from there he watched for an hour as the sunset dimmed its pink and purple lights behind the white-capped peaks.

John was startled as he saw his dead father's face take shape in a cloud formation looking the way his father had in the hospital bed when he was dying, and sudden tears caught John completely by surprise. He said out loud to his dead father, "Why did you love Larry and not me? I busted my butt to make you proud of me, but you never really loved me — never really saw me, only my brother!" The cloud picture dissolved, and John thought of his son, Wil, at Stanford, as distant as John had been from his father. He wondered if his own father had thought about him as much as he thought about Wil, and he vowed on that mountaintop he'd spend more time with his son and get it right with him, give Wil what he'd never gotten from his own father.

By the time John found his way back down from the high trail to the deserted train station, the darkness was complete. He barely caught the last cog train, and when he got to the Glion stop, the village was buttoned up for the night. He'd forgotten it was Sunday. He rang the night bell at the hotel and as he waited, he noticed a new queasy feeling in his gut. How long had that been there? He began to feel lightheaded and it crossed his mind that he might pass out. Answer the door! The minutes stretched on interminably, as he rang again and again.

At last, Celeste's sleepy, frowning face appeared in the small window of the door. Wakened from a sound sleep, she was silent and grumpy looking, but John was relieved to see her. When she let him in and turned on the hall lights, he impulsively gave her a five-franc tip. She smiled sleepily in response, said, *"Bon soir,"* and disappeared at the end of the downstairs hall.

Fighting dizziness and nausea, John started slowly up the stairs. By the time he got to his room on the third floor, it dawned on him that he hadn't eaten or taken his pills since breakfast. Since everything in town was locked up tight, he decided he'd tough it out. But then he remembered that some of the vitamins he took with his meds were food supplements — they might calm his hunger pangs. He took a full day's supply of pills, sixteen in all (he couldn't remember if he'd taken his morning batch), and washed them down with a large glass of water before he fell into bed exhausted.

A huge man dressed in black with a purple eye mask and flowing black cape charged across a high moonlit meadow of mountain flowers. John was terrified as he ran for all he was worth from the giant stranger. Suddenly, his foot hit a hidden stone, and he pitched forward into the knee-high grass, twisting in the air so that he landed on his back. When he looked up, the towering black figure was upon him with drawn sword descending toward his chest! John screamed and tried to scoot away on his heels and elbows just as the silver sword pierced his skin. The pain was unbelievably intense.

When John opened his eyes, everything was dark. He put his hand to his forehead and felt cold sweat. Then realized that he was in bed at the hotel. He'd been dreaming. As relief flooded over him, the pain hit again in the middle of his chest, burning like an internal fire, and John didn't need a cardiogram to guess what was happening. When the pain ebbed for a moment, he reached for the telephone on the bedside stand and banged on the cradle to raise the operator since there was no dial tone.

It seemed forever, and no one answered. Why hadn't he stayed at the Hilton in Montreux? As he kept banging on the telephone cradle, John thought of his father, dead of a heart attack at fifty, and wondered if this was how he had felt when death was coming for him. Then, at last, a sleepy voice on the other end of the line said, *"Oui?"* It was Celeste.

"Help," John said weakly as he braced himself for more pain. He tried to remember his high school language course — Spanish. *"Corazón!"* he gasped.

2

The Guide

Thick darkness surrounded them as Celeste's father and brother helped her drag John out of their ancient Peugeot pickup, half-supporting, half-carrying him up the path to the stone cottage clinic. Light shone around the outline of the figure standing in the doorway, the only physician on the mountain, the bent-shouldered, white-haired Dr. Charles Magie.

After helping John lie down on the examination table, the others left to wait in the outer room. John jumped at the touch of the cold stethoscope. He opened his eyes to a bright glare from the bulb in the ceiling and heard the clock on the little church's tower chime 4:00 a.m.

The old doctor mixed some white powder in a glass of water, gave it to John, and then began to ask him questions. He spoke English with only a slight French accent and his voice was calm and assuring. John found himself blurting out the account of his visit to Sam and then Sam's prescription to come to Glion.

At that moment an unbelievable drowsiness came over John, and he closed his eyes, feeling more at peace than he had in years. Something about this doctor made him feel hopeful and safe. Some sort of drug was flowing warmly through his veins. He was floating in a soft cloud. John chuckled in surprise and mumbled to himself, "I actually trust this old mountain goat!"

Ten hours later when John woke, the world looked as bright as the vivid flowers in the painting of a cobblestoned street scene in his white-walled room. For a few minutes he lay still, peacefully listening to the distinctive tick-tocking of a large clock that echoed from another part of the building. His thinking was still a little fuzzy, but he became aware that Dr. Magie sat in a chair by the window, reading.

"Ah," the doctor said. "You feel better?"

"I'm so glad you speak English — almost American," John mumbled, very relieved.

"Yes," said Dr. Magie, smiling, "I went to medical school in Boston. My name is Charles Magie."

"How's that?" John asked.

"Magie," the older man replied, "M-a-g-i-e. It's French, pronounced Mah'jhee."

For a few moments they talked about how John came to be in Glion and what had happened the night before. John was more alert than he had been the night before, but his thinking felt heavy and his talking slow, as if he had molasses in his mouth. Dr. Magie explained his findings from John's examination. "I can detect nothing wrong with your heart physically. The pain you experienced seems to be from acid in your esophagus from all the pills you took on an empty stomach. I gave you some Zantac to neutralize the acid and some Valium to help you relax and sleep. You were very restless. You've slept for ten hours. You must have been extremely tired."

"You mean I'm all right?"

Dr. Magie hesitated. "Well, I can't detect any toxic physical symptoms. If the pain recurs, there are some medical tests that would be advisable, but from our conversation when you came last night, I sense that . . . " he paused thoughtfully and continued, "something is not well with you."

Laughing, John said lightly, "I perceive you are a prophet."

Dr. Magie smiled and calmly looked at John in an understanding way.

"Well," John said finally, "are you going to tell me what you think is going on?"

"It seems to me that your problem is not about physical lesions, but perhaps your life. A larger problem?" Dr. Magie stood and said, "You can rest here a while if you like, but you are free to go. My telephone number is on this slip if you should need to call. I have other patients to see now, but if you would like, you can come to my house after supper. We can talk by the fireplace in my study."

That evening, John sat with Dr. Magie in his book-lined study, looking into the dancing flames in the old fieldstone fireplace. An Oriental rug lay in front of the hearth, and above the heavy dark wood mantel was an oil painting of the sun rising above Lake Geneva. John felt that same cozy, safe feeling he'd felt in the doctor's clinic. Dr. Magie answered John's questions.

"Do you mind if I call you Dr. M.?"

The white-haired physician thought a few seconds and smiled. "No, I don't mind." Dr. Magie continued the conversation he'd begun with John in the clinic. "I think all is not well with your life in some way." He asked John if he'd like to talk about that — to tell him about his life. Within half an hour, John found he was confiding in this man who seemed more like an old family friend than a physician. He talked honestly about his brittle marriage and his unhappy business situation, trying to be both very honest and fair. When John had recited the events leading to his trip to Switzerland, he said, "Frankly, Dr. Magie, I'm at a loss. I don't know what to do next."

John vividly recalled going to his father-in-law's office to tell him about the doctor's diagnosis and recommendation to go to Switzerland. Robert Latner shook his head. "For God's sake, buck up, boy, and get back to work. I'm almost thirty years older than you are, and I've never missed a day! No one in this family has ever been a quitter...before." Then the older man looked down at some papers on his desk, his way of dismissing people.

John felt anger rising in his chest. He wanted to tell the old man to take a flying....But this was Carol's father, and Wil's grandfather. Thinking of Carol and Wil, he bit back his retort, carefully closed the door behind him — so he wouldn't slam it — and stalked out.

A lifetime of training not to talk about family secrets stopped John from giving Dr. Magie these details. But John did say that he had a lot of anger about Robert Latner's sarcastic response to John's taking time off work for his health.

"Even though I know this arrogance and need to control are Robert Latner's problems, I'd still like to punch him out. And I know that does not exactly reflect great emotional maturity," John smiled sheepishly. "I feel as if my life is just fouled up. I love Wil as much as a father can love a son, and I love Carol more than anything else, but I can't communicate with Wil, and I can't get in touch with any sexual feelings about Carol any more. I feel terrible, but no one can find anything wrong." John felt vulnerable, amazed that he'd been so forthright. "That, basically, is my story, Dr. M."

Dr. Magie frowned into the flames darting up the sides of the charred pine logs. He waited so long to speak that John thought he might not have heard what he'd said. Finally, he looked up with a kind smile. "You seem to be an intelligent man with great abilities, but I don't hear any concrete dreams or goals for your own personal life. When you talk about yourself, I sense a great sadness, as if your heart is breaking because you haven't heard it calling to you to wake up and live for your own dreams."

John raised his eyebrows and then slowly nodded his head in agreement. "That's probably right. When you say that, I know it's true, but I don't even know where to begin to find out what I want to do with my life — even tomorrow." He paused and swallowed hard. "What do you think I might do to get off dead center?"

Dr. Magie looked out the window for a few seconds. Then he said, "John, I believe that inside each person there is a very creative and intuitive source of personal wisdom. But the fast pace of life and the overwhelmingly cognitive structure of education in the Western world causes a great number of people to grow up distrusting, and eventually burying, repressing this intuitive inner wisdom. I believe that information from your own inner wisdom can lead you to your own vocation, your own intrinsic dreams for the future. If a person is not in touch with his or her own inherent purposes, he or she will become attached to — or be co-opted by — someone else's goals. Sometimes that is unavoidable, but sooner or later, one's inner wisdom may rebel and send signals or warnings to that individual's consciousness through emotional or physical symptoms. These messages are intended to inform that person's conscious mind of the increasing distance between one's inherent self and the direction one is headed with his or her vocation or lifestyle."

John thought about what Dr. M. said. "Do you mean that my depression and my heart symptoms may have been attempts by my inner wisdom to tell me that I am getting farther and farther away from who I really am?"

Dr. M. just shrugged his shoulders slightly and raised his eyebrows, saying nothing.

"Maybe," John said thoughtfully, "that's what Sam suspected, but didn't have words for." John laughed and shook his head in wonder. "Good Lord, maybe I'm having a midlife crisis."

Dr. M. nodded without smiling, "That could be true. If it is, you will soon feel great relief from facing it, and you will feel more 'in touch with yourself.' "

"I do already," John said simply. Then, "How can I get information from my inner wisdom that I have repressed regarding my own specific dreams and goals?"

Dr. M. looked at John in silence, letting him savor the new insight into which he had just stepped. "For a few moments, John, I want you to play a game with me. To begin, we are not going to focus on your vocation, your relationships, or your personal goals, but rather on what overall state, personal attitude, or inner experience you'd like to have as a result of all your efforts. Do you have any idea what that overall hoped-for state would be for your personal life?"

After a few seconds, John said very definitely, "No question." He laughed, "It's peace of mind. But I don't have a clue how to get it."

"I think I can help you find out," Dr. Magie said quietly, "if you're willing to suspend your disbelief and do exactly what I will suggest for the next few minutes."

John looked at Dr. Magie and felt a silent warning bell of skepticism go off in his stomach. He was very cynical about trying to drum up any real practical happiness and serenity. On the other hand, this wise old man had pinpointed and described in detail the source of John's excruciating and mysterious life problems after listening to him for less than an hour. Though the statistical chance of their meeting was astronomically small, yet here he was. "All right," John said, sitting up straighter. "Let's go for it. What do I do?"

Dr. Magie went to his desk, picked up a ruled legal pad, a pencil, and an eraser. "Here's the game," the doctor said. "It's called, 'Life Dreaming.' "

3

Surprise Contact with an Inner Ally

~~~~~~~~~~~~

"The world of our intuitive and creative inner wisdom is not located in the noisy part of the brain, where language, logic, numerical solutions, and rigorous philosophical reasoning reside. The magical intuitive inner wisdom seems to live on the shadowy rim of the unconscious mind, the place from which sleeping dreams awaken. But when, as children, we get embarrassed, shamed, and ridiculed for trusting our intuitive inner wisdom or not being able to explain something we know to be true, we unwittingly imprison out intuition as an untrustworthy guide in the blackness of the unconscious mind where we cannot get at it by ordinary means."

John suddenly remembered one August night when he was a short, skinny six-year-old boy. He was sitting on the front porch at home with his father and his brother, Larry. His father was drinking beer and John had said, "Daddy, I think I'd like to be a movie actor when I grow up." His father and his brother started laughing. Through his laughter his father said, "You'd never make it as a movie star. Better learn to sell used cars." John remembered the burning shame as Larry said with mock seriousness, "Easy, Dad, Sean Connery was probably an ugly little runt too." John's father slapped his knee as he and Larry had laughed at John until tears came to their eyes. John hid his face and ran out into the night.

Dr. Magie noted John's skeptical and detached look and continued, "As you are no doubt aware, the unconscious is a sort of a storehouse for filing thoughts, ideas, and experiences that remain a part of us, though not in our conscious mind. One of the strange things Freud postulated about the human mind was that there is a 'censor' that guards the door to this part of the mind. This gatekeeping censor also sometimes prevents us from getting facts, names, or dreams that we want or need out of our unconscious mind and into our consciousness, where we can use them.

"For example, many times in school when taking an examination, I could not recall some fact that I needed, a fact that I knew very well. However, after handing in my exam and walking out of the room, the fact would spontaneously materialize with great clarity in my mind."

Dr. Magie smiled. "The censor had withheld, and then released the information I wanted.

"Another example of the capriciousness and power of the censor took place years ago. I had a very unpleasant argument with my wife, and I had not acquitted myself well at all. Just as I pulled out of the driveway after the argument, the censor released into my consciousness a brilliant, telling remark with which I could have easily won the argument — but which I had not been able to come up with before I left the house.

"The unconscious is also the prison of our inner wisdom, once we have denied its validity and repressed it. So," Dr. Magie continued, "to begin to retrieve specific information from our imprisoned inner wisdom when we want it, we must first distract the censor. We do this by playing a little game."

John started to object to this foolishness, when the doctor reminded him of his agreement to suspend his disbelief and do as he asked. "The censor is usually intractable. But like a parking lot guard, if the censor thinks I'm only playing an unimportant game, it may relax and 'go back to reading the paper.' When that happens, in a few minutes I can sometimes get an incredible amount of information from my unconscious mind past the censor — all kinds of awakening ideas and dreams and goals. As strange and unlikely as it may seem, this is how our little game works."

Dr. M. got up and handed John the legal pad, the pencil, and the eraser he had been holding. John took the paper but left the pencil in Dr. Magie's hand. "Thanks, but I have a pen."

Dr. M. insisted, "No, you should always do Life Dreaming using a pencil — with an eraser. It's easy to misunderstand or write down something you later realize is not right for you. And remember, your inner wisdom is flexible, and with it you are increasingly free. New ideas will come to you in the midst of this process. You can learn to flex and change. And you own the eraser."

John squinted at Dr. M., for it had never occurred to him that such fluid flexibility could be a sign of wisdom.

"First, I want you to put your overall experiential goal for your life — 'Peace of Mind' — at the top of a blank sheet of paper. Then I'm going to check my watch and give you exactly ten minutes. During that time I want you to write everything you can imagine that you could do, obtain, or become that would contribute to your peace of mind. Things you'd like to do before you die, specific vocations, places you'd like to visit, things like: be a banker, go to Australia, go skiing in Austria, be a school teacher, or meet a great sports hero — like your cyclist, Lance Armstrong." John smiled at hearing that this Swiss doctor in a tiny village on the mountain used an American athlete as an example of someone he might like to meet.

Dr. Magie continued, "Some of your dreams may be about material things you want to purchase or own, some of which might seem terribly materialistic, shallow, or larger than you feel you deserve. But list them anyway.

"Many people resist putting their real dreams on paper because they are afraid they will be shamed by their inner critical voices or by anyone who might see their dream list. But to free your inner wisdom, you must ignore those critical voices and list what you'd honestly like to do, have, or become. This self-honesty is the first step in contacting the inner wisdom. List everything that comes to mind that you'd like to do that you feel might contribute in some way to peace of mind about your life.

"Some of the things you write may seem bizarre, even immoral or criminal — but just write them and go on!" Dr. Magie smiled encouragingly at John. "You can always cut things out later if you see that they contradict a deeper value. Don't stop to think about the things that come to you or make any evaluations or corrections. Just keep writing. No one will see this list except you, unless you choose to share it. Remember, you can change it — you own the eraser. But for now, play. This is the game of your life!"

"But I've made lists like this before and nothing much came of them," John objected. "This idea has been floating around a long time."

Dr. Magie smiled. "That's right, it has." The smile vanished as he continued, "But the problem for many people has been that they did not have any specific guidance as to how to turn their dreams into specific goals. Besides, as I will explain later, the time constraint is very important to the specific technique we're using."

"But what if I'm the kind of person who puts a dead mouse in the punchbowl of every party given for me?" John asked.

Dr. Magie squinted at John not understanding. John laughed, "What I mean is that sometimes I have sabotaged myself and kept from succeeding because of some crazy feelings that 'I don't deserve to,' or 'I'm being greedy,' or 'I'm getting a big head.'"

Dr. Magie nodded. "Good point, but I'll show you some ways you can change those habits and get beyond the tyranny of those negative inner voices so you can accomplish your dream goals. That's why this approach is different. Just begin now by making your list. We'll deal with those problems later."

John shook his head, smiled a doubtful smile, and agreed to make the list. The doctor looked at his watch and said, "You have exactly ten minutes to list everything that comes to mind that you'd like to do before you die. Go! And write quickly."

Feeling a little foolish, John began writing. Dr. Magie sat across the room at his desk, looking at some correspondence. He glanced up occasionally to see how John was doing.

At seven minutes and twenty-three seconds, John said, "I can't think of anything else."

"You have to continue," the doctor said with authority. "Write some extravagant or out-of-the-question things you might secretly want to do, like train lions, be a movie star, buy a Rolls Royce, or fly a jet plane. Keep writing something. You may have to make things up, but do it. You're breaking loose a tightly bound inner prisoner. Go!"

Although there were a few seconds between each item, John kept writing until the ten minutes were up. He had just listed something when the doctor said, "Stop."

John took a deep breath and exhaled, "I'm amazed," he said, "at how many things I listed after I had wracked my brain and thought I was finished."

"It is surprising, but because of the pressure of the deadline, you don't have time to think, just respond. Somehow that opens a crack in the door of the unconscious mind, and all kinds of things start flowing out — unbidden, so to speak — many of them from your beleaguered inner wisdom." Dr. M. smiled broadly, "Near the end of the time, if one doesn't continue to focus on writing positive dreams, some people slip into their lifelong habits of evaluating the possible negative implications of their thoughts, and the censor may wake up and close the door. However, once this ten-minute process is begun, most people find a crack in the door will stay open. Over time as they practice, they can have increasing access to the information they're seeking for their lives from the inner wisdom."

Dr. M. breathed deeply, "Maybe the jailer is still withholding information from you. Why don't you just sit still a few minutes and relax? See if anything else occurs to you that you'd like to do before you die."

A few minutes later, John looked up at Dr. Magie and put down the pencil. After he finished looking over his dream list, he handed it to the older man.

"Now," Dr. Magie said, "renumber the list in the order of importance to you."

"Why?"

"By doing this you are switching to the cognitive, organizing part of your brain where you can plan and focus your best thinking on those dreams."

John said doubtfully, "Dr. Magie, I don't honestly think these things are from any deep part of me. I think I just made them up. Most of them are too ordinary to be coming from some deep inner wisdom."

Smiling, Dr. Magie asked, "Where did they come from then? You could have selected anything for this list, but under the pressure of time, you intuitively selected these particular things, and when you finished, you could think of no others important enough to list."

"But how can I know if these are really important to me?"

PEACE OF MIND

1. Vocation — accomplishment in a business I could enjoy that doesn't involve my father-in-law

2. Build a cabin for our family on a fishing lake

3. Trips to Paris and London

4. Being loved by my wife and son

5. Financial security — paying off debts, including the house

6. Stature in the community — helping community grow in healthy ways

7. Visit Alaska and fish for salmon

8. Time by myself

9. Spend more time alone with Carol, doing fun things

10. Health: getting in shape physically

11. Being a better father — spend more one-on-one time with Wil

12. Taking some three-day weekends

13. Non-business time with friends

14. Four weeks' vacation per year

15. Go as a family to Disney World

16. Visit Tahiti

17. Find ways to improve my emotional life

18. Find out how I foul up my life and relationships so I can quit doing it

"The next step will show you how to find that out. After prioritizing the list, you are going to change each of these dreams into a concrete and specific goal, and then make a plan for checking one or more out in the real world — to see what it will take to accomplish each of them. As you go through the checking process for each item, step by step, you will experience either a growing sense of excitement and enthusiasm, or you will lose interest in that goal, perhaps altogether. The checking process itself — and the release of creative energy for achieving the goal — will tell you your true feelings about each dream, and how important it actually is to you. This is the practical way you begin to discover which things are really from your inner wisdom."

John held his hand up to stop the conversation while he thought a moment. "Are you saying that this process actually releases new energy into your life as you begin to investigate your dreams?"

"Indeed," Dr. Magie replied. "In fact, the crucial thing I have learned about finding and committing to reach a dream is this: When one focuses on, investigates, and makes a serious commitment to accomplish a life dream, it seems that God gives that person's life a huge injection of positive motivational energy focused on accomplishing the goal that the dream produced. Dreamers seriously moving toward their goals become passionate and alive in a way that creates health. Their whole experience of life changes remarkably and is often heightened. They feel fulfilled somehow, even before actually reaching their dreams."

"Okay," John said, "let's go on. I'm not totally convinced, and this is really strange, but I'm getting interested."

The large clock in the front hall struck the half-hour, and Dr. Magie looked at his watch and then his appointment book. "We'll have to continue this tomorrow. Would 4:00 p.m. be all right?"

EXERCISE ONE
Summary of Steps for Awakening Your Personal Dreams
for the Rest of Your Life

Note to Reader: If your primary purpose in reading this book is to awaken and go for your dreams — individually or in a small group — it may be more beneficial for you to stop and do this exercise now. Or you can read the rest of the book and then complete the exercises. Whenever you do them, it is helpful to find a quiet place where you are not likely to be interrupted. Take a pencil, eraser, and paper with you.

1. Identify the overall experiential goal for your private life. (John's was peace of mind.) For many, the overall state or goal is something like happiness, security, or serenity. This is not incompatible with scientific orientation or a relationship with God. In fact, this process has helped many discover what God-given aptitudes and desires they have buried or ignored.

2. Write on the top line of a clean sheet of lined paper: "Things I'd like to do before I die that would contribute to my overall goal state (e.g., happiness, peace of mind)."

3. Using a timer or clock, spend ten minutes forcing yourself to list everything you can think of that you would like to do that would contribute to your hoped-for experience or state of mind. Use a pencil. Work fast. Don't stop. You can list bizarre items or anything that comes to mind that you'd like to do that would contribute to your overall goal. Don't change or edit your list. Just put down whatever occurs to you. Let yourself include things that may seem extravagant or self-indulgent or simple and prosaic as they occur to you.

4. When the ten minutes are up, take a few more minutes to list any remaining things you can think of that you would like to do before you die.

5. Renumber the list in the order of importance to you (e.g., number 4 may be the most important, so renumber it as number 1).

6. Rewrite the list in the new order on a clean sheet of paper.

7. Destroy or discard the first list.

8. Examine the reordered list, realizing that these are all the things you want to do for the rest of your life. (It is amazing that — for many people — this list will not change much over the years.)

4

The Alchemy of Transforming Dreams into Concrete Goals

The next afternoon, Dr. Magie handed back to John the list of his dreams. "All right. As I said, take your list and renumber the items in the order of their honest significance to you. Do not prioritize them according to how you think you should feel about them, or how your parents, wife, therapist, or minister might think you should. Remember, this is your game, so put the list in the order the young boy inside you would honestly like to follow if he had the freedom to choose. Putting your dreams in the order of their importance to you is very important. It tells your mind that you truly are getting serious about trying to accomplish your own dreams and not the imposed dreams of others. This is a step into the kind of integrity it will take to reach your large goals."

The doctor told John that he wanted him to try to do this reordering in ten minutes. "Putting new numbers by every item on the list according to their according to their attraction to you. Don't be a perfectionist. If you can't decide whether something should be fifth or sixth on the list, just put one number down and then the other. This is not science; it's intuition. It doesn't matter which is fifth and which is sixth. Just choose one, and then pick the next number to be reordered. The idea is to work fast and trust the process. Go!"

Noticing that John wasn't quite finished in ten minutes, Dr. M. said, "John, it's working. The locked door of your unconscious mind is cracked open now. Some very important information has already come to you. Realize that: relax, and flow with the game. Take a few more minutes to finish reordering your list."

When John had reordered the list, Dr. Magie said, "Rewrite the list on a clean sheet of paper in the new order, and then throw the original list in the trash can." John frowned inquisitively, to which Dr. Magie replied, "It's surprising, but when you go to the trouble to reorder and then rewrite the whole list, your inner wisdom says, 'Good Lord, we're really going to do it this time. He's actually planning to accomplish these dreams!'" John shook his head but did as he was told, genuinely surprised to find that the simple act of destroying the original list and focusing on the reordered one gave him a strong, but unexpected feeling of accomplishment as well as hope. As he examined the rewritten, reordered list, he felt that his life was already more ordered. The prioritized list was:

PEACE OF MIND —
IN ORDER OF IMPORTANCE

1. New Vocation — accomplishment in a business I could enjoy

2. Being loved by my wife and son

3. Health: getting in shape physically

4. Financial security — paying off debts, including the house

5. Spend more time alone with Carol, doing fun things

6. Being a better father — spend more one-on-one time with Wil

7. Go as a family to Disney World

8. Build a cabin for our family on a fishing lake

9. Stature in the community — helping community grow in healthy ways

10. Time by myself

11. Non-business time with friends

12. Trips to Paris and London

13. Four weeks' vacation per year

14. Taking some three-day weekends

15. Visit Tahiti

16. Visit Alaska and fish for salmon

17. Find out how I foul up my life and relationships so I can quit doing it

18. Find ways to improve my emotional life

"Okay," John said, "I've reordered the list. I'm fascinated by what we've uncovered, but how does that change what's going on in my life now?"

"John, by your own admission, your reality — your present life — is flat, and you are depressed. You've lost touch with the kind of creative energy and focus that brings the meaning and activities of life together." Dr. Magie shook his head. "I'm not telling you that dreaming automatically causes happiness, but I am saying that dreaming points the way to happiness and can bring new hope. I'm about to show you how turning your dreams into specific goals can kindle — or as you Americans put it — jump-start your motivational energy and launch you on a journey that can lead to fulfillment — and in your case, peace of mind!"

Dr. Magie stopped and thought a few seconds. Then he said, "Would you like to stop and have a cup of tea?" John was surprised to realize that he really did not want to. He wanted to move on. "That's a change," he said to himself, but he realized the older man might want a break.

As they stepped outside with their tea, John shivered. He hadn't gotten used to the alpine chill of early evening. Looking down at the sparkling water of the lake below, hundreds of feet down the mountain, John was surprised that he noticed a number of details. Ordinarily, he just saw the overall picture and then got back to the task at hand. That evening, his eyes followed a fishing boat sailing for shore almost as if it were a tiny white snail crawling on the blue and silver of the lake's surface.

Back inside, Dr. Magie picked up where they had left off. "When you begin translating dreams into specific goals, John, you are changing the internal reality of your life. You are beginning to put *living contemporary* people and dreams with energy attached to them in motion on your inner stage. You are preparing to move from fantasy into the objective world, preparing to step out of your stalemate and realize your dreams.

"The next step — isolating and investigating goals — is how dreams are translated out of the shadowy, semi-articulate language of speculation into the crisp real world of behavior, building materials, and relationships. In the private world of 'day-dreaming,' one can't fail. But when the dreams 'go public' as the dreamer attempts to achieve the goals, the fear of failure can suddenly drop into one's mind full-blown. That's why so many people continue to be only dreamers all their lives. Actually going for specific dreams can be frightening. But at the onset of the fear of failure, the increased motivational energy, sense of challenge and feeling of adventure released through this process can make all the difference as to whether one moves forward toward fulfillment, or stays stuck."

"Hmm," John said, remembering all the times he had made plans to leave Carol's family's company, only to stop when the fears jumped on him, fear of failure or of being rejected by Carol's family or by Carol herself. "That makes sense," John responded. "How do I pick a goal and work on it?"

"Choose the one on your list that seems most important to you personally. Don't pick one you think you *should* choose, but one that excites you and brings happy images at the thought of your accomplishing that dream."

John was very thoughtful, and then admitted, "It's strange, but even though I can make decisions fast about the business, I am having trouble choosing something 'just for myself.'" After some more reflection, John finally said, "My first choice is 'New vocation: accomplishment in a business I could enjoy.' But what do I do now, to find a 'right' new vocation so I won't become a 'successful misfit' again?"

"Take a clean sheet of paper and write at the top: 'New Vocational Possibilities,' Dr. Magie instructed. "On this page, list as quickly as you can all the vocations that pop into your mind that you think you might like to do for your life's work. You have ten minutes."

He wrote quickly and the time went by fast. John came up with a list which, when reordered, was as follows:

NEW VOCATIONAL POSSIBILITIES

1. Commercial realtor in Denver — putting together deals to build hotels, condos and shopping centers

2. Consultant concerning operating a business

3. Stock broker; investment counselor

4. Consultant for new product development

5. Public relations man for a large corporation

6. Operations manager for a large corporation

7. New business developer for a large corporation

As John looked at the reordered list, he realized with unexpected certainty that becoming a commercial realtor was exactly what he wanted to be. As he came to that conclusion, a flood of facts came to him. The business climate was good in Denver after several bad years, and all the signs were that the real estate business was coming back on track. He also had heard positive news from a friend in Orlando, Florida, who was doing very well in the commercial real estate business. John's mind began to race. He knew a number of the leaders in Denver's business community. He could even see in his mind's eye some choice locations that might develop into major deals. The sky was the limit!

He made notes and then showed them to Dr. M., who smiled and asked, "Where do you suppose those ideas came together from?"

John laughed then, "Don't tell me 'from my inner wisdom.' But it is remarkable how this process is working for me. I can't imagine why I couldn't see this by myself, before I came here."

"Actually, it's not unusual. Many people have a dream they can't afford to see because it is so strong that they would have to risk everything that represents their present security and social identity to pursue it. And before awakening the dream as a possibility, they don't have a strong enough desire to consider it seriously. Most people will not change until the pain and restlessness caused by not pursuing the dream is greater that the fear of what might be lost. Before you came here, you could not risk that kind of change. But after your 'heart pain,' you were ready to look and see what was possible. Just now, you learned an important secret about your inner wisdom: The power and insights often come after the commitment is made to risk changing."

John felt energized. Gone was the molasses-like mumbling and morose expression. He was alive, sharp, and energetic! "Well, however it happened, I know that if I can work it out, being a real estate developer is exactly what I want to do as the vocational part of my life. What's next? Do I 'just do it,' as the ads say?"

Dr. M. laughed. "No, John. Before even making a commitment to accomplish your goal, there are some things to examine to see how your proposed goal 'fits' you."

"Fits me?"

"Yes, before moving forward it's often helpful to do two things. First, in order to see how this vocational goal relates to the other dreams you have for your life, let's look at your earlier prioritized list of goals again. This time we want to see how many of your other life goals are compatible with your being a commercial real estate entrepreneur. In other words, how many of the items on your list of dreams do you think you could possibly accomplish if you were a commercial real estate developer?

So John and Dr. Magie talked at length about how many of John's other goals he could imagine meeting if he were to become a commercial realtor and developer. Finally John whistled aloud, "Why, I could meet them all!"

"That's not surprising. The inner wisdom you are tapping is a reflection of what you are as a whole person inside, including those parts of you that got buried along the way. Those buried parts were threatening to certain relationships or to an adapted image of who you felt you had to be to gain approval. Now, to see why you have been so frustrated, look at the list of your life goals in light of your present job. How do you feel when you are doing it? How many of your life goals to bring peace of mind that you listed can you imagine accomplishing if you keep working in your father-in-law's company, as you are now?"

After a few minutes of studying his reordered list, John looked surprised. "Why, I could hardly do any. Maybe three things on the whole list. I am completely bogged down and can't get away to do much of anything for myself without major conflict. Even though I don't like our business, I am almost completely absorbed in making it successful. Maybe I have a need to show Carol's dad that I'm as smart as he is — or maybe show *my own* dad, even though he's dead. Whatever it is, I've spent most of my time obsessing on things other than the goals I've just discovered for my life. Frankly, I quit 'dreaming' altogether years ago. I haven't had time or energy for much of anything but work."

John stopped talking and a thoughtful silence filled the room. Then he said to Dr. M., "Maybe shutting out the dreams and messages from my inner wisdom is how I got so burned out and depressed — along with working at a job that drains me of passion for life rather than producing it." John began to feel a surge of hope, but stopped himself and said bluntly, "Dr. M., is this real?"

Dr. Magie raised his eyebrows and nodded slowly, as John asked him, "When you first did this, how long was it before you knew that you were dealing with the authentic dreams of your life?"

Dr. Magie smiled. "I'm not sure. All I know is that during the months, and in some cases, years, following the creation of a list like this, neither I, nor most people I've led through this process, have had to change the list more than ten percent. That's strong empirical evidence that using this process uncovers things of lasting importance to the dreamer. It has worked out that way for many people.

"Besides, most of us who have used this approach very long have found we come to know intuitively when we are doing the "right thing," the thing that is congruent with who we discover we truly are be- coming. The crucial thing right now is for you to know that, whatever you discover about the feasibility of your being a commercial real es- tate developer, you have truly begun an incredible and life-enhancing adventure!"

John nodded his head, smiling. He realized at one level that this could be some sort of illusory experience, but it was the first time he could recall having a deep awareness of congruence, of beginning a whole new chapter of his life that had his own name on it. If this were true, he had at last uncovered what he wanted to do with his life. He had a vocational goal, and he saw clearly and specifically what his personal life goals were as well. He understood how his new vocational goal related to the other life goals he felt would bring him peace of mind.

Suddenly, John turned to Dr. Magie. "Just a minute, Dr. M., this is too easy. Life just can't be this easy."

"Eh bien, mon ami, I did not say this would be easy. I said it is *simple.* Once you start moving toward accomplishing your dreams, you will have to do a lot of hard work, and overcome more resistances than you can imagine at this point. The difference is that when you are awakening something that comes from the wisdom of your own deep inner self, you will likely receive a great influx of positive energy, of passion, and confidence to help overcome the fears and doubts. This energy and passion will make the work seem easier than it is, because you will be happy and drawn to finish what you are doing.

John looked at his list again. Although he was skeptical about how comprehensive his list was, he realized with awe that for the first time ever, the things he wanted to do for the rest of his life might be were before him in plain view. He had been given a game plan for the rest of his life, a kind of checklist to avoid getting involved in unrelated ventures that might be attractive but could sabotage his real life goals. Here at last was a way to say no to things that were not his to do.

Seeing his dreams materialize in the light of his consciousness from the murkiness of his unconscious, dreams to be achieved in the real world that had the marks of reality all over them was eerie. However, John also realized that Dr. M. was right: accomplishing the clearly defined goals from his dream list would not be easy. The question was, were they *possible — do-able —* by him?

Dr. M. looked at John thoughtfully and said, "John, I know this is a lot to assimilate. Why don't you relax this evening and let your feelings catch up with your mind." He looked at his watch. "You can still make a late dinner."

As John left Magie's home and walked down the shadowy, deserted cobblestone street to the hotel, he felt as if he were a boy again, intercepting a pass, weaving through the iron street lampposts, as if they were opposing tacklers, as he tried not to step out of bounds on the edges of the circles of light they etched on the cobblestones. He was happy, really happy. He was also out of breath when he reached the hotel, and found himself humming Carol's favorite song on their honeymoon, "In the Mood."

5

The Plan:
Hologram or Blueprint?

~~~~~~~~

The ancient grandfather clock chimed five as Dr. M. opened the front door. The smell of pine logs burning was pungent and almost palpable. "Come in, John, come in." He stepped back and gestured toward the study door. "Did you have a good day?"

John took off his coat and sat in one of the deep maroon leather chairs beside the yellow and blue flames dancing in the stone fireplace. "Well, yes — sort of a bad news/good news day. The bad news was I couldn't reach Carol last night or today, and my secretary couldn't locate her either. I was disappointed, to say the least, but I sent an e-mail telling her I was very excited about our future and would call her after our session tonight. The good news is I think I saw a new world yesterday, one in which I . . . belong somehow. And I want to share that with Carol, because I think she might be able to find her 'place' there too."

After a slight pause, John looked up at his mentor and said, "Dr. M., how can I find out whether or not my new vocational dream is feasible without quitting my job or spending a great deal of money?"

The old physician smiled as the American bypassed any further amenities and came right to the point. "All right, John, let's begin to explore that right now. For most business people, the investigative process I am going to show you is the most surprising and useful aspect of the whole dreaming process — a non-technical way of evaluating if a dream or business proposal to see if it is feasible.

"First, write your vocational dream, Becoming a Commercial Realtor, at the top of a clean piece of paper. By doing this, you are taking the first step in changing the ephemeral mental vision of your dream into a concrete goal that can be evaluated and accomplished in the world of actuality. In this process, what I'm calling a 'goal' is a concretized dream described on paper."

John obediently wrote at the top of a clean page:

Vocational Goal: To Become a Commercial Realtor in Denver — Putting Together Deals to Build Hotels, Condominiums, and Shopping Centers

"Good. Now take ten minutes and list everything you can think of that you will need to know before you can open an office as a commercial realtor in Denver."

In ten minutes John listed:

1. Talk to Bill Castle in Denver and find out what is involved in setting up a commercial real estate business (what kind of experience I'd need, etc.).

2. Call Charlie Sawyer in Orlando, where things appear to be going strong.

3. Check on what kind of financing I'll need after I finish this investigation.

4. Have a preliminary visit with banker friend, Ron Townsend.

5. Check on the commercial real estate market and financial climate of the commercial real estate business at this time in the U.S. and in Denver.

6. See about feasibility of selling my stock in the Latner Company.

7. Find out if I could apprentice with Bill or someone else some way. Are there short graduate level courses or seminars for prospective commercial real estate developers?

8. See an attorney to determine under what sort of entity we should operate: corporation, limited partnership, full partnership, individual proprietorship, etc. Get costs and tax consequences of doing each.

9. Real estate license or other credentials: requirements, costs, time involved to acquire.

10. Office space, equipment, employees (secretary, accountant, etc.).

11. Other equipment and information: truck, computers, plats, city development maps, etc.

12. Financial requirements and resources:

    a. Add total estimated start-up costs (from individual costs of each item investigated). Add "screw up fudge-factor" for errors.

    b. Find a creative business accountant and tax attorney experienced in commercial real estate.

    c. Determine our personal financial needs:

        (1) Draw up a personal budget for a year by examining last year's personal financial records to determine how much we spent on each area of our lives; then estimate how much we could cut expenses and how much income we'll need per month for next year.

        (2) Determine how much income we can take from interest and stock/retirement income, etc.

    (3) Could we take out a second mortgage on our house?

    (4) Could we borrow against the company stock? How much?

    (5) How much could I expect to earn the first year in the commercial real estate business?

13. Talk all this over with Carol, telling her about Dr. M. and the process.

14. Ask each of the people I talk with (above) to suggest someone else to whom I should talk, and what else I need to check.

"Stop," Dr. Magie said, "Your ten minutes are up, John. What you have just begun is the start of translating your dreams into reality. Look over your list and see if anything else occurs to you."

As John did this, he was surprised at how many specific details he had listed about starting his new business.

"Now," Dr. M. instructed further, "In ten minutes, renumber the items on the list according to the order in which you want to investigate them, and when you've done that, discard the first list."

When John had finished, Dr. M. handed him a loose-leaf notebook and some lined paper. Then he said, "This next step provides a concrete, manageable way to structure your investigation, which otherwise could become a chaotic, unfocused nightmare. I want you to write each of the fourteen items from your new, renumbered investigation list at the top of a separate page. Then you can make notes and jot down questions about each item to be evaluated on the appropriate page, adding more pages when necessary.

"When you put these pages in order in your loose-leaf notebook, you will have compiled the skeleton for a book titled *The Feasibility of Establishing a Commercial Real Estate Business in Denver, Colorado.* Your list of fourteen things to investigate will be the beginning of the table of contents, and each chapter title will be an item on the list, about which you will gather specific data, including the financial requirements related to each aspect of your business extended to the right hand column of each page. In this way, John, if you do the investigation diligently, and the results are positive, when you finish your investigation, you will have organized a financially viable plan that a banker will take seriously. If you are conscientious and thorough, you may well know more about the feasibility of starting a commercial real estate business in Denver than almost anyone else in Denver, including people who've been in the business for some time." Dr. M. smiled at his protégé.

John had taken in everything Dr. M. said, looking up from his notes with an expression both incredulous and cynical. "I see how I can take this list of questions and others that will be revealed during the investigation and find out all I need to know about opening this business.

But what I'm really amazed about is this: How can it be possible that it took only ten minutes to discover my dreams and another short period to come up with almost all I will need to begin a course of action to evaluate the feasibility of starting a viable and complex business? There is nothing in my education or experience that says this could happen."

"It does sound impossible, John. But remember your inner wisdom knew of your longtime but unconscious interest in this business. The fact is that in ten minutes, your inner wisdom, like a computer, collected from your lifetime store of knowledge and experience what you've assimilated and already know, and pointed you to what you need to know to at least begin evaluating your goal. Then it delivered to you a comprehensive vision of many of the important aspects of a startup business, couched in terms of specific questions you particularly would want to ask. So what we have is a preliminary action plan for investigating a substantial venture.

"The speed and focusing in this way are not magic. In fact, becoming conscious of what questions need to be answered about almost any proposed action, and prioritizing them for a concrete evaluation can become a normal process of your ongoing business as you learn ways to listen to and trust your inner wisdom. The resistance you feel about believing in this process is common. It's difficult to believe one could dive to the heart of important questions about life and its problems in a few minutes, but that's because most people have not been educated to value intuitive thinking or to understand, access, or even believe in the viability — or existence of — your own personal inner wisdom. Most of us have been trained that only cognitive, logical processes and theories are viable means of evaluation.

"Our ten-minute game allowed you to suspend your disbelief long enough to get concrete, usable information from your inner source of wisdom, and if you had known less than you do or more, your questions would still have started at the front edge of *your* knowledge. That's why the process works for both sophisticated people and beginners in the any field. The leaps we can make with an educated intuition may indeed seem out of this world, as they say. But this rather incredible experience you just had of uncovering and organizing information in the evaluating stage may reinforce your willingness later to keep going and implement your business dream in the face of difficulties.

"Even with all the scientific investigations of neurologists and psychologists, our understanding of how to utilize the creative potential of the intuitive way of knowing has been left, I believe, almost completely untapped."

"But," John said, "why don't brilliant people use the intuitive method presenting truth?"

"Ah, but they do. It's just that because people are educated to trust only the cognitive, theoretical methods, they don't notice when great men and women use the intuitive methods to get things changed."

"Who's done that — used intuitive methods to change people's thinking?"

"Well, two who come to mind at once are Sigmund Freud and Jesus Christ. Freud used a series of case histories — stories — to support his conclusions rather than the current theories about the mind. And Jesus used intuitive stories — parables — rather than the theory of law. But as strong as both teachings were, the resistance of the cognitive thinkers was *enormous!*"

John, I'm not really sure how the ten-minute game does what it does. But I have learned through a great deal of experience, that the process the game sets in motion can and does work for people whose intuitive minds have not been too badly bruised or starved by an overemphasis on theoretical scientific approaches to problem solving. For some people these simple ways of thinking will become part of a different way of examining and solving problems in all aspects of life and relationships. However, for those people who cannot suspend their disbelief long enough to take these seemingly simple steps, this approach will continue to seem impossible, and even naïve.

"It may be that the ten-minute game 'distracts' what I have called the censor, that stubborn inner guardian who keeps us from accessing our unconscious mind to get information we need. Sometimes, as you have experienced, when the door is cracked, the precise information the seeker needs to know practically jumps out on paper. Over time, with practice, the inner wisdom can begin to guide one — in an incredibly short time — to more simple, reasonable solutions to all kinds of complex problems. As we learn how to track our inner wisdom, we begin to make discoveries that can lessen our fears, help us to relate with people more realistically, change our attitudes, and bring pleasure to whatever work we do.

"The process may appear trivial to an educated, philosophical mind, because the game is so simple, like child's play. How could truly important information come so quickly and easily? But as you will see, much of the information you have discovered is not only psychologically sound but reality-oriented information tailored specifically for you."

"Wait," John said, "that's part of my question! How can this information be so 'tailored' for me? For instance, in my business planning there are a lot of other questions I could have listed and didn't. The ones I 'perceived' as you say, were the ones I intuitively know are the right questions for me to ask."

"John, I know we are getting into some deep ideas, but I believe our inner wisdom is a sort of gathering and storage place for information that is particularly relevant and applicable to each person. For example, when Mme. Magie and I both read the same book, she gets things out of it that I miss completely, and I make what I consider to be exciting discoveries she doesn't even notice. Her inner wisdom abstracts and gathers what she needs, and mine stores what I need. In other words, each one of us is given a private storage place for that particular part of any piece of information or event most pertinent to us. That's why your dream list describes dreams that are important to your intrinsic self. Your dreams are expressions of your own inner wisdom, things that you may not even be aware of until, or unless, they are revealed to you in the dreaming process."

"Good Lord, Dr. M., it sounds like you are saying that the reason the inner wisdom I am discovering seems so usable, so 'tailored for me,' is because my brain somehow abstracted and predigested it all for me from all the volumes of things I've read and hundreds of experiences I've had. That's about the most amazing thing I ever heard! How did you ever figure that out?"

Dr. M. threw back his head and laughed. "Well, John, I'd like to say it was a brilliant idea I conceived, but in fact discovering this was accidental. A few years ago I counseled someone I'll call Alice, a very indecisive twenty-one-year-old young woman. I tried for months to help her learn to make decisions. Although Alice was extremely intelligent, she was withdrawn, non-communicative, and thirty-five pounds overweight. Her parents had sent her to me, because she could not decide about taking even the smallest action. Apparently, her family made virtually all her decisions.

"Finally, after a number of sessions, in which she was listless and evidenced almost no imagination or creativity, I was stymied. Following an intuitive hunch, I decided to ask her if she would be willing to play a simple game with me. It occurred to me that if she, on her own, could discover a dream to which she was attracted, she might be able to make a decision to consider trying to accomplish it. I told her only that we were going to play a game about finding one's dreams and goals. I limited her to ten minutes to help her suspend her disbelief that she could ever make an important decision. To my surprise, the ten-minute dream discovery game immediately triggered Alice's enthusiasm.

"But Alice's reaction while making the dream list was different from anything I could have predicted. Almost at once I realized that something about Alice herself changed in a way I couldn't understand. Alice began writing quickly, and it appeared she wasn't just playing a game to attempt to fish ideas out of her imagination or her memory. To me, it seemed as if she had made some sort of intimate contact with someone or some source I couldn't see — from which a flood of specific information was coming.

"When the ten-minute period ended and Alice had finished her dream list, she looked up and beamed. I don't know what I expected, but I certainly did not expect to see her come alive before my eyes. And when I read her list, I could hardly believe some of the dream-goals she came up with. I can remember a number of them vividly. Some were vocational. One dream was to go back to school and prepare to become a teacher, to teach sixth grade or to counsel girls in trouble. There were several trips she wanted to take: to Paris to sightsee, and to New York to see musicals, shop at Bergdorf-Goodman's, and see a professional basketball game.

"But as surprising as these were, what fascinated me most — and that is why I'm telling you this, John — was that several of her dreams had to do with specific things she wanted to change about herself. Things like get a physical examination to see why she was so tired and listless, get into some kind of weight loss and exercise program to help her develop some self-respect, tell her mother she was sorry she had been such a bitch the last couple of years.

"The fact that Alice uncovered in this brief time what she needed to do in order to fulfill her other dreams was a striking surprise to me. Since I had not anticipated Alice's reactions, I watched carefully the way the ten-minute exercise changed her subsequent progress in our counseling and I paid attention to what developed in Alice's life.

"As she trusted in, committed to, and acted on what had come to her, she no longer felt alone inside. The fact that she could make decisions about her life, gave Alice the courage to move away from the control of her parents. The happenstance of my asking Alice to play a game with me was amazing good fortune, but I had no idea we would discover a process that could help many other people."

John was silent. He had never considered there might be a source of valuable, usable knowledge and guidance inside himself that he could access and apply to the real world. After a few minutes of reflection, he looked up at Dr. M. and asked quietly, "What's next? I feel like you've dropped me on the yellow brick road without a map. I need some guidance!"

With a twinkle in his eye Dr. M. replied, "One of the secrets of accessing inner wisdom is that you have to move — take some steps — before you get guidance, John. Even God can't guide a stationary object. Tomorrow we'll look at some possible next steps you can take so you can go home and move toward evaluating your new adventure."

As he walked back to the hotel, John felt better than he had in years, as if he had at last begun a crazy adventure that was his own and not his father's — or his father-in-law's. He couldn't wait to call Carol!

EXERCISE TWO
Steps for Changing a Dream into a Specific Goal
and Investigating Its Feasibility

1. Write the first dream you want to explore at the top of a clean sheet of paper.

2. In ten minutes, list all the things you can think of that you'll have to know or do before you can accomplish or clarify that dream goal.

3. Rewrite this list of tasks on a clean sheet of paper in the order in which you want to investigate the items. Discard the original task list.

4. Put each item on the list to be checked at the top of a separate page in a loose-leaf notebook. Number the pages to correspond to the numbers on your reordered list. Put in extra pages on which to note your findings behind the page for each item.

5. Work through the reordered list by checking with people who have appropriate expertise or knowledge.

6. As you finish talking to each person you check with, you may want to ask if there are additional people they would suggest you talk to about any of the other items about which you think they may have expertise or contacts.

7. When you finish checking on each item, you can get cost estimates and record an estimated cost for each item in the right hand column of each page.

8. As time goes on, go through steps 1–4 above for each dream on your list you want to investigate to help determine its feasibility.

6

A Mouse in the Punch Bowl?

John felt like an excited teenager filled with hope and hubris who couldn't wait to share his dream with his sweetheart bride. The minute he rushed into the lobby, he placed a call to Denver in the phone booth. As he waited for the overseas connections, John's mind was filled with a kaleidoscope of glittering images of successfully completed shopping centers, of getting off a plane with Carol on a Bermuda vacation, of a cabin on a small fishing lake in the Rockies. And he wanted to blurt out the wonder of what he'd learned about the inner wisdom, and how to discover what was really important in life — and accomplish it! But when Carol didn't answer any of the three numbers he had for her — including her cell phone — John felt his excitement change to disappointment and then concern. "What if something has happened to Carol? But everyone knows how to reach me in Glion?" Then John felt anger rise from his chest to his face. Where the hell was she? This was not like her at all to be gone two days in a row and not call. Then John remembered her cold eyes and — her silent treatment — looking straight ahead when she drove him to the airport. "Maybe she has stepped across a line and doesn't care anymore." He knew he was being melodramatic, but he felt confused and deserted. Then, standing there in the old phone booth, he recalled something he had said after Carol locked him out of the bedroom the night before he went for his check up, "Maybe I don't care either."

John stepped out of the phone booth and shook his head to clear his thinking. He felt depressed, drained and lonely as he walked down the hall toward the dining room. He needed a drink. Suddenly he was aware of the loud happy hour noises coming from the small crowded bar ten feet ahead. He stopped and looked over the swinging doors. An accordion player was holding forth, playing and leading a few customers singing, in a vain attempt to penetrate the swirling French conversations and laughter.

The scene reminded John of a happy hour at the country western bar near his office. He smiled and pushed the door open.

After two double Scotches at the bar while observing the familiar but indecipherable Saturday night conviviality, John felt the knot of anger and fear in his chest melting. He bantered with the bartender, Paul, who spoke English, and introduced John to Swiss Schnapps. Time disappeared until his stomach reminded him he hadn't eaten since breakfast and he was ravenous. Checking his watch, he saw it was 8:30 and stood to go. Paul said, "The dining room is crowded now." John nodded his thanks, left a slightly excessive tip, but decided to try his luck anyway.

When John stepped into the candlelit dining room, François, the maitre d', saw him from across the room. Smiling broadly, he approached him and said, *"Ah, bon soir, Monsieur Martin.* Herr Bruner and his wife have checked out and the dining room is full, but a woman who speaks excellent English said she would be happy to have you join her as a table companion since the parties at her table have also left today." He raised his eyebrows expectantly, as if he were personally involved in the request, "Would sitting with her be satisfactory?"

Inwardly, John smiled at François's enthusiasm, but his look was serious as he nodded and said, "Yes, François, it is very kind of the lady to offer to share her table and interpret the menu for an easily confused monolingual American."

François led him through the subdued but scintillating musical sound of French dinner conversations, accented with the light bell-like tinkle of silver touching china. The Schnapps and Scotch John had in the bar transformed the high-ceilinged dining room: dozens of soft candlelights became magical fireflies lighting a fairy king's hall.

Many of the silver-haired vacationers who filled the room looked up at the handsome American as François navigated the magic chamber of white tables. John, feeling effusive, nodded to one and all.

He thought, "Well, life is so good I can be nice and listen to one lonely old lady for an hour. Besides, maybe she can give me some clues about where to shop for a nice gift for Carol in Montreux." François arrived at a table next to one of the huge lake-view windows, now a black mirror reflecting the dining room, and in his most elegant and polished maitre d' manner, gestured formally at John as if he were a visiting diplomat, "Madame Fontaine, may I present Monsieur Martin from the United States?"

John froze. His dinner partner by the window was one of the most beautiful women he had ever seen. Clear blue eyes, the color of the lake below in the morning sun. Coal-black hair pulled tight into a bun with a diamond-jeweled comb. Her low-cut black dress was severe but in perfect taste, revealing a remarkable, slender figure. She looked to be somewhere between thirty-five and forty-five.

"Bon soir, Monsieur Martin," she said.

After a long pause, John laughed and shook his head, "Forgive me, Madame. I was . . . distracted. It's gracious of you to agree to share your table with someone who obviously has such difficulty speaking."

He could not remember being so surprised — or tongue-tied — in a long time, but since he was also high, he felt no shame or awkwardness about his reaction.

The wine steward brought a bottle of wine, looking unsure as to whom he should present it. Madame Fontaine interceded, "Monsieur Martin, the wine has been brought for me, but of course I cannot drink a whole bottle. Would you rescue me and share it?"

John nodded at the steward, who poured a small amount into his glass. John tested the wine; it was excellent and no doubt expensive. Had he just been 'had' for the check? Not that he cared, but as if she could read his mind, Madame Fontaine quickly apologized. "I hope you'll forgive me if I have put you in an uncomfortable position. You see, the wine was ordered automatically on my behalf. It's . . . a tradition." Caught off guard again, John watched as she wept briefly into her small handkerchief. Obviously chagrined, she shook her head and eventually whispered through her tears, "I'm so sorry. Please forgive me."

"It's all right," was all John could think of to say. Then — "Would you like me to move? I don't want to impose on your privacy."

"No, no, please don't leave. I'm sorry about my emotional outburst. You see, my husband and I came here on our honeymoon twenty years ago. The first night, we discovered this wine, and we loved it." She stopped talking and idly touched the wine bottle with her forefinger. "My husband bought several cases from the young couple who owned the hotel. He asked that it be stored in the hotel wine cellar."

"Each year we've returned on our anniversary to celebrate with our special wine . . . until this year. Before he died in January, my husband requested that I come one last time to drink our wine." Straightening in her chair as she tried to control her emotion, the lovely widow unexpectedly drained her glass and said to John. "My behavior is inexcusable; I have imposed upon your kindness and spoiled your evening. I thought I could handle this by myself but it seems I was mistaken." She looked squarely into John's eyes, "I was wrong to use you in that way; I hope you will forgive my presumption."

John saw the pain and sadness in her eyes behind her bravado and his heart went out to her. Although warning bells were going off inside his head, he responded softly, "On the contrary, I feel honored to share this important time with you."

He could see how vulnerable this very sophisticated woman was — and how tenacious — to fulfill her dead husband's request. As they sat in silence, the reflection of the candle flame in the window was the only movement in the table-sized, private space they shared. By the time dinner arrived, John felt himself strongly attracted to this mysterious dinner companion. He wanted to hold her in his arms and comfort her, he wanted to make love to her. Ashamed of his disloyalty

to Carol at some level, and at the idea of taking advantage of this griev-
ing woman's vulnerability, he cursed himself as a voice deep inside him
whispered, "Go back to your room and call Carol now." But he didn't
move and instead, when Madame Fontaine touched her wine glass with
her forefinger, he poured them both more wine.

"Thank you," she said. "My name is Claudette."

"My name is John."

They began to talk about their childhoods, and the schools they attended. Claudette laughed when she said, "I actually went to Vassar for
a few months, when I was seventeen."

"What happened?"

She laughed, "I got homesick and came home. That's when I went to
the University of Paris, where I met my husband-to-be."

"Would you like to talk about him?"

Claudette looked down at her hands in her lap for a moment. John
couldn't remember ever seeing anyone so lovely. Claudette looked up.
"Jean-Pierre is — was — his name. I was eighteen — a very spoiled child,
I'm afraid, having just come home from Poughkeepsie, New York. I was
having a coffee at a sidewalk café with a girlfriend, Marie, when this
tall, strikingly attractive young man sat down alone at a nearby table.
He had black curly hair, dark eyes and appeared to be several years
older than I. Ordering coffee, he began to read the newspaper. He was
so handsome I felt my heart beat faster and my face flush. I was almost
dizzy. It was what we call a *coup de foudre* — literally, a thunderbolt. You
call it love at first sight. I felt foolish being so smitten, but there was no
question in my mind — *this was the man I would marry.*"

Marie, my friend, asked me, "Are you all right?"

"Shh, be quiet. He's coming this way." She turned and saw the man
walking toward us.

Smiling she said, *"Bon soir, Jean-Pierre."*

"I almost fainted as he kissed her hello, and laughing, she said to
him, 'Sit with us. This is my friend Claudette who may expire if you
don't speak to her.'"

He smiled and pulled up a chair, "Since I'm reading for a medical
degree and will soon be a physician, I am against most people's expiring.
Would you care to discuss your symptoms?"

"That was twenty-three years ago; we were almost never apart from
then on. Two years later we were married in Notre Dame. Jean-Pierre
had a medical practice for a few years, and then a fifteen-year business
venture with his grandfather, Blaise Fontaine."

Time passed unnoticed as John and Claudette shared a small world
that she peopled from her past. Eventually she said, "But what about
you, John Martin?"

John told his story of being raised in Colorado and meeting and
marrying Carol — about his plan to enter the commercial real estate

business in Denver. He added, "We have one son now at Stanford University named Wil."

They were both quiet for some seconds, when Claudette said, "We have two children, now almost of age." Claudette faltered and finally could only hold her glass out unsteadily.

John poured what he realized vaguely was the last of a second bottle into their glasses, and with wine-induced boldness, he stood up, glass high in a toast, "Here's to the future of the lovely Claudette. May you awaken from this night of pain, and accomplish your unspoken dreams in the coming new chapter of your life."

She looked at him, blue eyes wavering, and they were both aware that by now they were very drunk. "That's the most beautiful thing I have ever heard: that it might be possible for me to recover and achieve my hidden dreams — in fact, that I might even *have* dreams again someday."

"I believe you can." John said, although at that moment he couldn't remember exactly how that could work. Out of the corner of his eye as he sat down, John saw that the dining room was empty except for the two of them and François, who came over and paused respectfully. "Madame, may I assist you?"

John held up his hand and said as steadily as he could, "No, thank you François, I'll see Madame Fontaine to her room."

François squinted at John and started to object politely. But rising unsteadily to her feet, Claudette held the edge of the table and said, "Thank you, François, for everything, but I shall not require your assistance," smiling warmly at the maitre d', but offering her arm to John.

7

Get Ready, Get Set...

～～～～～～

The next morning, John acknowledged Dr. M.'s warm greeting with a brusque nod as he walked past the old man down the hall and into the study, flopping into the leather chair and staring into the unlit logs stacked in the fireplace.

By the time he got to his room the night before, he had forgotten all about calling Carol and when she called him this morning, she was not happy. John was so hung over that he could hardly hear her through his splitting headache, her icy voice was piercing. "Where the hell were you until after 1:15 a.m.? I called at 9:00 p.m. and 11:30 p.m. and left messages. You said there are no movies in Glion and no TV in the rooms!"

After a hailstorm of further accusatory words, John said, "Carol, I'm sorry, but there are other people here who are trying to sort out their lives. I was helping one of them last night who'd had a death in the family." Having managed to tell almost the truth, John felt some strength and then anger. "Besides, Carol, I've been trying to reach *you* for two days and nights, and no one even knew where you were. Where were *you?*"

Carol was still cool. "John, I *returned* those calls." It had not occurred to him to check at the desk after he couldn't reach Carol the first night. He had just kept making more calls to their home number.

John mumbled, "Well, I didn't remember that they don't have a modern telephone system here. I didn't check at the desk."

In no mood to tell Carol about his new dream of quitting his job and becoming a commercial real estate developer, he certainly did not want to talk about the person he had had dinner with the night before. So he just changed the subject, "The work with Dr. M. is going great. I'll give you a full report tonight."

～～

Absorbed in all these thoughts, John finally looked up from the fireplace and said, "Dr. M., if I quit my job, all hell will break loose for Carol. Her father is given to emotional abuse anyway, and punishment for any serious infraction of his plans could be lethal. Plus, I sat in the hotel dining room and drank wine until late. So I was pretty hung-over when Carol's call came this morning. And it didn't go well."

"I'll tell her about the new vocational dream tonight." Then he switched to his all-business voice. "I'm definitely going ahead with my investigation of the commercial real estate business because I am more convinced than ever that this is the next step for me. That's true even though I already realize it will take a lot of time to do the necessary investigation we came up with yesterday."

Dr. M. nodded slightly, simply listening as he poured John a cup of coffee, and the silence between them grew.

A voice inside his head urged him to tell his mentor what had happened the night before when he had dinner with Claudette, but he could not risk damaging their new relationship, so he went back to his dream search.

"Let me ask you something, Dr. M. What if, after a thorough investigation, it turns out that becoming a commercial realtor is not a feasible choice for me?"

Dr. M. looked at John, got up and lit the fire. "That happens once in a while. Your inner wisdom has no way of telling what the current business climate is going to be, only what might be suitable for you, according to what you have read or experienced in the past. Because the conscious communication with this wise inner part of yourself is new, you will inevitably get some garbled receptions at first. We can talk about the source of that confusion later, if it becomes necessary. If your first choice is not feasible after a careful investigation, I think you can still be grateful: the investigation will have saved you from another depressive period of being a 'successful misfit' in the wrong business. In that event, you could investigate your second choice of being a business consultant."

"What if I investigate all the choices and none of them is feasible?"

"Hmm, that happened only once in my experience with this process. When I was in medical school in Boston, a man I'll call Harry came to me. He had a good job which he didn't dislike, and at which he was doing very well. He worked for a growing company owned by his first cousin's family, but when he turned forty he became depressed. He confided to me that for the past six years he had been tormented by the fact that he hadn't left his job and followed a dream he had of going to seminary to become an ordained minister. When he came to see me, Harry was at a crisis point and was miserable.

"I asked him where he would go to seminary, if he went. With no hesitation he said, 'There is only one place I would go: Harvard Divinity School that's part of the dream.'

"As it happened I knew the registrar there, the father of a classmate of mine in medical school. So I said, 'I think I can help you' and was able to make an appointment for him to talk to the registrar that afternoon. The following day when I saw him, Harry looked relaxed and happy, leading me to ask optimistically, 'You got accepted?'"

"He laughed and said, 'No, as a matter of fact, the registrar implied that with my grades, I couldn't get into Harvard if my father built the school a new building.'

"So having checked out what he thought he wanted to do, Harry found it wasn't feasible, but in simply *doing* the *investigating*, Harry resolved his nagging guilt about not pursuing what he thought was his true vocation. He was able to stop obsessing about it, and went home and threw himself into his old job with new enthusiasm.

"Once he'd checked out his other dream and had *chosen* the business he was in, Harry came to love his career in business. It was sad he'd spent six years in misery which could have been avoided with one simple phone call."

"So whether your dreams are feasible or not, the point is that what you learn while you're checking them out can bring you a new perspective and a new approach to whatever you do next."

Looking at the list of questions he'd made before the session, John said, "I'm pretty convinced I can accomplish my number one goal of being a commercial realtor, or if not, at least one of my other vocational goals. But once I get started and really focus on my work, it's always hard for me to remember my other priorities, like some of my family goals on the list I showed you. How can I keep my non-vocational goals in view?"

"Good question, John. I discovered some simple ways to keep my primary vocational/financial goals moving and help the unconscious mind work on my personal goals at the same time."

"What ways?"

"One thing is to take a loose-leaf notebook and put together a dream book."

John held up his hand, and laughed. "A dream book?"

The older man smiled. "The motivational part of the human mind seems to respond to pictures more strongly than to written words. So I found pictures in magazines or travel literature that represented each of my dreams. In your case, the pictures might be of beautiful commercial real estate developments, of places you want to visit, of a family spending time together, of the sort of cabin you want to build on a lake, or of working with the city council — something inspiring that represents each of your goals. I have a separate page for each dream, and I attach actual pictures that represent the dream. One woman, whose first dream was personal financial freedom, cut out a picture of a magnificent American bald eagle gliding over a mountain pass, and pasted it on the page titled, 'Personal Financial Freedom.' So you can be creative with this dream book and the images in it. In fact, every morning I take five minutes to look through my dream book and it's surprising how many times just looking through those pictures of my own 'accomplished' dreams gives me a palpable surge of motivation and confidence to move forward."

John nodded, "What about when you're traveling?"

"I've found it helpful to list all my prioritized goals on several index cards and carry these cards in my wallet wherever I go. Reading through the goals at least once a day, aloud if possible, takes only a few seconds, but for me, it is a powerful motivator and keeps me conscious of my other personal dreams. When I'm working at home I take a few minutes when I wake up or just before I retire to simply look through my dream book and visualize my dreams as being already accomplished. These small habits fix all my goals firmly in my mind, so they become a part of who I am and what I do. The constant presence of my dreams in my everyday life helps me remember to do what I can every day to fulfill them, and reviewing or revisualizing my goals every day sends a message to my unconscious mind that this is our agenda. As I've continued that discipline my inner wisdom often sends me unsolicited hints about how to reach my dreams even faster."

"I'm sorry, Dr. M., but that sounds a little simplistic." John's hangover made him more impatient than usual. "How has doing these things you're suggesting made any *practical* difference in your life?"

"Hmm, well, of course I don't know what the specific effect of any one of these practices is, but when I visualize my goals every day I have noticed that they seem to 'attract' solutions or actions as I go about concentrating on other things. For instance, in my dream book I put a picture of a family being happy together in a beautiful vacation spot. I found by looking at that picture every day, I thought about my own family more — what they needed and wanted — and began to do more thoughtful things for them and be with them more — without even trying to change my old habits. One morning after spending time looking at that family picture, I planned a spontaneous surprise vacation trip for our family on the Riviera, which ended up being a huge success for all of us. For me, looking at those pictures was a significant part of my doing that."

"How do you keep from getting overcommitted with projects and invitations to do other things?" John challenged the doctor.

The older man laughed, "Well, keeping a list of my dreams and focusing on them regularly has not cured my compulsive nature, but it has curbed my lifelong habit of making too many commitments. When anyone approaches me with a proposal that demands a substantial commitment of time or money, I tell the person I'll consider the proposal and get back to him. Then, when I can be alone, I study my dream list on the index cards before I reply. If the proposed commitment is not going to move me closer to one or more specific goals on that list, I turn the proposal down without further investigation.

"It's incredibly helpful to know what is mine to do — and what is not. If I accomplish the goals on my dream list, I'll have a serene and happy life. If I try to do too many other things — even if they're attractive, good things — I get overwhelmed very quickly."

"But what if the interrupting proposal has a high probability of making a substantial profit?"

"Of course, you can always take on the new commitment if you want to. But more often than people realize, it is precisely the good and attractive activities or projects people get involved with that are unrelated to their major goals that turn out to be the cause of their failure to achieve their major dreams. By having a list of everything I want to do before I die, I have become a much more decisive person. I have saved much time, and reduced the agony of indecision.

"Of course, I always try to stay open to additional opportunities that might be a part of my life, but by looking through this list day after day and taking time to listen to my inner wisdom, I've come to trust that the list truly represents my real vocational and personal purposes, so I try to remember at all times that I will be very happy if I accomplish just those goals that are already on my list. I can always add a goal that begins and continues to flutter around in my mind when I am looking at my dream book or my list, but truthfully, I haven't felt the need to add very many.

"A friend who has discovered his goals and used his list to consider new proposals once told me that making a few big decisions and commitments has saved him from having to make dozens of small decisions about other possible opportunities. I find that true for me as well.

"The second advantage to reading my dream book every day is that my unconscious begins to send its specific agenda to my conscious mind. One of my goals was to visit Sweden, mostly because my college roommate was from Sweden and talked about it all the time. I'd had opportunities to go, but it had never been convenient. Then, about six months after making my dream book, I received an invitation to do a series of lectures in Stockholm. At the time, I was busy, but when I looked at my list and realized that here was a chance to fulfill my life's dreams of doing more public speaking as well as visiting Stockholm, I said yes, and the result was my wife and I had a wonderful trip to Sweden, which I probably wouldn't have had if I hadn't been in touch with my dreams."

Dr. M. stopped a minute to let his words sink in and then asked, "How do you feel right now about your future?"

A picture of an angry Carol flashed in John's mind. "You mean my vocational future?" Dr. M. frowned, but nevertheless nodded.

"My vocational choice seems like a feasible adventure," John told him. "Just deciding to check the possibility of being a commercial realtor feels as if a trusted relative of mine has given me a map of where I want to go. And ideas about this dream have been blossoming like popcorn popping since I decided to investigate the commercial real estate dream. So it's not like daydreaming, because I have concrete tasks to do that you gave me."

"Not quite, John" the old man said, still standing. "I gave you no content or destinations. You discovered what you are going to do by getting in touch with and awakening your own buried dreams. These are all your ideas, John, your dreams!" Walking toward the front door, Dr. M. said, "Since the dreams came from your own inner unconscious, your inner wisdom can give you a more relevant kind of guidance, and," the doctor paused, looking at John directly, "even protection from tempting opportunities and unexpected changes that could sabotage your efforts."

Suddenly alert, John asked, "What do you mean, protection?" in a tone that made Dr. M. stop and turn back.

Looking keenly at John, he said, "As you proceed to actualize dreams that came from your unconscious, you will learn to know and listen to your inner voice as it speaks to you about other areas of your life and relationships that may be disrupted by your change of direction and intense new focus. Although there will be difficulties and perhaps some conflicting and negative messages from people close to you, urging you not to risk, you can learn to win these battles and keep moving — if you have enough desire to risk facing whatever comes up on the way."

As Dr. M. opened the front door, John felt his confidence in the commercial real estate business returning and yet, he also felt somewhere deep within him that he and Carol were not right somehow. John started to dismiss the thought until later, as he had always done, but something stopped him. "Since I'm leaving in the morning, there's . . . something I need to talk to you about what happened last night — before I see Carol." Dr. M. looked at John a few seconds and then nodded and stepped back from the open door.

Two hours later when John came back to the hotel, François was standing by the small front desk wearing his topcoat, beret in hand. "Madame Fontaine left this for you," he said handing John a small envelope, and before John could thank him or give him a tip, François turned and left.

EXERCISE THREE
Making and Using a Dream Book*

1. Title a photo album or loose-leaf notebook "Dream Book."

2. Put a copy of your dream list on page 1.

3. Write each dream at the top of a separate page.

4. Tape a picture or make a drawing that represents your meaning of that dream when accomplished.

5. Each morning or evening, spend a few minutes looking through your dream book. Visualize your dreams as being realized and your enjoying each dream as it becomes real.

---

*If you decide to keep your dream list with you on 3 x 5 cards so you can refer to them daily, you can list all your dreams on one or more cards. Read through the list at least once a day, visualizing each dream as being accomplished, and experiencing your feelings about that.

8

Go!

As he stepped into a cab to take him to the airport, John wondered about the hope he had found and whether he could really become a commercial realtor. He also wondered if his father-in-law would cut Carol and him out of his life if John didn't stay with the family business. The old man was tough and certainly capable of doing that. When he thought about Carol his mind rubber-banded back to the beautiful Claudette. Could he make Carol believe the truth: that his strange evening with Claudette was only an attempt to help her fill an obligation to her dead husband, an attempt that had gotten out of hand? Should he be honest and tell her what happened — and that he was never going to contact Claudette again? But the mental picture of Carol's obsessive jealousy stopped him. He had told Dr. M. about Claudette and his strong attraction to her, and what he could remember about their getting drunk together. Since he had decided never to see her again, the questions about telling Carol seemed academic and unnecessary.

John looked at the small beautiful handwriting on the envelope in his hand. He was tempted to tear it up unread, but then slipped the envelope in his inner jacket pocket. He would consider whether to read the letter after he got on the plane to New York.

As the cab driver transferred his bags from the cog train station, John looked at the brilliant day. He would always be touched by the beauty of the morning sun on Lake Geneva. As they rimmed the shoreline, Claudette popped back into his mind, taking him completely by surprise. He was looking into her eyes as she said, "That's the most beautiful thing I ever heard." And as hard as he tried not to, he kept reliving parts of the evening with her.

He turned his thoughts to the exciting new things in his life. By finding out what his dreams were, he had discovered a positive, doable world, with concrete goals that were authentically his to guide him and spur him on. Now, the depressed, confusing, emotional jungle he'd been in when he arrived in Switzerland had vaporized. He knew the problems were still there, but he wasn't afraid of them now. And he wasn't alone. Dr. M. had stepped into his corner. John read his dream list and focused on his new goals, and he was suddenly happy again. Even the

long security lines at the airport didn't bother him. He spent the waiting time reading through his dream cards and imagining the dreams
being fulfilled. As he thought about what he'd learned, John could imagine his inner wisdom cheering him on — right there in the airport. He
caught himself whistling "Yankee Doodle" as the security guard waved
him through. John shook his head and laughed. At least he could tell
Sam that his prescribed trip to Switzerland had worked: the patient was
certainly no longer bored or depressed.

—ᴍᴍ—

When he was settled in his aisle seat with a cup of coffee, John decided
it would be childish not to read Claudette's letter.

> Dear John Martin:
>
> Thank you, thank you!
>
> You had no way of knowing, but you saved my life last night.
> I had a number of Seconal tablets in my purse and was planning
> to commit suicide by ingesting them with the last glass of wine.
> That's why I was so emotional when you came and listened to
> me. Your understanding presence gave me hope — and saved me."
> John pulled back from the letter and continued reading. "You were
> like sunshine: sensitive, strong and passionate and our time to-
> gether dissolved my fear and pain for a few hours when they were
> overwhelming me. I will never forget your sensitivity, your love.
> Thank you.
>
> I don't want to be presumptuous, but the next time you and
> your family come to Paris, I would be honored to have you come
> to my home for dinner so I can express my gratitude for your help
> to Mrs. Martin and your son.
>
> Gratefully,
Claudette Anton Fontaine
>
> PS: Some months ago I inherited a substantial sum of money, much
> of which must be invested. Would you consider a request to in-
> vest in your new business venture? If so, please let me know what
> the procedure would be; and, if you approve, my attorney will
> contact you.
>
> CAF

9

Dream Killers — and Angels

"What do you mean, you're going to be a commercial real estate developer?" Carol blurted, obviously angry. "We don't have the money to do that!"

"Wait, wait a minute, Carol. I'm sorry I dropped that on you so unexpectedly. But I'm not rushing into this. I've made a plan to check the possibilities carefully before we jump into anything and in fact, I'm exploring this so we can all have a better life. I'd like to show you my plan for checking out the new business."

Carol squinted her eyes and looked at John as if she had never seen him before. Her fears flashed a warning, but she had always wanted him to stand up to her dad, and an inner voice whispered to her, "John really seems different somehow since he got back from Europe. This might be the right thing."

"All right," she said skeptically, "I'll look at your plan. But no promises."

An hour later, Carol marveled at the careful thinking John had done. She looked up at him, tingling feelings dancing across her skin, as she recognized the impulsive cowboy, 'Killer' Martin, once again. The man she had married.

"I can tell how important this is to you, John, so I'll go along with the feasibility study. But we have to come up with the finances to eat — and then there's tuition for Wil's college for one more year. He says he wants to work this summer and start paying us back, as much as he can."

John felt tears in the corners of his eyes when he held her. "Honey, don't worry, we'd have to have those bases covered before I'd consider opening a business. And... I want you to know that I... I've never loved you as much as I do right now."

The next twelve weeks flew by as John checked off the items on his list to investigate his new career goal. Moreover, as he and Carol talked about each step, they had never been as close. One evening at supper about three months later John said, "It won't be easy, but the reality is we can do it!" He smiled, eyes shining as he held out his business plan book. "It's time to talk to your father." As Carol had watched John's every move, she was surprised at his quick, decisive actions. Whenever

John ran into something new that he had to know about or do before he could move forward; e.g., get a real estate license, he put it at the top of a clean sheet of paper, listed everything he would have to do to take care of it, and then checked it all out. John looked at his watch, "Hey, I'm late for a meeting at the bank." He smiled at Carol and gave her a playful kiss on the neck and ran downstairs, saying over his shoulder, "Love you!"

After John drove out of the driveway, Carol sat, thrilled by the new life in him. His depression had lifted, and he had found the courage to leave the Latner family business. But she also felt fear. Carol knew what a proud, cold and unforgiving tyrant Robert Latner could be when his will was thwarted — she'd watched him financially squash Dennis Walker, the man her mother had married after Robert had left her. First, Robert had falsely defamed Dennis's character, and then he squeezed him through his creditors until he went under. At the time, Carol had believed her father's denial that he acted from revenge. She had always needed him to be the white knight he claimed to be. But now the memory rose in her mind, adding to her fear.

The next morning, John walked into Robert's walnut-lined corner office, but before John could say anything, the old man leaned back in his chair and said, "Switzerland, eh? How's that Swiss stuff, son? Must be good: you look like a new man... or was it French?"

"What are you trying to say?" John quickly realized his father-in-law was trying to throw John off balance and it had worked like a charm.

The old man nodded, looking innocent, "Well, about a month after you got back we got a confidential call, from a private investigation company in London inquiring about a 'John Martin.' You applying for a job in Europe?" The old man had a look of wide-eyed innocence.

"What the hell are you talking about?" John blurted.

"I did a little checking on my own through my old adjutant in World War II, George Ingram, now with the CIA European Division." John shook his head in disgust, but Robert was on a roll. "John, it's amazing what kind of information the CIA can come up with."

"Come on Robert, get to your point. I've something important I need to talk to you about."

The old man held up his hand in mock fear of John's anger. "Okay, I know your time is valuable, and I wouldn't even bother you with this, if the investigation from Europe wasn't about you." Robert raised his eyebrows as if asking for permission to continue.

"So, Robert, who is it that wants to know all about me?"

"Well, you'll never believe this, but the source of the inquiry is one of the largest French conglomerates, a world-wide holding company with headquarters in Paris: Fontaine Industries. The inquiry apparently originated from a very high official in the home office. Know anyone in that outfit?"

John felt weak and said nothing. Did Robert know about Claudette Fontaine? He waited to see what Latner really knew about his connection, if any, with Fontaine Industries — and what connection Claudette might have. But the old man quickly dropped any pretense of calmness and began to rage at John, "What the hell are you trying to pull, some slick maneuver to sell out my company to an outfit owned by Frenchmen — a bunch of Frogs?"

John silently exhaled a sigh of relief. He could kick Claudette for instigating a check on him, though he figured it was probably coming from a legal department because of Claudette's expressed interest in John's company. It was plain the old man didn't know anything about his meeting with Claudette in Glion.

"No, Robert, I'm not planning any deal to sell your company out from under you. What I am going to do is start a commercial real estate business in Denver that won't be competitive with you in any way."

"What do you mean you're going into the commercial real estate business?" Latner roared, his face flushed with anger. "It's been a disaster area for five years — everyone knows that." Then he sneered, "And where do you think you're going to get the capital to start a business you don't know beans about? Without me, you haven't got a pot to pee in."

John felt the blood rushing to his face — a familiar mixture of shame, anger, fear, and frustration from boyhood when his own father had ridiculed his dreams — but he managed to speak evenly. "I've done a lot of checking and worked out the finances. I'm not here to ask your permission or borrow money. I just want to tell you that I'm going to leave and try to build my own business. The guys in my office are good and well trained, so I'm not leaving you in the lurch. There won't be a drop-off, and I'm giving you two weeks notice, if you want it. This is about me and going for my dreams, Robert. It's not about you. I'm grateful to you for giving me a chance to work here, and for all I've learned from you."

"Yeah, you sure are grateful," Robert sneered, "running off and leaving the business I've been building for you and your family. Well, get this straight! You and Carol are *on your own* financially starting *right now!* And don't think either one of you is going to inherit a dime from me. Disloyalty is one thing I will not countenance! I can't believe your ingratitude, and," he added sarcastically, "your ignorance about what's going on in the business world." He swiveled his chair around so his back was to John, and picked up the phone. "Elizabeth, help Mr. Martin find his way out. Box up the personal stuff in his office and *mail* it to him."

John was taken off guard by the intensity of Robert's anger and a little surprised at his open threat to disinherit Carol. Although John was totally prepared to be on his own, the encounter still raised his anxiety level. In addition, the fact that Claudette's husband's company was a major conglomerate and that its legal department had reached clear to Denver to investigate him was unsettling.

That night Carol said, "Honey, I've never in my whole life been afraid about not having enough money until now, and it's awful!" Even though she disliked her father's tyrannical ways, because of his substantial estate, she had always felt secure financially. "You know, John, I'm so naïve. I watched him abandon Mother when he divorced her, but I keep expecting Daddy to be my father and love me no matter what. I can promise you though, if he said he'll disinherit us, he'll do it." Carol began to sob. "He's always been fanatically jealous about anyone who threatened to leave him. But I can't believe he's so out of touch that he wouldn't know his love and understanding are much more important to me than anything material that he could leave us."

John held her, and she was grateful they had done their homework, and had a plan. John was grateful that Carol had been an A student in accounting. If they both cut their overhead by careful spending, they could make it for a year or two. They had their savings, and John hoped to have income from moonlighting as a consultant for his old friend, Bill Castle, who owned Castle Developers, the most successful commercial real estate company in Colorado. Carol began looking for a part-time tax accounting job, and in addition, would be keeping their own company's books. They hoped that by the end of a year John's new business would begin to be profitable.

It wasn't long before John discovered a tract of land for sale that was perfect for a shopping center. He got an option to buy it, and to his delight learned a new highway which would connect the tract to the freeway was approved the same week. John arranged for financing through Bill Castle. In the process of working out the deal, he showed Bill his plan. Bill said, "I want to talk to you when you get this acquisition buttoned up."

About two weeks after the purchase of the shopping center site, John and Bill Castle were having lunch. Bill and his wife, Fran, had been friends of John and Carol's since college. Rumor had it Bill had made an enormous killing by getting out of the market just before the dot com bust.

"John, I think it's great you're making a break for it. Don't worry about what your father-in-law said. A lot of people don't know this, but it's a great time to be in commercial real estate in Denver."

"Thanks, Bill. I'm really pumped. And my learning curve is straight up. Although," John laughed, "I guess that's no surprise since I've just started."

Bill smiled. "I know what Robert Latner is trying to do to you. He talked too loud at the club the other night. And I've got an idea of how to stop him. Why don't you come help me out for a while? We're buried right now and could really use you. You can develop your shopping center project, and you'll be operating under our umbrella. Robert knows I'm big enough to shut *him* down if he messes with me. Besides," Bill's smile broadened, "if you're going to learn the business, you might as well learn from the best."

—*uu*—

After working night and day with Bill for a year, John had a good grasp of what being a commercial realtor involved. Carol had run the daily construction schedule for the shopping center project and helped John restructure the part of Castle Developers he was working in. Bill was amazed at both their abilities, but especially John's process for creating sound action plans in a few minutes. John loved what he was learning from Bill about real estate, but was surprised at how difficult it was to avoid discouragement and stay focused on his own dreams at the same time. He stayed energized by keeping his dream list with him and looking through the cards every morning and evening.

But other problems arose at home that John hadn't counted on. Carol was happy he was out of the depression he'd been in when he went to Switzerland, but she wasn't as ecstatic as he was about the challenges of the business and their new life. It seemed to John that she was jealous, even though his romantic interest in her had been reborn with his enthusiasm for his work and life in general. Since they'd started making some significant money, Carol's anxiety about the financial future had eased considerably, but something about his energy for the new business seemed to frighten her. They began to argue again, and she became jealous when he stayed late working night after night — even though John's secretary was a totally straight arrow and seldom there after work. If any little thing went wrong in the business or at home, Carol exploded at John.

For example, John got a chance to buy a tract of land by a lake for a very good price. Since having a cabin on a lake was important on his dream list, John broached the subject with Carol. He intended to put a down payment on the land, so that someday they could build their dream cabin. The property was a good buy, and he knew the vacation developers were moving toward that tract, but Carol didn't know anything about the rest of John's dreams — just about the business. She immediately shot down the land-purchasing idea. "Are you crazy? We're not exactly rich, John! Good lord!"

Her retort shocked and stung him. Early in their marriage she talked about how wonderful it would be to have a family cabin. She'd always had access to her father's cabin in Estes Park, and John knew she missed going there since they'd left Robert's business, so her adamant refusal to consider the purchase of land for a cabin confused him.

"What's the matter with you, Carol? We're doing well financially."

But Carol couldn't hear good news. When things went well, it was as if she'd made up her mind they were destined to fail, and if they were succeeding, that she was being left behind somehow. Her attitude was irrational and self-centered from John's point of view. He knew she was crucial to everything he was doing and affirmed her often, but after a number of angry, tearful encounters about the land purchase, he backed off. Then it dawned on him that maybe Carol wasn't excited about the future because she was living *his* dream, but didn't have any dreams for herself — just where he'd been when he went to Glion. Dr. Magie had warned him that even if he was succeeding at his new vocation, personal problems could sabotage his dream. John picked up the phone and placed a call to Glion.

The old doctor listened understandingly to John's account of all that had happened, the good and the bad. "John," he said, "You may be right about Carol. When a husband gets in touch with his dreams and starts to fulfill them, and his new enthusiasm and happiness can be a threat to his wife, especially if she's not in touch with her own dreams and goals. Of course, this is also true if the roles are reversed. And it's not at all uncommon for one mate to unwittingly sabotage the other's dream in order to keep the enthusiastic one from 'running away into the dream.'"

"That sounds exactly like what's happening to us. What can we do?" But before Dr. Magie could reply, John asked, "Could we come together to see you? Things aren't good between us. The argument over the cabin is just one example. We're in a relatively slack time in the business waiting for additional financing, and I have airline miles for two round-trip tickets. Can you make time in your schedule for us?"

10

Sharing Dreams
with Your Partner — Scary!

Carol loved Montreux, and as the cog train went straight up the mountainside to Glion, she took stock of her reflection in the window: midlength blonde hair, blue eyes. "Still pretty," she thought. At 5'7" she usually wore a size ten dress, although lately she'd bought a few twelves. She hated the few extra pounds that had showed up these past few months, but she knew she'd probably never be satisfied with her looks. John still seemed to find her attractive, but inside she was afraid and insecure. Always handsome, he'd gotten even better looking over the past months. She looked at his image reflected next to her own: tan and trim, he'd been lifting weights and running again. And his new freedom and confidence had done something incredible for his presence. All her friends had noticed. "Good Lord!" she realized for the first time, "I'm envious of his new look! I'm even afraid this crazy guru he's found may somehow take him away from me!"

The future seemed uncertain as Carol took stock of her situation. On the plus side, she trusted John and his abilities. His courageous stance about leaving her father, and his new, serene optimism made her feel more secure about the future than she ever had before. And it helped that Bill said John was a natural at real estate. On the other hand, her father hadn't returned her calls or Wil's in a year. And she had no financial safety net without a connection to him.

One night two weeks earlier she'd awakened, sweating all over, from a dream of walking out of bankruptcy court. All their friends were on the street in front of the courthouse looking away and snickering. It was humiliating. She sat up in bed and was wide awake the rest of the night. She finally decided, "If worse comes to worst and the business fails, we might have to sell everything and live in a mobile home in the forest." Looking over at John's handsome face on her pillow she thought, "Doing that with John might not be all bad."

"But if the business succeeds, what if he gets a big head about it? Or worse, what if some cute young thing comes along when he's vulnerable — and we're fussing — and he notices she doesn't have the extra five-pound midwaist donut I can't get rid of? What do I do then? I know I shouldn't pick at him and point out everything I think is wrong with him. I know that approach is self-defeating, but I can't seem to stop it."

Carol shook her head, "What's the matter with me? I got what I wanted — John's not only out of his depression, he feels great about life! Why do I feel worse? I bitched about having to take care of him and Wil, but now it feels like they've cut me loose from caring for them and I'm not needed any more. Everything I do seems random and disconnected. I've always felt so 'together' but lately I wonder if I'm losing control."

—*nnn*—

Carol was brought back from her reverie by a clanking noise as the cog train slowed to a stop. Through the window, she saw a willowy young woman and a little boy smiling and waving a warm welcome to them. As Carol stepped down from the train while John was getting their bags, the woman said in careful English, "Good morning, Mrs. Martin. I am Celeste. *Enchantée.*" Carol nodded at Celeste, as her young brother held out his hand to shake hands with Carol.

A distinguished older man whom Carol knew had to be Dr. Magie stepped forward, smiling, with a bouquet of purple and white mountain flowers especially for her. "It's good to see you," he said. "I am Dr. Charles Magie, *Madame,* John has told me some very good things about you."

"Thank you," Carol smiled.

John and Dr. Magie shook hands, while Celeste saw to their luggage.

"I'm looking forward to getting to know you, Carol, and hearing how your dreams are doing, John. I thought you would like a few hours to get unpacked, have lunch and rest from your flight. If that meets with your approval, we could meet together at five this evening."

John looked at Carol, who nodded her response.

Later that evening in Dr. M.'s study, he told them his way of getting to know couples was to spend forty minutes alone with each person, and then an hour with all three meeting together.

—*nnn*—

After the individual interviews, they were all seated in Dr. Magie's study. He talked a little about what he'd heard each of them say, and then added, "What I'm about to tell you won't solve all your problems, but communication and closeness can increase remarkably as a couple shares in the manner I'm going to describe to you.

"Some years ago, a skeptical German merchant and his discouraged wife came to me for counseling. The wife watched over her husband very carefully, and seemed ready to nip in the bud any signs he might try something that could make him succeed enough that he wouldn't need her.

"First, I took the man through the process of discovering his personal goals. He came up with a list of dreams and a new vocational venture that he decided to investigate. Then I asked the woman if she would like to check out what her dreams might be, in the same way her husband had, so they might understand each other better. She thought about it and said she guessed she would. As it turned out, it helped both of them."

He directed his kindly eyes toward Carol. "Your situation is not the same as that couple, but I'm wondering if you would like to do this, Carol?"

Taken by surprise, Carol looked away from Dr. Magie who waited patiently in silence, listening to the crackle of the logs in the fireplace.

Carol had never known anyone who listened as sensitively and perceptively as Dr. M. did. During her talk alone with him earlier in the evening, she had felt she could trust him almost immediately. After a few desultory remarks about her background, she found herself wanting him to know her. She told him of her college dream to be a writer and shared some of the intimate details of her life, including the discouragement she felt about her marriage to John. Now, as she pondered the question of exploring her own dreams, she found it easy to believe this man could help her, too. Besides, though it was hard to admit, she knew John was a different person, far happier and more together, since he'd found some direction for his life after talking with this man.

The constant knot of anxiety in her abdomen had been growing for months, so she was ready to try almost anything. She twisted her wedding ring around her finger, feeling her fear level rise as she gathered her courage. "Yes," she said at last in a quiet voice, "I'd like to do that."

The next evening Carol came to the Magies' home without John, who was to join them later. Madame Magie opened the door. "Welcome Carol Martin, we're delighted you're here."

A few minutes later Madame Magie excused herself, leaving Carol alone with Dr. Magie in the big leather chairs in the study before a cheery fire.

"This evening can be the beginning of a fascinating adventure. Have you thought much about specific dreams and plans for the rest of your life?"

"No, actually I was taught it was selfish to spend time thinking about myself that way. As I told you earlier, in college I had a fantasy of becoming a writer some day, and even took a second major in English literature. But since John and I married, I've focused on John's life, and later Wil's. I thought that was the way it worked."

"Ah, yes. But tonight I want to give you a gift — the freedom to discover and awaken your own dreams, which may or may not be connected to those of John or Wil. I want you to let your imagination soar and however difficult it may be, to focus on what dreams are specifically yours.

"Most people who've been through this process have no idea how to begin to find their own dreams," Dr. Magie said. "Many have been taught it's selfish to think about themselves. For a great number of people, however, getting in touch with dreams in this way is a maturing and life-changing experience which brings them into deeper interaction with people close to them — and themselves. So try not to be afraid to dream big dreams. In fact, big dreams bring with them greater energy and sometimes, the passion, power — and necessity — to integrate one's entire life."

"Dr. Magie, I'll go through this process conscientiously, but I have a lot of skepticism about discovering anything very significant."

"That's all right," Dr. Magie said. "If you're willing to suspend your disbelief for an evening, we can proceed." He gave her a pencil and a lined yellow pad.

Dr. Magie explained the ten-minute dreaming process, and after an awkward moment, Carol began to write. Almost immediately, she felt a stirring of excitement about the things she was listing that she wanted to do. After ten minutes, she was entranced. She thought of several of her friends who might like to try doing this. A career interest she'd put aside many times rose to the top of her priority list. She'd put it aside because she didn't think she could do it, because her mother had taught her a woman's job was to support her husband — period. In the end, her reordered list was as shown on the following page.

After completing the reordering of the things she wanted to accomplish with her life, Carol crumpled her first jumbled list and tossed it in a nearby wastebasket. "This is fun," she grinned. "I feel like a kid who's asked for too much at Christmas — as my mother used to tell me I did before Dad's business became successful." Then she added seriously, "Have many women used this dream search process? This could do more to free women to find vocational fulfillment than anything I've ever seen."

Dr. Magie smiled. "Many people — men and women — have never dared to look for their own dreams because they were told they shouldn't want so much. But in order to reach your potential, you must push your horizons and find dreams big enough to motivate you to go through the risks and work involved in fulfilling them. Because most nations are dominated by male leaders who make the laws and create the opportunities, women have less access to such opportunities." After some instruction about picking and checking some specific dreams, Dr. M. set another appointment with Carol.

CAROL'S GOALS TOWARD HAPPINESS
(REWRITTEN IN ORDER OF IMPORTANCE)

1. Write a book to help people with the process of living.

2. Help Wil get settled after graduation (hopefully in the Denver area).

3. Health—get back in shape: diet, rest, exercise, and checkups.

4. Give more money and time to help abused wives and children and other causes relating to people in pain.

5. Go to the health club at least three days a week and run on alternate days for thirty minutes.

6. Get the kitchen remodeled.

7. Spend more quality time with John — who seems to be slipping away.

8. Come back to Switzerland and spend a week or two with John sightseeing and hiking in the mountains (actually, since I'm only dreaming: spend more non-business time alone with John when we're home, too).

9. Go to graduate school or other classes or conferences to learn more about writing.

10. Look into ways to help underprivileged families through our church. Look into the possibility of attending church again even if I have to go alone.

11. Get home mortgage paid off.

12. Stay in closer contact with relatives—answer mail.

13. Sail to England (see museums and tour lake country, etc.).

14. Sail to France on the newest version of the Queen Mary and see the Louvre Museum in Paris.

15. Visit John's mother more now that she lives in Denver and John's family members in Connecticut at least once a year, and see if I can relate better to them.

16. Buy a piece of sculpture by Charles Umlauf.

17. Take three one-week vacations a year — at least one without Wil.

18. Build a cabin on a river in the mountains.

19. Spend some time in Santa Fe looking at Indian art.

20. Get a massage at least once a month (I'm ashamed to write this — it's so self-indulgent, but having had a few, I know regular massages would be wonderful).

21. Someday buy a convertible for me.

Then he called John in to join them and said, "In the process of achieving dreams, sometimes it can be helpful for each person in a marriage to know what the other is dreaming. Knowing where your partner is coming from can make communication much more clear. If you'd like to try this, perhaps you could each take a turn at telling the other some of the dreams on your list."

Carol looked at the heavy walnut baseboard around the study and then finally asked, "What would be involved? This is frightening to me."

Dr. Magie said, "I know this isn't a natural procedure for some people. As I have guided other couples in the early stages of sharing dreams, I've found a few guidelines that help.

1. No interrupting the one sharing

2. Neither person can ridicule with laughter or funny faces what the other says

3. No negative comments about the other's dreams or how the other's behavior is affecting one

4. No advice unless asked for

5. Sincere encouragement and congratulations for trying and failing — as well as succeeding — are important.

After explaining these ground rules, Dr. M. asked if they would like to read some or all of their lists to each other. Neither had seen the other's list, and they were both curious, but each was hesitant about being so vulnerable, especially Carol.

"I'll try," she finally said, "If we can also put in the rules that neither of us can hold the other to these dreams. At any time we can decide to change our own dreams, or add to them, or decide not to do them. And neither of us can impose a time schedule on the other for accomplishing any of the other's dreams."

John agreed, "That sounds good to me." Carol looked at him hard to make sure he understood she was serious.

Dr. M. said, "If you decide to continue this practice when you get home, these ground rules should be written on an index card. Always keep the card where you can both see it when you're sharing and discussing your dreams." He reached into his pocket and pulled out a card with the five ground rules for sharing printed on it and laid the card on the table in front of them. "Now," he said, leaning back in his chair. "Each of you has five minutes to read from your dream list. Who'd like to go first?"

Carol wanted to get it over with before she changed her mind, so she volunteered. John sat back quietly in the big leather chair with his hands resting on the arms and listened respectfully as she read from her list. As she realized John wasn't laughing at her or her dreams she gained courage. In fact, his surprise and obvious approval of several of them amazed her, especially the one of going to graduate school to study writing. When John's turn came, Carol listened intently as he shared what she now understood from her own list-making experience were his deepest, most honest hopes about his life, and the ones about having more time with her almost brought her to tears.

When they'd both finished, Dr. Magie said, "Sharing your dreams is a way you can begin to understand each other's heart's desires — the things each of you wants to do with your life and what your priorities are. That way, Carol, if John brings up a subject that normally would seem ridiculous to you because you have no interest in it, you can listen and understand that it's a part of his dream. The same would be true for you, John. And instead of looking incredulous, as if the other had lost his or her mind for suggesting such a thing, you can listen, hear each other's dreams, and help to implement them — if the other one wants help — even though the dream may not be something you're particularly interested in yourself. Of course, if the other person's dream contradicts one of yours, or is similar but differs in some ways that are important to you, you'll have specific issues to negotiate.

"Do either of you have anything you'd like to ask or say to the other about what you've heard? You can ask for clarification, but remember, neither of you can trivialize or negate any dream of the other."

Smiling, Carol shook her head. "You know, John, I'm really amazed you want to spend more time with Wil and me, and that you'd really like to go to England. I've wanted to go to England for years, but we never talked about it. Now maybe we can make a plan to try to get there someday." Dr. Magie listened quietly as this sort of intimate connecting happened several times during the ensuing minutes.

John looked thoughtfully at his wife, "I think I've been putting you down with regard to your going back to school to study journalism because I had no idea you were serious about wanting to be a writer. I felt you had a good thing going with raising Wil and all the volunteer work you do. I didn't realize how much you wanted to write until I saw your eyes light up and heard the tone in your voice as you read that item on your list. I'm sorry I didn't support you in your dream to write."

Carol was moved by John's words, and felt tears welling up in her eyes.

After a few seconds, Dr. Magie cleared his throat. "My experience has been that an unexpected result of sharing dreams is that the process can be one of the best ways for couples to foster love and mutual support."

John squinted his eyes and cocked his head. "Could you say more about that, Dr. M.?"

EXERCISE FOUR
Ground Rules for Sharing Dream Lists or Specific Goals
(or Problem Issues) with Another

1. After both persons have completed the initial process of discovering and prioritizing their dreams, and they want to share their dreams, they agree to the following rules during sharing times:

Ground Rules for Couples' Sharing

1. No *interrupting* of the one sharing

2. No *laughing* or *making funny faces* at the one sharing

3. No *negative comments* about the other's dreams, or how the other's behavior is affecting one

4. No *advice* unless asked for

5. *Sincere encouragement* and congratulations for trying and failing, as well as succeeding, are important

2. The abbreviated version of these ground rules written on an index card should be kept in sight of both partners when they're sharing and discussing their dreams. If either breaks the rules, the other can point to the card in a non-blaming way. This is sometimes difficult for the one who has broken the rule, but it is very important not to use sharing as a time to control or put down the other person.

3. After one person shares dreams, the other may only ask clarifying questions or make positive comments. Neither can speak negatively about the other's dream or about how the other one is implementing it. No advice can be given unless requested.

4. Sincere encouragement and congratulations for trying and failing, as well as for succeeding, should be offered as often as possible.

5. Either party can apologize for past belittling or ignoring of the other's dreams, if appropriate.

6. Each agrees that neither will hold the other to the dreams read, limit the dreams or goals to the original lists read, or try to impose any sort of time limit (with the exception of common or mutual dreams.

7. Partners can negotiate the priority of common dreams, agreeing to specific actions and timetables when working on common goals.

8. When unresolvable conflicts arise, the partners may consider going together to a counselor for help, together if possible. If not, one person may want to get help separately — and should not be shamed or discouraged by the other.

11

Intimate Surprises for the Adventurer

Dr. M. said to Carol and John, "The sort of listening and supporting that couples experience while achieving their dreams can be powerful forces in developing lifelong intimacy in their relationship. For example, Carol, you may interpret John's nonjudgmental listening, even in those simple exercises, to be a strong indicator and expression of his love for you. And a partner who feels 'heard' is likely to want to help the other fulfill his or her dreams. But when couples haven't shared their dream lists, sabotaging and criticism of ideas can occur for reasons that aren't apparent to either partner. A good example, John, is what you said about not taking seriously Carol's wanting to go back to school. Until she shared her dream list, you had no idea how important going back to school was to her.

"Another example might be building that cabin by a lake you mentioned in our conversation, John. When the opportunity arose to buy a tract of land for it, you were ready to commit because of recent financial successes in your business. But, Carol, because you hadn't heard how important building a family cabin was to John you objected even though it's an important dream for you, too.

"As strange as it may sound, if I don't know what *my* dreams are, I may still feel fear and even sabotage a dream of my wife's that's in conflict with a dream of *mine* — even though I'm not *aware* of that dream as being one of mine too." Dr. Magie paused and a sad look came over his face. "I did that with Mrs. Magie several times before we made and shared our dream lists. By becoming aware of our own dreams and the other person's, and having our lists in order of importance, my wife and I can now negotiate the priority of various items on the lists and other things in our lives. Also we can move more quickly with less conflict when unexpected opportunities come up to realize one of her dreams, one of mine, or a common dream."

Carol interrupted. "My gosh, you're right! That's exactly what happened in our arguments about the cabin. I wanted a family cabin, and I knew Wil would love it, but I had two problems when John wanted to buy the land. First, I dreaded spending any extra money until John's business got more secure. And second, I had envisioned a cabin high in the mountains by a *stream* with lots of trees. I couldn't picture the cabin in a pasture by a lake. Also, John's desire to buy the land irritated me because here he was, about to build a whole second home, and I've been wanting to have our kitchen remodeled for five years. I was afraid we wouldn't have money for both, and I'd lose out."

"Wait a minute," John said. "You never even mentioned the kitchen to me!"

"Well, I certainly did mention it once, just before you came to Switzerland the first time. You said remodeling the kitchen was out of the question because you didn't know what you were going to do, and we might have to sell the house. Then, when you got home and started realizing your dreams, you suddenly wanted to build a cabin. I was furious, since I assumed you remembered how important remodeling the kitchen was to me, and were ignoring my wishes."

John looked at her thoughtfully and turned to Dr. Magie. "Whew!" he said, smiling. "I'm just beginning to see what you mean about how going for your dreams can affect marriages." He turned to Carol. "Honest, Honey, until I saw your list today, I hadn't even thought of the kitchen; it always seemed okay to me and I'd forgotten your wanting to redo it. I'd be glad to remodel the kitchen before we build the cabin. Would you be willing at least to discuss options about the cabins on the tract I discovered?"

Carol nodded, but a bit hesitantly. "Okay . . . "

"The tract is in a beautiful location on the edge of a mountain meadow with all kinds of trees around it. The cabin is on the bank of the stream, just where it flows into the meadow and the lake. The price is good because the owner really needs the money. Would you at least go look at it? If you truly don't like it, we'll say no. I didn't mention the stream and trees because I didn't know they were important to you."

"Are you really serious that we can remodel the kitchen before we build the cabin?"

"Sure," John said enthusiastically. "We can use the *existing* cabin on the tract for a while. Then, as we spend time there, we can decide whether to redecorate that one and build on, or junk it and start over. But we can definitely get the kitchen at home remodeled now." John paused and looked into Carol's eyes. "Carol, I really want you to get your dreams met, too. By making the down payment on the land, we can nail down the place and be paying for it each month. The way things are going with the business, we can probably do the kitchen next month, though we may have to wait a couple of years to build a new cabin."

Dr. Magie smiled. "This is how you can look at both of your dream lists together and begin the joint adventure of negotiating and meeting the goals you each have."

"But what if I have a goal he isn't interested in?" Carol asked.

"Do you have a specific example?" Dr. Magie asked.

Carol studied her list for a few seconds and said, "Ah, going to Santa Fe to look at Indian art. I know you wouldn't like that, John."

"Right," John laughed. "That wouldn't be high on my list."

"Well, it isn't high on yours either, Carol," Dr. Magie pointed out, smiling. "In fact, it's almost last. But the point is, by having your priority lists and understanding the other person's priorities as well as your own, you can negotiate options to getting dreams met. Do you have any ideas of how to accomplish this dream of going to Santa Fe?"

Carol thought. "I could go with my girl friend, Fran. She loves Indian art too, and," she smiled at John, "Bill, her husband, would be even less enthusiastic about doing things like that than John is."

"You could do that," John offered. "But if it were really important to you that I come along, I could go check out the commercial real estate business in Santa Fe while you went to the museums — and I could write the trip off. Then we could have candlelight dinners together and maybe do some skiing or hiking together in the mountains, depending on what time of year we went."

"You'd do that?" Carol asked.

"Yeah, It'd be fun."

Carol smiled, "John, you're beginning to sound like a very wise man."

Dr. Magie said, "This is how uncovering of your life goals can help you begin to communicate more effectively as a couple. You're noticing John's 'wisdom' because you're each getting in touch with your inner wisdom and beginning to use it in your relationship. But this isn't always an easy way to live together. There'll still be conflicts that appear to have nothing to do with your goals. You may also be surprised by some unresolved childhood issues that can surface as you grow toward your dreams."

"Like what?" Carol asked.

"Oh, fears of failure...control issues...jealousy. But having some common dreams and helping each other realize your individual dreams can reverse a lot of the critical, negative, shaming interactions that often happen in marriages. And, of course, dreaming together can help you both focus on the positive aspects of your present and future life as a couple, and as individuals within your relationship."

"Has this worked for many of the couples you've worked with?" Carol asked.

"Not all, but many. Some people are too afraid to dream. Others are afraid to share their dreams for fear of ridicule or sabotage. They have a deep, often unconscious defense against failing or being revealed as inadequate. Still others are fearful about a mate's suddenly beginning to take responsibility for his or her own future. It's threatening to have a formerly bland but predictable partner getting excited about something that seemingly has nothing to do with you. Some problems like this may relate to childhood abuse issues in the life of a husband or wife. And psychological counseling may be indicated.

"But even in some of these cases, the attempt of both parties to discover life dreams and goals can start a process that leads to better, more honest communication and a more positive atmosphere in a marriage. The discovery that one's inner wisdom is an important and neglected asset can be helpful in all kinds of ways. In some adults there are critical, abusive and shaming inner voices that have drowned out the voice of inner wisdom since childhood, so some people need the help of a psychological counselor before they can trust the dreaming process, their spouse or their inner wisdom.

"Sometimes," Dr. Magie smiled gently as he continued, "the process leads people to go to a counselor to find out about how to deal with their strong fears about their marriage, their mate, and their own right to dream and achieve their own goals.

"One shouldn't blame a spouse who can't risk sharing this way — or try to force such sharing. All I've been saying is that sharing what both partners have learned about themselves and their dreams can often be helpful and synergistic. With the aid of this ten-minute technique, couples can begin to understand and respect, not fear, their own and each other's dreams. A side benefit is that couples who talk at this level don't usually undermine each other's goals or compete as much in other ways. Actually, however, only couples who truly want to develop a deeper love and trust are likely to choose to share at this level."

"As a matter of fact, the main thing this simple dream-accomplishing technique has done for many couples is to allow them to begin to see a picture of their mates' heart, that sensitive arena of hopes, dreams and visions of happiness. When two people who share in this way want to have a loving and supportive relationship, the process almost always changes the atmosphere of the relating, toward increased intimacy. I've seen some couples move from a divided, adversarial stance into authentic and caring intimacy within a few months.

"The point I'm making here is that although many individuals awaken and achieve their dreams, it is sometimes very helpful to have someone close to share with in this way. A partner or small group of dreamers can enhance people's chances of reaching their dreams and, at the same time, improve the quality of their relationships in ways they couldn't have imagined."

12

A Daily Interpersonal
Communication Process for the Journey

———*///// ////// //////*———

"Dr. M.," John said, chuckling, "Are we having fun yet?"

Dr. M. looked puzzled.

"Well," John said, "the idea that we're going to get our communication straightened out and move from verbal sparring to intimacy sounds great, but the actual hard work of doing that seems pretty grim to me. When do we start having fun?"

The older man chuckled. "Once Mrs. Magie and I had both committed to reaching our individual dreams together, we learned an important secret. It's well known that when people commit and focus on a stated goal, they're more likely to reach it. But it is less well known that they are also more likely to be as happy in the process of moving toward the goal as when they actually reach it. So the answer is, she and I found ourselves happier together as soon as we specifically committed to reach our goals, whatever it took. For one thing, we could laugh about some of our foibles and that was certainly new."

"Should we make a time to specifically commit to reach our goals?" Carol asked.

Nodding, Dr. M. said, "There aren't any rules about that, but when Mrs. Magie or I have thoroughly investigated a large goal and decide to go after it, we always meet and discuss goal and what will be involved in achieving it. If both of us are agreeable, then the one whose goal it is simply says, 'I commit to give everything in me to reach this goal. I will not quit.' "

"Do you make that kind of commitment to reach every goal?" John asked incredulously.

"Oh no, just the ones that are *most* important to us. But the point is that once we have made such a serious commitment that's when the 'fun' begins for us. Our commitment sort of cleared the decks of our lives and we rolled up our sleeves. That's when a lot of positive changes took place for the two of us, and when we started building a daily interpersonal support system to keep us focused and moving forward."

"How does that kind of support system work?" asked Carol.

"What I called a daily interpersonal support system is any regular, daily, affirming interaction between two individuals in an ongoing personal relationship that allows both parties to air feelings, hopes, dreams and progress or blocks to reaching their goals. A strong condition is that we can share the real pain and fear, for instance, without being shamed, corrected or attacked. When couples or two good friends, or even a small group of friends make a serious commitment to realize their dreams, this act of commitment often triggers the fear of failure in one individual as well as the fear of desertion in a partner. Since such fears are normal, having safe ways to express them to each other often takes the negative intensity out of the fears and allows people to get past them and even laugh at the ridiculous lengths we go to keep from facing our fears and moving on to the business of discovering dreams and achieving the goals derived from them."

After a few seconds of considering what Dr. M. had said, Carol added, "My second question has to do with the actual sharing." Carol paused to think. "I don't really know how to share my innermost thoughts very well. In my family we just talked about surface things and not what was really important to us." She looked at John. "I'm afraid to talk to you about my dreams without Dr. M. present."

John nodded. "I know my parents meant well, but for our own safety and happiness they discouraged us kids from trying anything risky or too difficult. Consequently, when one of us expressed a dream that involved aptitudes that one of our parents didn't have, they often said, 'That's an interesting idea,' or 'We want you to do what you want to, but . . .' and they would give us reasons our dream wouldn't work. Then they'd suggest something else they thought we should do. I know they only wanted to help us learn to keep our dreams within reason, but their fears and limitations kept me from dreaming much at all, especially thinking about anything 'outside the box,' so to speak. I played football because it made my dad proud of me, and I guess it gave me an appropriate place to work out my frustration and anger."

"So that's the complex that built 'Killer' Martin?" Carol smiled.

John took a deep breath. "As a young boy, I needed the love and approval of my parents more than I needed to go for a dream. My mother has always had health problems, and I felt responsible for being with her when she needed me. I became fearful of taking emotional risks, which is the reason I stayed in your father's business for so long," he looked at Carol, "That is until I couldn't stand it any more! I had quit dreaming for myself and pushed my own life goals into the basement of my mind, until I wasn't aware that I had any dreams at all. And Carol, I don't want Wil, or you — or me — to have to live that way any more. I always worked hard to win, and so I could make a living. But without concrete hopes and dreams of my own, I was bored out of my skull and secretly afraid I'd never find my own place in the world."

After a few seconds, Carol cleared her throat. "When I was a girl, my family, especially my dad, teased me or flat-out told me I couldn't make it when I told them about a dream of doing something outstanding. By the time I was sixteen, I had quit dreaming, too, though I was an A student by then and received lots of encouragement from my teachers. Ultimately, I just followed in my mother's footsteps as a mother and housewife. As you talked, John, I realized I had buried my dreams even from my own sight, just to avoid the pain of being teased or shamed for dreaming. But maybe by using this technique for awakening our dreams, we can learn to give each other the real support our families never could." All three were silent.

Quietly, Dr. Magie said, "This room was just filled with a message from your inner wisdom, Carol, about how your dream search together might provide the personal nurturance you missed as a child." Carol nodded, and Dr. M. continued, "That's what happened to Mrs. Magie and me. I remember distinctly the June night I told her I was going to take some time to write a book. I feared she'd disapprove, and I expected her to say, 'Oh, come on. Let's go hike up the mountain. We've wanted to do that for days,' or 'We've been locked up in this place for two weeks. Can't we go to Geneva for the weekend?' But instead, she said, 'I'm glad you're getting at that dream, Charles. I want us to take some vacation time together, but why don't you go ahead and take the time you need now to work on your writing, and we'll take a vacation together in the fall.'"

Dr. Magie seemed genuinely moved by the memory. "It would be difficult for me to tell you what Mrs. Magie's support meant to me after being raised by a father who thought the only important things for a man to do in life had to do with succeeding in the army. And her support of me has made me enthusiastic in supporting her in a new venture: in Montreux she's beginning to tutor children with learning disabilities."

"How do we begin learning how best to support each other?" John asked.

Dr. Magie stood, walked over to the window, and turned around, "You can begin this period of sharing by deciding to set aside twenty minutes every day for two weeks. This is how the twenty minutes would go. One of you can share for five minutes, and then allow five additional minutes for feedback and questions from the other. "For instance, John, you talk uninterrupted, for five minutes about your life, thoughts, feelings, and progress on your dreams while Carol listens.

"Then, Carol, you say, 'What I heard you say was . . . ' and in five minutes you repeat in your own words everything you heard John say during his five minutes. At first, it's very difficult to recall everything the other said for that length of time. And it's embarrassing to admit your mind wandered. But this exercise made me realize for the first time how poorly I listened to Mrs. Magie.

"Then you, Carol, have five minutes to share what you choose to communicate about your life while John listens, and then he has five minutes to repeat in his own words what he heard you say. This time for disclosing thoughts and feelings about problems and progress relating to your own dream list, and of being heard by someone you love, can bring significant renewed hope and energy for your dreams — and your relationship. The total time of sharing and feedback is twenty minutes for you as a couple to share information and receive feedback about your dreams.

"Listening for five minutes without interruption and being able to re-call everything that was said is very difficult at first. But since listening is crucial to authentic intimacy, the feedback period is a necessary and effective way of learning to be intimate. It's amazing how often we don't hear what our family members are trying to tell us. Knowing you're going to give feedback can improve your level of attention and mem-ory quickly, and you often hear people outside your relationship better. Your demonstration that you heard your spouse or friend accurately is usually more encouraging and affirming to him or her than one who has never done this exercise could imagine. However, if your feedback makes clear that you misunderstood what your wife or husband was trying to say, the spouse who shared can interrupt your feedback to clarify what she or he said.

"This feedback period is not a time to evaluate or comment about the content of what you heard — just repeat it accurately. If you can't repeat everything in your own words, apologize and ask to hear it again.

"But," Dr. Magie stopped and held up his right forefinger for emphasis, "for this sharing to be intimate, healthy and supportive, it's necessary for both people to follow the ground rules I mentioned earlier. A card on which these ground rules are written — no interruptions, no funny faces, no advice, and so on — should be placed between the parties during the sharing and feedback to protect each person's vulnerable inner child as she or he is sharing.

"The important thing to understand is that these five-minute sharing times are monologues, not dialogues. The purpose of the sessions is for *each* of you to have five minutes a day without interruption to express your happy and sad feelings and be heard about what you're doing individually.

"Sometimes after the twenty-minute period is over, one or both of you may want to *affirm* or *encourage* the other, and that can be extremely helpful. But if one of you — say it's you, John — wants to give some *suggestions* or *advice* about what Carol said, then you must first ask Carol if she would like to hear a suggestion. At that point, Carol can say either, 'Okay' or 'No, I'm not ready for that right now.' You both have to understand that these are the rules of the game. It's not an insult if Carol, or you, John, is not ready for outside advice, thoughts, or opinions. Remember, one of the primary reasons many people are out of touch with their dreams and are not able to share easily within their marriages is that someone discouraged, shamed, ridiculed or ignored them as children (or in other relationships) when they shared their feelings or spoke of their hopes and dreams. Because of these kinds of earlier experiences, your sharing partner may not be ready to risk receiving suggestions yet."

Mrs. Magie and I found that if we each shared five minutes after breakfast each morning, and had up to five minutes each for feedback and questions, we both had plenty of time to say what was on our minds, since we kept up to date by sharing every day."

"Does anyone really have the discipline to do this kind of sharing every day?" John laughed, shaking his head at the idea.

Dr. Magie looked at John thoughtfully before replying. "Actually, most people don't, John, but Mrs. Magie and I do this virtually every day, and several couples we know do it, too. We're not legalistic about it, and of course we skip some days. At times we've stopped for several months, when the habit of listening and sharing was well established — but I don't think many couples will stay committed to twenty minutes a day of regular sharing. They'll do it only if they're in enough pain or isolation, or if they feel a great enough longing to be intimate, to love, be loved, and be heard."

EXERCISE FIVE
A Daily Interpersonal Communication Process
(Approximate Twenty-Minute Format)

Couples may decide together the length of time for sharing. The following description assumes five minutes sharing and five minutes responding by each partner. After a few meetings, the time for various parts of the exercises may be lengthened or shortened. It will be helpful to get a stopwatch or timer with an alarm. Read aloud the ground rules for couples' sharing on page 78, Have a three by five card with the five ground rules on it placed in plain view between the sharing parties. Note time, or set an alarm for five minutes.

1. The first person shares for five minutes, as the other listens carefully without interrupting. The person sharing talks about his or her own feelings and dreams, but not about the other person or the other person's dreams.

2. After alarm goes off at the end of five minutes, the listener has up to five minutes to try to reflect back in his or her own words what was heard.

3. After this feedback, reset the alarm for five minutes. The second person shares, followed by feedback from the one listening for another five minutes.

After both partners have shared and given feedback, affirmation or encouragement may be offered. But if someone has suggestions or advice, that person asks if the other person would like to hear those suggestions. If the answer is no, the person with the suggestion does not insist. The purpose of this exercise is *not* problem solving but learning to *share safely* and to *hear accurately* what your partner is saying.

13

Intimacy 101: Listening and Loving, Interrupted by Life

mm mm mm

"Dr. M., what do you do," John asked, "if your spouse doesn't *ever* want suggestions?"

After a pause, Dr. Magie said, "Marriage partners should proceed gradually. Some of the private material being shared is important and precious to the little child part of any spouse. If after a five-minute time of sharing and responding, your mate tells you that she really doesn't want the suggestions you're ready to offer right then, don't insist or act injured. Just acknowledge you heard what she said.

"When my wife first told me she didn't want a suggestion I wanted to make to her, I felt hurt and thought she had shut me out," Dr. M. said sadly. "I forgot that before we started learning how to talk to each other about our dreams, she hadn't been telling me *anything* about her goals, and almost nothing about her feelings, because I constantly tried to fix or manage them. Being a physician and counselor, I had myriad ideas about how she could correct her plan or behavior at almost every point.

"Years before I had learned that counselors don't often do well when they try to act as counselor to their own family members. But I learned through this process that my job as a *husband* also is not to fix or change my wife regarding her quest for her dreams, but to hear her and love her. After I learned that — for about the sixth time — and quit trying to instruct her, she occasionally started asking me for suggestions.

"It didn't take long for us to learn how much it damaged our relationship for one of us to jump on the other's problems or dreams, to fix, improve or give advice on how to implement them, without the other's invitation. Even if the suggestion might be helpful, it tends to shame the other person, and this shame can block a person's ability to hear much of anything accurately. And when either partner feels shamed, the magic, intimate feeling of security and closeness can disappear in an instant, along with the increased positive energy and passion the couple was experiencing. On the other hand, when there isn't the fear of being fixed, sharing can provide real strength to the one sharing."

"Wait a minute," John said. "We're both busy people now that we've started our new business. What do I do if Carol wants to keep talking about something that comes up *beyond* the twenty minutes, and I've got to get to a business meeting?"

Dr. Magie said, "It's important for you both to be able to tell each other, before the sharing starts, if one of you has to go to work or has an impending appointment without the other taking that as a personal rejection. And if the one not leaving indicates there is something important not yet discussed, it is helpful if the one having to leave will suggest a specific time to talk later. For instance, 'I have to leave now, but could we talk about this sometime after 8:30 this evening when I get home? If not then, when will you be free to talk about it? I'm really interested and would like to set a definite time to discuss this with you.'

"Another thing that may happen is for one person to bring up a loaded issue from the past like, 'I still haven't gotten over the time you insulted me in front of my family at Christmas five years ago by making fun of a mistake I made with my boss. I often think about the shame and anger I felt.'

"This dream-sharing time is not the time to bring up such things. But if something emotionally charged should pop out in the morning sharing time, I've found it best to set another time to talk about the painful issue, if either partner feels the necessity to discuss it more. However, as time and the experience of sharing goes on, both people can often let their mate express such things as the pain of a past occasion without having to react, get defensive, or respond at all, except to offer an acknowledgement of how what happened was painful. When a couple reaches this place, they're much more secure with each other, because they realize that everybody has unfinished pain about past events and that voicing such pain in a non-shaming way does not destroy the relationship. Mrs. Magie and I found that just five minutes of sharing time each per day, and five minutes of being listened to led to a much more comfortable atmosphere in the rest of our marriage."

"Thank you, Dr. M." Carol was very touched by his vulnerability in sharing his life as well as his wisdom with them. "I realize you worked us in at the last minute, and I want you to know that these sessions have already changed my life — and our marriage."

John added, "You are something else, Dr. M. Thanks again."

After their evening with Dr. Magie, John and Carol spent several hours at the hotel talking with each other about their dreams and how they might improve their relationship. In the midst of their discussion, John remembered that Carol's dream list included spending some vacation time traveling in Switzerland. He said, "Carol let's start realizing dreams right now. How about a week traveling in Switzerland?"

"You mean on this trip?"

"Why not?" John looked at his watch. It was 10:00 p.m.

Since it was seven hours earlier in Denver, John made arrangements for Carol to realize her dream of traveling in Switzerland while they were still in Europe, and to help fulfill one of his dreams: to spend more non-business time with her. A few phone calls to the office and their home and they were free to travel for a week in Switzerland, which he announced to her with glee as he hung up the telephone.

Carol could hardly believe it. "You mean *right now*, starting today?"

John nodded, looking suave, and Carol backed up in mock amazement. "Who is this handsome hunk before my eyes?" she exclaimed, fluttering her eyelashes. "Are you planning to have your way with me if we go away together?

"You'll just have to wait and see. If you play your cards right...."

Giggling, Carol picked up a pillow and began pounding John, who covered his face with his arms until they were both weak from laughing. Later, as they lay beside each other in the dark, holding hands and looking out of their picture window at the white moon high above the silver tips of the tall fir trees below, Carol whispered, "John, I don't think I've ever felt so peaceful — and so close to anyone as I do right now."

John whispered in the dark, "Me, too."

Rinnng! The sound of the old telephone suddenly filled the room.

John abruptly sat up on the side of the bed and groped the bedside table for the receiver. "Hello? Yes, this is John Martin. What is it, Celeste? Okay, please connect him." John put his hand over the speaker and said, "It's Bill Castle." Then uncovering the mouthpiece, "Hello, Bill."

As John listened, his face tightened and he put his left fist to his mouth, as if blowing into it on a cold day. "Thanks, what time is it there? Okay, please tell her we'll start home on the first plane we can get space on tomorrow. I'd appreciate your letting Wil know tonight. I'll call you and him from the Geneva airport about our arrival time. Yeah ...yeah...thanks again. Tell her we're coming and we love her." John hung up the phone.

Carol asked, "What's the matter, Honey?"

"It's my mother. She's had another stroke and she isn't expected to make it this time."

Carol put her arms around John from behind him on the bed and laid her head on his shoulder. "I'm so sorry, Honey!"

John patted her arm, "Carol, we'll come back for our Switzerland second honeymoon trip as soon as ... "

"Don't worry about that, John," Carol interrupted, "Your arranging for us to make the time to go right now means we're in a new world in our relationship. I know we'll make the trip when the time's right, so the exact date isn't a problem. What did Bill say about your mother?"

On the cog train down the mountain in the predawn darkness, John watched the dark forest flash by behind the image of his face in the window. "Damn," he thought, "I'm no kid anymore, but I sure wasn't ready for Mom to die." He wanted to weep because he'd never really talked to his mother about what was *real* in his life. But he couldn't weep — too much training to "be a man."

John shook his head and automatically pulled his brief case out from under the seat in front of him. He'd already checked to make sure they could make American flight 49 from Paris to Dallas and on to Denver. He'd call Wil from the airport to let him know their arrival time. He began to do a ten-minute plan about what he'd need to do when he and Carol got home.

14

Born in the Ashes: A Dream Team

The funeral had gone better than John had feared it might. The sermon had been short and he was relieved that his mother's minister had restrained himself from hell and damnation preaching.

After John and Carol thanked their friends and the few relatives who'd flown in, everyone left, and John finally sat in the reading chair next to his and Carol's bed.

Carol sat on the arm of the chair. "You okay, Honey?"

"Yeah, I'm fine," John sighed clear to his toes. "Just a tad tired." Staring at the wall across the room for a few seconds, he said, "You know, I was disappointed Mom died before we got home. There were some things I wanted to tell her and ask about."

Carol nodded, "But it's wonderful she was clear enough to write that letter telling you about her faith and that she'd miss you. She really trusted God about her dying."

John nodded, "Yeah, I didn't dream she had that kind of faith, and I'll bet Dad never knew it either."

"Actually, you and your dad would not have been the easiest people to talk to about God."

"That's sure right. But it's strange…even though I don't have that kind of belief, I'm glad she did."

John pulled his Palm Pilot out of his shirt pocket and turned to the appointment section. "Did you call the Salvation Army people about coming to get Mother's stuff?"

Carol knew that was the end of the funeral talk. Uneasily but firmly, she said, "No, and I'm not going to until your mom's sisters go through the house and get what they want. That's what your mother requested in the letter she left for me in the hospital. She also listed some things I might want. And besides, I don't think we ought to rush around and clear her out of our lives. Why don't we sleep late and get some rest? We've had a 'no sleep' night, an overseas flight, a house full of relatives and friends, and a burial. I'm exhausted."

"Me, too," John admitted. "I'm glad one of us has some sense now. I sure don't. I want you to know I'm going to get Mom's estate cleaned up fast and then really start hitting the ball to get our business off the ground, so you won't wind up like my mom did when my dad died suddenly leaving her without the financial freedom to do what she wanted to do."

"Honey," Carol said, "I'll work right beside you, but I want *you* to know that I'd a *lot* rather have more years *with you* than a zillion dollars without you because you killed yourself working."

"Like my dad?"

Carol looked at him a long time and then nodded.

John looked up at her and frowned. Then he smiled and said, "Come here and sit on my lap. I have something important to tell you."

The next week turned out to be more stressful than Carol and John imagined. John was very resistant to dealing with any of his mother's personal things, and often dropped out of sight into his office.

Having been responsible for distributing and disposing of her own mother's personal effects, Carol knew what to do, but John's disappearance into their business still felt like a desertion to her, although he bristled at that suggestion and declared again he was getting the business going for her.

Two mornings after the funeral, Carol was walking through the boxes and furniture in John's mother's house with a notebook and pencil, making a list of everything. There was a column for what could be done with each, a daunting task. She was startled when the doorbell rang.

On the front porch were three of Carol's women friends who had known each other since high school, a quarter-century before. They were dressed in jeans, and carrying cleaning equipment. Carol stared at them in surprise for a few seconds.

"Well, can we come in?" Cynthia asked. "We miss you and your e-mail is obviously broken, soooo. . . . "

Carol dabbed at her tears as she opened the door. "Oh, thank you," she said sniffling. "I seem to be overwhelmed, what with being behind in our new business — and now this," and she spread her hands indicating all the half-filled boxes stacked around the living room. Her three dear friends gathered around her and gave her a group hug.

Later as they stopped working and ate the lunch they had brought, Carol looked around the kitchen table. Cynthia was a middle school teacher. Carol smiled as she saw how neatly she'd placed the take-out subs and salads at each person's place.

Dorothy, who'd been working hard at bringing things to Carol to be sorted, but also was clearly managed the project, asked Carol, "You want me to call now and get a couple of Jaunty Janitors to come clean the carpets and windows after we're through with the packing?" It was easy to imagine how Dorothy had gotten to be a senior VP at Northridge Bank, and still be a rabid advocate of women's rights.

Carol laughed, "Not yet, Dorothy. We ought to make sure all the breakables are packed and gone. You know how awkward men can be." Dorothy nodded.

Jenny glanced around the kitchen like the Realtor she was. "The market is good for houses this size, but if you want to sell it fast and for top dollar, it should be in move-in condition."

"There," Dorothy said, "I knew we should do heavy cleaning. Maybe we should get that women's executive cleaning service. What's their name?"

Jenny smiled, "Well, it's not 'The Merry Maid Willing Worker Girls."

Everyone but Dorothy laughed. She just said, "Damn, I hope that's not a real business name."

As the four women worked together over the next few days, they asked Carol about her trip to Glion and what she learned from "the amazing Dr. M." about finding and accomplishing dreams. In fact, they had all been surprised that Carol and John had left the security of the Latner family business. Dorothy had heard at the bank from John's partner, Bill Castle, how well John and Carol were doing. Carol told them about Dr. M.'s process for discovering one's dreams, and the exercises for dealing with personal and relational problems that can sabotage the work of achieving dreams and goals.

Cynthia said, "Carol, would you take us through that process? I really need a new challenge. I'm sick and tired of being sick and tired of my job."

Dorothy said, "I'd like to do that, too." And Jenny nodded.

When they finally finished moving John's mother's personal property out and had cleaned the house, Carol took them to the Metropolitan Club for dinner to thank them and celebrate. While they were having coffee Carol said, "I've been thinking about your wanting me to take you through the dream discovery process. Would you all like to meet for a sort of introductory session? First, I'd take you through the process to see if any of you would like to get on this adventure with us — to awaken your dreams. Then we can decide if you want to meet once a week to actually start achieving goals you came up with."

Jenny said, "We thought you'd never ask!"

Dorothy and Cynthia said, "Yes! When do we start?"

They were thrilled. Carol seemed to have changed in so many positive ways since John and then she had met Dr. Magie.

Getting her date book out of her purse, Carol said, "What evening would be better, Wednesday or Thursday — or Saturday morning?"

15

Birthing a Non-Business
Dreamers Group

The reason Bill Castle was telling everyone who would listen that John and Carol Martin were doing great things for Castle Developers was that John had become the top acquisition representative for new projects. Not only that, but after Bill had confided in John a number of organizational problems that surfaced as a result of Castle's rapid growth, John and Carol redesigned and implemented the company's financial structure and procedures. Along with his work for Castle, John also made two lucrative deals for Martin Industries in accordance with his agreement with Bill. Besides the shopping center location, John purchased and then sold a tract in the mountains that was perfect for a restaurant looking for a site, positioning the Martins to have the financial security to go on their own soon, at which point they could focus on building their company, Martin Industries, into what John dreamed it could be. Carol was great at catching the details of financial planning and cash flow for Martin Industries in addition to her work as a contract consultant for Castle in restructuring financial procedures. They were busy but happy, and through it all kept having their twenty-minute report-in sessions, which allowed them to know each other's security thresholds and preferences better than they ever had, and to deal with most problems with much less conflict.

Meanwhile, Jenny, Dorothy and Cynthia did not let Carol forget her promise to meet with them about their dreams — and hers. Their initial exploration meeting was held at Carol and John's house on a Saturday morning just four weeks after John's mother's funeral. Jenny, Dorothy and Cynthia each brought friends or associates who also wanted to go through the dream identifying and achieving processes, and each one in the group of thirteen agreed to meet for six weeks before dropping out, if they decided to commit to the adventure after Carol's presentation.

Carol looked around the living room at the thirteen women in their thirties and early forties. She had never felt comfortable sharing important parts of her personal life with other women, and she had butterflies in her stomach. "Before we begin the Dreaming Process, we are going to take a few minutes to begin to get to know each other. Dr. Charles Magie from Glion, Switzerland, who taught my husband, John, and me the dreaming process I'm going to describe, encourages an intuitive approach to working in groups, and I will use some of the methods with you that he taught us. To help us to become more comfortable with each other, and suspend our disbelief in order to uncover our buried dreams, I am going to ask you to follow exactly the instructions I'm about to give.

This sharing time won't be invasive, since you can participate or pass on any subject. First, take a moment to get into groups of three with two other people you don't know. After you introduce yourselves, each person is to take *two minutes* to talk about her childhood — anything good or bad that happened when you were a little girl. Two minutes, no more. I have a digital timer and will signal when two minutes are up."

Carol laughed good naturedly, "If you don't take the full two minutes, the group can ask you anything it wants to and you have to answer." They knew she was being facetious, but that made it more like a game.

Then she explained, "When the buzzer goes off to end the first two minutes, stop even if you're in the middle of a sentence, and go on to take *one minute* to tell about the happiest experience you can recall. This happy experience can be recent or from your past. You may not be able to recall a happy experience, but tell your group whatever, in retrospect, seems like a happy experience." Carol stopped, and then said, "I'll go first.

"When I was a little girl, I was very lonely. I had one brother who was six years older, and I was sure my father loved him more than he loved me. He used to take my brother hunting and fishing, and I wanted desperately to go with them. I'd cling to my father's leg and put my legs around his ankle, and he'd have to carry me like an iron boot. But he would shake me off, slam the door, and say, 'You can't go. You're too little. You'd get hurt.'

"I'd cry and go to my mother and ask her if Daddy loved me. She'd say, 'Of course, he loves you.' I could tell she was embarrassed, but she said, 'In five years your brother will grow up and want to play baseball with other boys. Then it'll be *your* turn to go fishing with your father.' So I waited and sure enough, my brother did start playing baseball, but then my father became a baseball fan. He watched my brother play every game and even went to practices. He'd lost all interest in hunting and fishing. Later he was killed in a motorcycle accident."

Carol looked a little sad and lonely, but she continued, "I thought if my own father didn't love me, who would? At about that time in my life, I must have made an internal decision to go for achievement since I couldn't seem to get Dad's love by just being myself. I became an overachiever as a student to try to get some kind of attention and love. And even now...." Just then the timer went off and she stopped midsentence.

Then she said, "The happiest experience I can recall happened recently and had to do with a close relative who was widowed about five years ago. I had been alienated from this woman for several years, because I suggested that, due to her health problems, she might want to go into a retirement center. My thought was that she could get the medical help she needed on a regular basis there. She got angry at me and told other members of the family that I had hurt her deeply.

"This last week I was visiting her in the retirement center. As I left, she said to me, 'I love you, and I want you to know that I'm aware you had a lot of pain as a little girl because of your relationship with your father. I'm sorry I couldn't reach out to you then. I was too afraid. But you've been good to me, and you were right about my moving into this place. I couldn't have taken care of myself at home.'" Right then the timer went off, and Carol said to the group, "That's the happiest experience I can recall in recent years."

As each person told the other two in her group about her childhood, Carol timed them until everyone had taken their two minutes, and then their one minute. When they were all finished telling their happy experiences, Carol stopped the discussions and asked that they all take a minute to tell the others in their group how they felt about each other. They were surprised, but almost everybody said they felt closer to the others in their small group than they did to some people they'd known for years in business settings or even church. Because that intimacy had developed in the small groups in approximately ten minutes, the whole larger group was ready to work together on the ten-minute dreaming process.

Before continuing, Carol asked for questions. There were none, so she explained a little about inner wisdom and about how people often repress their hopes and dreams in their unconscious minds. Then she told how the ten-minute dreaming process can divert the censor so we can recover our own now unconscious life dreams.

During the next forty-five minutes, Carol directed the women to choose an experiential goal like happiness or serenity, after which they went through the ten-minute process of listing and numbering all their dreams. Finally, they put their dreams in priority order and threw away the original lists.

"What do we do now?" Cynthia asked in her middle school English teacher voice. "I'm excited! I didn't have any idea I wanted to do some of these things, but now I want to know how to get them actualized!"

Mr Crutchfield — Homemaker SSS Teacher
older lady — not to attractive
loves teaching 9 yr. old boys

Carol sighed and smiled nervously. "Before I answer that, Cynthia, I want to tell you all that groups have always scared me. I've been afraid that if I shared personal things, I'd make a fool of myself and be rejected — or that someone might tell what I'd said outside the group. But John and I have been doing a two-person sharing session a few minutes every day for some time now, and it's helped me a lot in expressing myself. So I thought we'd do the same thing here — just begin to talk about going on this adventure. We can help each other meet our goals by sharing some of them, but we won't discuss any we're not comfortable with sharing, and we won't necessarily get into many specifics about those we do share. I just want to provide a place where as many of you who want to can share some of what's happening to you and what you're feeling as we all try to accomplish our own dreams."

Dorothy agreed, "Women I know share mostly opinions. I think I'd get a lot out of hearing how other people are feeling as we go through this process. You might not guess it to look at me, but I'd find it a lot less threatening to do this together than to try it on my own."

Jenny commented, "Yeah, we don't share many feelings in real estate either — and besides, I need someone to make me accountable. Alone, I tend to put my own dreams aside as being selfish, or at least not important enough to give priority to. I'm excited about being able to come back to all of you to share the good things as well as the bad. I think knowing I'll be coming here and sharing every week will give me motivation and courage to try things I probably wouldn't on my own."

Cynthia thrust her fist into the air, at the same time exclaiming, "Yes! — If you guys keep trying and coming back, I know I'll be more likely to take my dreams seriously."

A housewife named Bobbie said, "This is scary for me, but I'm excited, and I really want to do it."

The excitement in the room was almost palpable as Dorothy said, "Where else could we share what happens to us on this dream quest? In most of the conversations with people I work with at the bank, it's not appropriate to share personal dreams, much less change them into goals and work to achieve them as we're going to do. And when I was growing up, my family never even mentioned the idea creative vocation of dreams — especially for women. I guess that's why I never took my own dreams seriously."

"What are the rules?" Cynthia asked. Everyone laughed. Cynthia blushed and snapped playfully, "Well! I've been teaching for eighteen years, and I just know there have to be some rules."

Carol patted Cynthia's hand. "As a matter of fact, Dr. Magie did have a few suggestions." The others laughed, but picked up their pencils as Carol continued.

"The first rule is confidentiality. That is, each of us agrees not to talk outside the group about what's said here, or even who comes to the meetings. Dr. Magie says confidentiality creates the safe atmosphere we need to be honest in what we say." She looked at each of them for signs that they understood and agreed.

Everyone nodded their heads, except Jenny, who looked somewhat troubled. "What is this, a secret society?"

Carol shook her head, "No, Jenny. But it is personal and intimate, and intimacy requires privacy. And a lot of groups I've been involved with in the past didn't feel safe because there were no rules of confidentiality. Dr. Magie taught us that talking about your dreams too much with people who aren't exploring their own dreams almost encourages criticism, and that can defuse your focus on the dreams. Also, if they tease you, it puts you under unnecessary pressure to achieve your dreams or makes you want to quit. It's hard enough under the best conditions to keep dreaming and believing you can accomplish your dreams. But in this group, you'll be safe, and you can always choose not to share anything that's too scary or personal. But the idea is to keep what is said here in the group."

Carol read the "Ground Rules for Sharing" from the index card Dr. Magie had given her and John. When she finished, she put the card on the coffee table near the center of the room.

Cynthia brought up another concern. "I'm not very good at groups, but there's something I really want to say. It may sound strange, but I'm not even sure if my dreams are appropriate."

Carol said, "I know how you feel. But I can tell you, the only way I could figure out whether my dreams were realistic was to talk about them in a safe atmosphere, before I investigated them in the real world!" Everyone sat quietly, and Carol knew they were all wondering if their dreams were realistic. "I'll tell you what," she sighed, with a little anxiety. "I'll read from my dream list first. My fear is that you won't think these are good dreams, but Dr. Magie said to be honest when I listed them, and this is what I came up with. If we're going to do this, I might as well show you what I mean."

After Carol read her dream list, an intimate silence filled the room because she had risked being vulnerable. A few seconds passed before she took a deep breath and asked, "Feedback, anybody?"

"Way to go, Carol!" Dorothy exclaimed. "Your dreams sound wonderful and freeing to me. I can see I was afraid to put down some things because they might sound superficial or grandiose. I was ... conservative. I'll bet that comes from my childhood experience. My mother always reminded me that I was 'only a woman.' She'd say, 'Don't hope for too much, honey. That way you won't be disappointed when you don't get it.' I'm going to add getting a massage at least once a month to my list, too." Several of the other women nodded and a friend of Jenny's said, "I can't believe how I've been brainwashed not to want anything for myself."

"Yeah, but what about loving our neighbor as ourselves?" Cynthia asked.

"That's the problem," Carol said. "A lot of us *do* love our neighbors as ourselves. The trouble is I never learned to love myself, so I'm a pretty poor neighbor lover."

Jenny had been sitting quietly, but at this point she spoke up as though she could no longer hold back, "Dorothy, you and Carol are out of my league! You're talking about getting massages and flying to Switzerland when all I'm dreaming about is paying off the mortgage on my condo. I hate to tell you, but I've always been a little jealous of your lifestyle, Carol. That's just where I am." She paused, shrugged, and after an embarrassed silence ventured, "I must say, though, that for years I've wished I could go on one of those Club Med singles' cruises for two weeks in the Virgin Islands." Just as a wistful smile started to appear on her face, she caught herself and frowned. "But isn't it dumb to dream about things you can't afford to do?"

Everyone looked at Carol.

Shame swept through Carol at first, the old shame she'd always felt about being raised with money. But then she remembered Dr. Magie's ground rules for responding to someone else's sharing and her shame faded. Her composure returned, and she began kindly, "You're saying you've been jealous that I was raised in a family with money? I've always felt a little guilty about that, as well, and I've tried to look at people who were really rich, richer than we were, to feel better about what I had. But I'm realizing in this dreams-to-goals process that I have to deal only with my own life to find my true dreams. Dr. Magie says the only way to avoid the criticism and bickering that can come with jealousy is for each one of us to focus only on our own dreams, without judging whether someone else's dreams are too large, too small or just inappropriate.

"All my life I've tried to squelch my dreams," Carol continued. "And all my married life I've been dishonest sometimes and kept secret things I really wanted. I've played it safe, not taking any risks. I hope in this group we can accept each other's real dreams. It's hard enough to express them. I'm hoping we'll be about encouragement, not fixing each other." She ended by smiling at Jenny.

"I can see how you might be self-conscious about having money," Dorothy commented, "and I've got to say that my main motivator to accomplish my first dream is *about* money: financial security. My motive is fear, because the plain truth is I'm afraid I'll be a financial burden to my brother and sisters when I'm old. I know fear isn't a very noble motivation, but evidently on this dream quest adventure, the name of the game is to be honest about our dreams. I hope we'll learn not only how to tell if our dreams are authentic and doable, but also how not to put down other people and their dreams."

Jenny piped up, "So are you saying we're supposed to encourage each other to do what each needs to do to check out our dreams and to learn what *God* has given each of us particularly?"

"Thanks, Jenny," Carol replied. "I would have said it differently, but that's the way I understand what we're doing. We're trying to find dreams that are all our own, not someone else's. And there's nothing in this about our dreams being noble or anything else. This dreaming process has already begun to change me in a healthy way. I'm becoming more aware and assertive, and less ashamed to want some special things I enjoy. And at the same time, I think I'm becoming more sensitive to other people and their choices — even when they're different from mine."

The group had set an alarm clock to help them limit the meeting time to an hour and a half with a ten-minutes early warning to allow for the next week's assignment. It beeped as Carol spoke. She asked for questions, and when no one asked anything, she took a few minutes to tell the group some of the things she'd learned about making a dream book, and how they could copy their dreams on index cards to carry with them and read every morning or evening. She suggested that during the following week each person who decided to commit to the six week experiment would either begin a dream book or list her dreams on 3×5 cards and then pick one particular dream from her own dream list. At their next meeting they would discover how to change that dream into a specific goal and begin checking it out.

While fixing supper later that evening, Carol's mind raced as she remembered the sparkle of excitement in the dream group members. She felt she'd made a strong beginning in calling her friends together. She felt confident that she would have a support group, even though John didn't want one and had already become preoccupied again with his business. But to her surprise, when John came home he seemed really interested in what had happened. The first thing he said was, "How did your 'Dream Team' session go, Honey? I thought about the meeting and hoped it went well."

—mm—

The results of that meeting were startling to Carol. Her telephone rang off its cradle. The women who attended had seen Carol's freedom to express her feelings and go after her dreams of learning to be a writer, and they expressed their gratitude for the caring ways she had reached out to them. Her sharing had touched them much more than she'd known.

The group continued to meet for six weeks, and then fifteen more women joined them for another six weeks, after a beginning orientation meeting Carol led. Several of the initial group shared with the newcomers what they were discovering.

A week after the second group of sessions Carol's phone rang at dawn.

"We've got a problem," Dorothy said, without any preliminaries.

Carol looked at her watch and asked, "What are you calling me about at six o'clock in the morning!"

"Oh sorry, but I got an idea that won't wait."

"What's so important?"

"You know how I told you after our last Dream Team meeting that all kinds of people have asked about joining our group and doing Dr. Magie's awakening process?"

"Yes."

"Well, I was at a meeting of the State Women's Coalition, and the President, Deborah Wainwright, told me she's been hearing about our group and what's happened to it. She's interested in having you present the dreaming process at the board's annual retreat in Aspen. They think it sounds like something that could help a lot of women to awaken and achieve their unspoken dreams.

"As a matter of fact, that's the proposed title for the statewide convention meeting in the fall: *Awakening and Achieving Your Unspoken Dreams.*"

"Whoa, Dorothy. Let me get this straight. They want me to come and present the process to the board retreat?"

"Yep . . . and well, if they respond to what you present at the retreat, they also want to talk to you about taking the whole convention — about five hundred women — through the process as the keynote speaker next year."

"You're crazy, Dorothy. That's not something for a large group of people."

"Why not? They could all do their lists at the same time just like we did."

"Well, I don't know. Someone would have to write a follow-up plan for small groups, if women at the convention wanted to move ahead and achieve their dreams."

"Yeah, that's when I told them that since your dream was to become a writer, you'd be the perfect person to write the small group follow-up plan for them, and . . . "

"You what?"

"Well, you told us you'd already started a small book explaining the way the dreaming process works. And, Carol, so many women don't have a mentor to help them get in touch with their dreams — much less encourage them to achieve them. This would be a great contribution to women everywhere."

Carol was silent, thinking about what Dorothy was saying. She hadn't told the group, but that was what she'd been talking about with her own new mentor — who was a writing teacher in the university graduate tutorial program she'd been working in for two years. They had talked about how to make the dreaming process accessible to people, and particularly women, everywhere. She'd already written some articles about parts of Dr. M.'s process and she had e-mailed Dr. M. for guidance.

"You still there?" Dorothy finally asked.

"Yes, let's talk about this at the Dream Team Wednesday night. Because if I do this, you and the others will have to help me do the planning and pull it all off."

"You'll do it then! I'll call you later."

EXERCISE SIX
A Ten-Minute Ice Melter Process
for Almost Any Kind of Group

This process requires approximately three minutes per person or more time if the group is small or time is not a problem. (It can be done with a large group in as few as ten minutes by using groups of three.) The overall group leader should share her or his experience first, in two minutes, being as honest and personal as is feasible. Use a stop watch or timer.

1. First sharing (two minutes): Share anything you want to about your childhood. (The past can be safer to share.) It often is helpful if some painful or uncomfortable experiences are shared, to set the floor of vulnerability appropriate to the group. Set the timer for two minutes. When it goes off, set it for one minute and move on to question two.

2. Second sharing (one minute): Describe the happiest experience you can recall. It may have been in childhood or last week.

3. After you as leader have shared for two minutes and then one minute, tell the group (or groups of three) to begin the two-minute sharing. Tell them that you will stop them at the end of the two minutes, and remind the person speaking to begin to describe the happy experience at that time. The leader will stop the sharing in two minutes and remind the person sharing to tell of a happy experience in one minute.

4. Again, at the end of the one-minute period, the timekeeper stops the speaker and the next person begins his or her two minutes and one minute until all three members of all groups have shared in this way.

You may want to tell the larger group that the person in each group of three who is sitting nearest to the front of the room goes first, and then they proceed around the circle clockwise. Remind the group that everyone is free to "pass without penalty" and not share her or his experience during this exercise.

16

An All-Pro Rookie

The five years after the death of John's mother were almost magical for Carol and John. The shopping center deal became extremely valuable when construction of the nearby highway bypass was completed, so Martins' income was even higher than anticipated.

They had built a beautiful home on the edge of the plain next to the mountains. Bill and Fran Castle and their teen-aged daughter were now close friends. And it was obvious that Bill was using his influence to advance John's career in every way he could.

A nationally syndicated writer did a glowing article in the *Denver Post* on John and Martin Industries. At nights and on weekends, Carol was deeply involved in training leaders for dozens of women's groups on the dream actualizing process through the use of a small book and exercise manual she wrote to meet the demand created by her speaking to the Colorado Women's Convention.

Three years after moving in with Castle Developers, while laying the foundation for Martin Industries, John had gone to Bill and said, "I'm ready to raise some new money and get my own business going. Working with you has been great. You've given me a crash course in commercial real estate, and," John laughed in feigned surprise, "somehow Robert has completely backed off from trying to cut me off at the knees. Being with you has been a great way to learn the basics without starving — or getting killed. Thanks, Bill."

Bill recommended a meeting with Arthur Bennett, an independent stockbroker who specialized in finding places people in high tax brackets could invest significant funds. He was the man with whom Bill had made his new fortune. John called him.

John didn't know how much money to try to raise for Martin Industries's initial venture. Bill and Arthur recommended forming a limited partnership and raising $3 million. Arthur said, "As general partner you will maintain control. Minimum investments will be $100,000. This way, the maximum number of people you'll have to deal with will be thirty. And if the first partnership goes well, you can either form a new limited partnership or set up a corporation and go public."

Bill chimed in, "If you set up a corporation, later you can offer the limited partners stock in the corporation for their partnership interests, a tax-free exchange. That way you get the partnership income as capital for the corporation, and the investors have already taken the tax charge-offs for their share of operating expenses to the partnership real estate deals. But could still benefit from the growth of the new corporation, and the stock would be a more marketable asset as a publicly traded company."

John nodded, "That's what I'd like to do. I'll run some numbers and scenarios for prospective investors in the initial partnership and get back to you."

Arthur said, "If the first projects succeed, capitalizing the company will be easy. Having prominent investors as initial stockholders will spread the word (and confidence) about the new ventures to "good old boy" groups all over the world. That synergy alone would almost assure adequate financial backing."

Three million dollars sounded like a fortune to John. Bill, however, assured him there were still enough tax advantages to the kinds of deals he planned to get involved in to interest a lot of people the three of them knew in high tax brackets. "And besides," Bill added, "the basic problem for wealthy people is 'trust.' They're more than a little paranoid about speculative new ventures, but a lot of them trust Arthur. They want to go with a manager who's talented, but also with someone they trust — and you're squeaky clean. They will go with you."

"You really think so?"

"Tell you what. So you'll believe me, I'm your first partner for a $100 K share!"

"Why?" John laughed, "I've never known you to be exactly sentimental about trusting people with your money."

Bill laughed, "You're right about that. But I'm getting old and tired, and investing with you instead of working sounds pretty good. If you play your cards right, I just *may* sell you my business some day and go trout fishing at my cabin. Actually, part of my reason," Bill said laughing, "is that you've picked up my instincts. That alone would make you a natural to succeed in this business. But one of the main reasons I want to invest with you is the business plans you've developed. That's about the most creative and simple, yet comprehensive system I've seen. I don't see how it can fail. Did you learn that from old Robert Latner?"

John laughed, "No, actually my therapist taught me."

"Your therapist?"

Yeah," John chuckled, "But I don't want to talk about that right now."

Bill laughed and clapped John on the back. He really liked John Martin, and he believed in him.

The first thing John did after he developed a proposal for the initial limited partnership was to spend some time with Arthur Bennet, who would be the key player for the first phase of his plan.

After talking to John at length, Arthur agreed to raise the money. "And I'm buying a $100,000 share. Bill showed me your business plan and what you did at Castle. I like what I saw; besides, my doing that'll be a good incentive to influence a number of clients I deal with to come along, since they know I'm conservative about this kind of investment."

Then came a jolt . . . right after Bill and Arthur had committed to buy shares, the economy in Denver took a serious downturn, and investment money seemed to dry up, something no one had counted on.

"Don't worry," Arthur said, "I've a network of clients outside of Denver — a group of investors in Europe who're diversified and wealthy enough to be impervious to the this trouble. The U.S. is still the best and safest place in the world to invest and preserve capital."

Carol's Dream Team had gotten very close. Two of them, Cynthia and Jenny, had investigated new vocations and were in the final stages of starting their new ventures. Carol's mentor was a widely published writing teacher on the faculty of Denver University who was brilliant and intuitive and understood the power of the dream system instantly.

Carol told the group, "I'm learning more than I ever imagined I could, and I'm happier than ever before!" Her work with Martin Industries blossomed, too. Using Dr. Magie's philosophy and methods, and counseling with him by phone several times a year, she and John were developing ways to get things done rapidly in all aspects of their business. And they were very much in love. Overall, life was about as good as it could get for Carol. The only fly in the ointment was that she had to curb her jealousy about John around most of their attractive women friends — except Fran, who was like a sister and the only one she talked to about such things. "It's not like I don't trust him," she confided. "He never looks sideways at another woman. I know it's irrational, but I get angry if he's even nice to anyone — always have." She shrugged.

One evening when John and Carol came home, there was a huge arrangement of roses on the coffee table in the living room. "Who in the world?" Carol said, looking at John for an explanation.

"How would I know? Bill Castle's the only one I know with enough money to send *that*."

Carol reached for the large card envelope. Inside was a note — and two plane tickets to Geneva with a Hertz car rental reservation. The note said, "It's time for our second honeymoon in Switzerland. Much love, John's Inner Wisdom."

17

Second Honeymoon and an Invitation to the Launching Party

mm mm mm

Carol shivered and turned off the A/C in the car. "Look at that sheer rock cliff!" she exclaimed pointing ahead as they came around another hair pin curve."

John said, "Yeah, looks like a giant cut it in one slice with a butcher's cleaver the size of a tennis court. And look how steep *all* the mountains are at this height, and how much snow is still on the peaks."

As they drove the winding mountain roads in the snow-capped Swiss Alps, they were like children on a first vacation. Either Carol or John wanted to stop at every village or overlook — and often they did. The first night they stopped at a quaint Swiss bed and breakfast. "Ah, you are honeymooners!" the owner said. John and Carol laughed, looked at each other and said, "Yes!" That night they snuggled together in a huge feather bed and after talking about what they had seen that day, they made love.

Two nights later in Zurich, after a candlelight dinner at a romantic restaurant on the lake, they were back in their room. Carol was undressing in the bathroom when, smiling seductively, she leaned out and said, "Hey, does all this remind you of anything from our past?"

John pretended to be trying to remember, but he shook his head. Then his eyes lit up. "You mean when we flew to Chicago to see the Bulls-Nuggets game?"

Carol laughed and shook her head. "You're so weird," she said, running out of the bathroom, grabbing up a pillow and attacking John. "I meant our *honeymoon,* you dope!"

"Oh," John said, catching her arms and pulling her on the bed with him, "I thought *this* was our honeymoon!" She quit struggling, and melted into his arms.

mm

The morning after their first night in Geneva, over bread, cheese, and fruit with hot chocolate in their room, John said, as usual, "It's eight o'clock. Do you want to go first?" They wound up flipping a coin and

Carol shared first. Even on their second honeymoon, they had agreed to use the twenty-minute check-in support system along the lines that Dr. Magie had described five years before.

"Remember on my list that I want to write a book that would help people live more sanely? I decided I was about ready to write the small book for women about the Dreaming Process, but I was reluctant to talk to you about it because I might not be able to write it, and you'd try to fix me so I could or would get at it." When John started to object, Carol put up her hand to stop him, and continued, "I'd felt excited and frightened when you suggested I go with you to see Dr. Magie, since I had read one of his early books, and it impressed me. But I worried even then that if I came to see him, you or he would try to tell me what my dreams *should* be, and I sure didn't want that! I was relieved that neither of you did that and that you still haven't tried to fix me. Now, watching the women in my group, and working with women all over Colorado concerning their dreams, I'm more excited about the future than ever." John looked puzzled, but didn't interrupt. "Anyway, seeing Cynthia, Jenny and many others find the courage to risk changing to accomplish their dreams has given me hope that I can research and write an important book on the intuition and be a good writer, actually helping people become free to do important things in the world. Dorothy has been elected President and CEO of Northridge Bank, Jenny quit real estate and is doing well as a stockbroker, and Cynthia is getting the financing together to open a private school for children with learning disabilities — all in less than four years!"

After both had spoken and given feedback, John asked, "Do you want any suggestions?" He thought he had some excellent advice for her about how to arrange a time schedule to pursue her book project.

Carol thought a moment. "No, not right now, I'm just starting to get serious about this new book idea, and I want to think about it alone for a while."

Realizing again that John's style was to "solve it when you see it," Carol knew that she needed time to begin processing by chewing on the ideas and digesting her thoughts before getting into solution mode, so she was taken back when John said, "Okay, I understand."

Carol looked at him in a way she hadn't before. Carol was thinking, "I never would have believed John could respond that way. He's really changed." She felt warm and safe with him somehow. It was a great feeling.

When their six days were over, they sadly returned their little Ford Escort honeymoon special. Disappointed they wouldn't get to see Dr. M. who was on the last week of a lecture tour in Japan, they had made reservations at a hotel in Geneva near the airport for their final night in Europe. John leaned over and kissed Carol gently on the lips. "You know," he said nodding his head, "you really do honeymoons well! How'd you like to fly away with me to the land of your dreams tomorrow?"

"Great," Carol said, looking at him with great affection through happy but tired eyes, "as long as the flight goes to Denver, Colorado."

While they were at the reception desk, John asked if there were any messages. There was a fax from Wil, and a telephone call from Arthur, who was at the Grosvenor House hotel in London. Arthur's message said, "Read your e-mail when you get this."

John got out his laptop to plug into the hotel message center, and said, "Tell me what Wil's fax says while I'm getting this started."

Carol said, "He's coming home . . . and wants to work in the company." She handed John the fax:

To: John and Carol Martin
Subject: Application for Employment

Dad and Mom: I've got three good job offers since completing my MBA, but I think I could learn more working at Martin Industries. How's your nepotism tolerance? I'd be glad to come for an interview to talk about positions and terms. (I'm coming to Denver anyway and would like to stay at home till I can find an apartment. Please advise about that.)

Wil

John was secretly elated. His relationship with Wil hadn't improved, but he hoped they had a mutual, man-to-man respect even though they still argued when they were alone together. He read the message twice and asked, "What do you make of this?"

Carol looked at him questioningly, "Looks like a job application to me."

"Do you think he's serious?"

Carol's mind swam with thoughts of Wil moving back to Denver. She'd missed him terribly, but knew he and John still got along like oil and water. "I think it could work if his office were in the other building." She was referring to the two-story office complex they had leased across from the original Martin Industries office. "He could start as Roger's assistant in acquisitions and learn the ropes of the new company."

"Yes," John nodded, "And he'd have a chance to settle in without being in my lap."

"Which would make it a little less . . . stressful for you," Carol agreed."

"What do you mean by that?" John snapped.

"Well, you two don't exactly have a 'Good night, John boy' relationship. I just think it'll go better if there's as much physical space as possible between you two until we see if Wil has grown as much as his grades indicate he has."

"Okay, let's do it. Will you write an answer we both can sign?"

Carol nodded and felt in her heart that somehow time would help the two of them get together. She asked, "What was your message from Arthur?"

John read, "John and Carol: Got your message from Geneva. Missed you when I called back. Sorry you couldn't come spend a couple of days en route to Switzerland in London to meet your twelve new English partners — 1200K that is! How about that? I am determined to celebrate with you because these guys have convinced some big honchos on the continent to join them in our partnership venture. Since I'm coming to Paris to sign them up, and you're going home via Paris, how about at least stopping off overnight for a celebration dinner at the George V to meet the newest members of your eclectic financial family? I've made reservations for you there and will catch the tab — for that and all required travel changes. This is the beginning of a whole new chapter in your lives — and, I suspect, mine — so be my guest. Do it!!! Answer at once. I'll handle the details. — Arthur."

John could hardly believe so many of the partnership shares had been sold, and he laughed out loud.

"What is it?"

"Well, it looks like Arthur's been hypnotizing people all over Europe. We've got almost a 'full scholarship' to play in Denver commercial real estate. He sold most of the shares, and he's evidently got verbal commitments from some of the people he's meeting in Paris this week."

"You're joking!"

John shook his head and then told her about Arthur's celebration plans in Paris. She thought a minute. "I didn't bring any clothes for that kind of evening."

"You can pick something up."

"John, you don't just 'pick something up' the hour before a dinner party at the Hotel George V!"

"Don't worry! We get in at 10:00 a.m. I'll ask Arthur to find out about the right places for you pick something up."

When Carol looked dubious, John said, "You're so beautiful right now, you could wear something from a discount store sales rack and look great." Before she could protest, he added playfully, "But you won't have to. We're in tall cotton, Mrs. Martin, and this is the way it's done."

18

May Day! May Day!
Fire on the Launch Pad!

wwwwwwwww

"Please fasten your seat belts in preparation for landing and make sure your tray tables are in their upright and locked position. Welcome to Charles De Gaulle International Airport — and to Paris, France." John looked up in surprise from his European edition of the *U.S. News*. The rich musical quality of the brunette flight attendant's voice was so much like Claudette Fontaine's that he thought for a moment she was there.

Carol said, "What's the matter?"

John shook his head, "Nothing." Although he had temporarily forgotten that Claudette lived in Paris, he would never forget the magical candlelit evening with the beautiful widow at Glion. As he thought about her, he remembered responding to her passionate, vulnerable letter of gratitude handed to him by François. He had politely declined her offer to invest in Martin Industries, since the company had only been a dream then, or as he had put it, "was not positioned at this time to accept outside investments." He'd thought his response would be the end of the relationship, until his termination session with Robert Latner revealed that she'd been checking on him. Since that time more than five years ago, he had received several notes — three, to be exact — congratulating him on awards or articles that had appeared about him or his company in various publications, including the *Denver Post*. The notes were always friendly, always charming and witty, but although he never replied to her correspondence, and she never referred to their meeting in Glion, the letters always had the faint scent of the perfume she wore that night that never failed to stir him more deeply than he could admit — even to himself.

Carol interrupted his thoughts, "Well, fasten your seatbelt, cowboy. I don't want to lose you splattered all over French soil." The lines through French customs in baggage claim were long and noisy, but then they saw Arthur waving at them from outside the customs area. Just then a Frenchman in a dark suit appeared saying, *"Monsieur et Madame Martin?"* He took them through a very short VIP line.

112

"Martin," Arthur said jovially, after he'd hugged and greeted Carol, "you'll never believe what's happened. These young French guys are heroes with their friends because they made a killing investing in the U.S. market with me." Without stopping, he looked toward heaven and crossed himself. "And they've asked if some of their friends could come tonight to meet us! We could sell another venture tonight, if we had one!" He seemed genuinely glad to see them and was already in such a festive mood that John suspected he'd started his celebrating a little early. Inside the stretch limo, the first thing Arthur did was to offer them drinks from the bar as they cruised through the blasting horns and shouts of Parisian traffic. He explained to Carol that the personal shopper of a family he knew in Paris was at her disposal for the day.

On the way to their suite at the George V, they were ushered through the ornate lobby filled with priceless antiques and stunning flower arrangements. They continued through a high gallery with large Flemish tapestries and more fresh flowers. Arthur pointed to a grand piano, "Every evening during cocktail hour, this great pianist plays Broadway show tunes and light classics." Although John and Carol had been to Europe, and Carol and her family had stayed at the Ritz in Paris when she was twelve, she'd never seen anything like the Hotel George V. As they got into the elevator, she was aware of feeling both excited and anxious. Their lives were changing very fast, indeed.

In the bedroom of their suite was a portable hanging rack containing a dozen beautiful size ten cocktail dresses, several more formal evening dresses and some sample accessories. The personal shopper was an attractive, conservatively dressed English woman about Carol's age, who had been in the fashion industry in Paris for years. From the moment Susan said, "Good morning, Mrs. Martin," Carol knew they would get along. She smiled at Susan and said to John and Arthur, "Why don't you two go in the living room. Susan and I have a lot to talk about."

Later that evening, when Carol, John and Arthur were waiting for the elevator going down to the private dining room, Carol said quietly to John, "I feel a little like Alice must have felt, stepping through the looking glass." The way he looked at her made her realize she really did look gorgeous.

Arthur had sent an envelope to their room containing an updated list of the names of the dinner guests but John hadn't had a chance to look at it. Now, as Arthur walked up and greeted Carol, "Whoa! You look — great!" John pulled the list from the pocket of his dinner jacket and was examining it when he stopped and grabbed Arthur's arm whispering to him, "What the hell is *this?*" Just then the elevator door opened and Carol stepped in ahead of the two men.

"What do you mean?" Then, seeing where John was pointing on the list, he smiled a broad victory smile, and said in a conspiratorial whisper, as he stepped in behind John, "That's my surprise. Four of the men who bought the last five shares of the partnership were high executives of Fontaine Industries, and they're bringing their new board chair, Madame Claudette Anton Fontaine. How's that for a coup? Fontaine Industries did $12 billion in sales last year." John looked at Arthur quizzically as the elevator door opened.

—*um*—

The private dining room was understated Old World elegance, with antique Napoleon silver and polished wood reflecting a soft light that seemed to slide across the surfaces of the dark wood of the side tables. Arthur welcomed the guests as they came in and introduced each to John and Carol over the background noise of a string quartet. There was an open bar and soon the French and English voices mingled into the universal sounds of laughter and cocktail banter. A waiter brought a martini. As the alcohol seeped into Carol's frontal cortex, the group seemed to homogenize before her eyes — they all became Frenchmen.

Between acknowledging introductions and laughing at sophisticated humor, she had been quietly looking the group over. The men were in their thirties and forties, younger than she had expected. Most of them were trim and handsome in dinner jackets, except one, who was about sixty, overweight and looked a little out of place though totally at ease — in his older style Tuxedo and unruly gray hair. Carol remembered that his name was Fontaine. Now she noticed that he seemed to be focused intently on her John, standing in every group that gathered around him. He was listening more than casually to what John said, or so it seemed to Carol. With his plump, unsmiling jowls, the man looked a little like a pit bull.

Free from her own island of curious admirers at one point, she noticed that the pit bull was actually focused on a sophisticated woman about her own age, a stunning brunette, in perfect black and diamonds. Carol had met her briefly with the older male Fontaine and thought they were a couple. Now examining the woman more carefully, Carol shook her head, and thought, "That's about the most gorgeous woman I've ever seen; she must be a French movie star or something." In fact, she could hardly take her eyes off the woman, and while at first glance everything looked normal, a warning bell went off inside Carol's head. The crowd around John shifted slightly, and she could see into the woman's eyes as she looked at John. "Good Lord," Carol said, "That woman is in love with my husband!" Her throat constricted and her eyes narrowed, but then someone stepped beside John, blocking her view.

"What?" It was Arthur, who was visiting with Carol while managing the party from the sidelines. John was relaxed but totally focused on the investors' questions.

"Oh nothing, thanks," she responded to Arthur's question, never taking her eyes off the woman in black. "It must be my imagination," she said to herself. But the longer she looked the more certain she was of the woman's attraction to John. And then she saw him smile at something the woman said. "These two are not strangers," her interior jealous voice said knowingly."Now that you mention it, Arthur, I would like another martini, please, dry, no olive." Arthur raised one finger slightly, and a waiter, who seemed to be assigned exclusively to him saw his nod, and disappeared in the undulating field of guests. Casually, she said, "Tell me more about the Fontaine woman talking to John?"

When Arthur saw the woman Carol was asking about, his face lit up. He nodded and said confidentially in her ear. "That's the surprise of the evening. That's Claudette Anton Fontaine."

"Who?"

"Oh, I'm sorry, we only knew she was coming at the last moment. She's the new Chair of the Fontaine Conglomerate, one of the largest holding companies in the world. The older guy is a cousin of her late husband. She could wave her hand and make us all very wealthy if she decided to go with John."

"Go with John?"

"If she decided he was suited to her purposes."

Carol looked at the woman carefully, "I think she's already made that decision." Beaming and nodding, Arthur didn't notice that Carol was doing neither.

Arthur said, "Ah, here's your martini." The waiter took the small linen napkin from the silver tray, and formally presented it to her, as the *maitre d'* approached them, "Shall we serve, *Monsieur?*"

Arthur offered his arm to Carol, who deliberately downed the martini in her hand, gave him the empty glass and said with a slight slur, "Thank you, Arthur, and I think I'll have another. This could be a long evening."

The dinner and wines were beyond excellent, and after dinner Arthur reintroduced John and Carol to the assembled guests, asking John if he would describe some of the opportunities he saw in commercial real estate in Colorado. John was charming, incisive and articulate, and Carol had never been more proud of him. Several questions were raised about new tax consequences for foreign investors in the U.S., and though Carol tensed at the first question, John had evidently included "tax consequences for foreign investors" in his action plan after hearing that Arthur intended to go overseas for money.

When John finished, the group applauded, and Carol commented to Jacques Fontaine, who was seated next to her, "The flowers are magnificent."

Arthur, overhearing her, agreed, "I don't know who does the flower arrangements at the George V, but they are said to be the most creative and beautiful of any hotel in the Europe." He nodded to the French people at the table, and shaking his head, said to Carol in honest appreciation, "The French are really something." He caught Madame Fontaine's eye, and nodding slightly to her.

Madame Fontaine smiled graciously and then shrugged and said in a slightly throaty voice, "Well, it not easy to admit this, but the artist who arranges the flowers for George V is Jeff Leatham, an American — from California, I believe . . . but it is possible that some of the flowers came from France." Everyone, including Carol, laughed.

Then she asked Carol, "If it would be appropriate with your schedule, I . . . we would like very much to show you some of the wonderful gardens of Paris."

Carol tried not to hate this charming, beautiful, and apparently sincere woman and her offer of hospitality, but she was quite high by now, after three martinis and wine during the dinner. Part of her actually wanted to accept the invitation, if only to find out what kind of a woman she was dealing with, but inside, she was seething. The possibility of this woman having a secret relationship with her husband was her worst nightmare, and her mind was a bubbling cauldron of irrational jealousy, fear and rage. There was silence at the table. Out of the corner of her eye she saw John listening to the conversation. "He doesn't look happy," she noted to herself. Her stomach was tense, throat constricted. Her thinking was fuzzy, and her vision blurred slightly, as she started to respond to Madame Fontaine's invitation.

But before she could say anything, John interrupted pleasantly, as he rose and moved behind Carol's chair. "Thank you, Claudette, but we have a very early flight out in the morning." Ignoring Carol's angry stare, he continued. "We would like very much to see the gardens of Paris, perhaps at another time, but I don't want our new partners to think we don't have the famous American work ethic. So, sadly, we have to leave."

After saying their good-byes to the new partners of Martin Industries and acknowledging the other guests, John led Carol toward the elevator. She was not at all happy at being hustled out of the party, however gently.

It was clear to her by John's actions that he knew she had exceeded her usual self-imposed 'one-cocktail-and-two-glasses-of-wine' limit. She also perceived from two decades of marriage that he could smell the smoke of her volcanic temper. Her contracted pupils and 'don't touch me' body language sent unmistakable signals that the coming eruption would be high on the Richter scale.

Oblivious, Arthur pushed the elevator button and waited while they entered. "I've got a couple of the new prospects to talk to. But I'll take you to the airport for the nine o'clock flight in the morning. American 79 to Denver via Dallas, isn't it? John nodded. Meet you in the lobby at 6:15?" John grimaced, but nodded. As the doors started to close, Arthur held them apart and added, "Thanks for coming. You two were *outstanding!*" And the doors came together, leaving them to ride up alone.

Carol fixed John with a fiery stare and snapped one word, "Claudette?" When the elevator stopped, she marched down the hall toward their suite, unlocked the door and went into the bedroom, locking it behind her. Filling the marble bathtub, she poured herself a glass of Champagne from the bottle John had ordered chilled for their private celebration in the room after dinner.

He knocked loudly, "Open the door. We've got to talk."

"Go away, Prince Charming. If you hurry you may still be able to kiss her awake."

"Don't be an ass. I love *you.* I was being nice to her because Arthur said she and her cousin — the fat guy, who's also her bodyguard — have bought the last four shares of the partnership: $400,000 worth. They've already signed up; Arthur closed the deal late this afternoon."

She didn't say anything.

"Open the door. I had no idea these two were partners till I saw their names on the list in the elevator — the list Arthur had sent up the room an hour before. Let me in. This is too important to stuff under the covers."

She unlocked the door and threw it open in one motion. Her eyes were blazing, "Isn't it customary to 'sweep things under the *rug?* Not the *'covers?'*"

He realized Carol was far beyond being rational, and was close to being out of control. He began to feel waves of nausea. He'd had several drinks too, and had feared women's rage directed at him since his childhood. Inside, his inner voice said, "Tell her the truth. It's the shortest way through this. "But he replied to the voice silently, "I can't. She'd never understand. And I can't risk losing everything."

"What's the matter?" she said, "Freud got your tongue?" She was calmer now, but her anger was sharp as a razor, "Let's start from the beginning. When did you sleep with Claudette Fontaine? That woman is in love with you. I'm not a wizard, and I was a little high, but I could see it in her eyes. Women's eyes just don't focus and shine the way hers did when they've just been *introduced* at a dinner party. I was hoping what I saw was about the martinis, but when you called her 'Claudette' as if you had known her for years, I knew." She was still hoping against hope that she was wrong, and he'd have an explanation, but John just stared at her, so she took another shot, "Where was it? Where were you together?"

John was in agony. This was a bad dream. He hadn't even thought about getting back in touch with Claudette. He was frightened by the intensity of Carol's anger, but he finally took a deep breath and said, "I met her in Glion, on the last night — the first time I was there. But I did not sleep with her — we just had dinner — in a crowded dining room — because the maitre d' seated us at the same table."

Carol looked at him as if he were thinking she was a fool. "What after dinner, cribbage? That's the night that I called your room until *1:15 a.m.*, and you never came in. I'm not a complete fool. And I know how you are when we've been apart a week — much less ten days. You might as well tell me about it, I'll find out anyway. If I have to, I'll ask her. And if I do, I'll know. It will show in her face. And if you don't tell me, I'll blow this whole deal with your partners. As Arthur said, 'It's all about *trust*,' Mr. Clean. Well, it is with me too!"

John had known for years how deep and irrational Carol's jealousy was. But he had never been in a situation like this, and the truth was so unusual that it sounded like a lie — even to him; but, he decided that he had no choice but to tell it.

"I know this story will be hard to believe."

"Try me."

He shook his head, took a breath and began.

"And why I didn't let François take her upstairs, I'll never know. . . ."

"Yeah, good question."

"I was pretty bombed, but she had lost her husband she was obviously very much in love with. I guess I just didn't want her half-carried up the stairs by a waiter. I felt like it was my . . . duty, somehow, to escort her to her room."

"Your *duty?*" John, who was looking down, remembering, nodded. "You *bastard!* What about your duty to me, your wife? Remember?" Her whole body a drawn bowstring, she wanted to pick up an andiron and smash his head with it. Her rage and shame coursed through her until finally, she said, "Shit!" and stalked over to the window and turned around. "Okay, tell me about it. Did you take her into your room, or hers?"

He said, "It wasn't like that. Although, I did carry her into her room."

"What *happened*, John?"

He shook his head. He was looking into the upper corner of their room wracking his brain to recall her bedroom that night. "All I can remember was carrying her through the door like dead weight." He remembered something, and said, "I do remember thinking how light she was to be so tall."

Carol slapped him hard across the face. "Wrong answer!"

"Listen, I was so drunk I could hardly stand up, and she had passed out and was snoring from the top of the stairway to her room. I don't think I could have done anything, even if she had been awake and wanted to."

She laughed a mirthless, sarcastic laugh. *"You,* Killer John? With a woman as beautiful as Claudette? You could have risen from the dead and made love to her, and we both know it. Just *admit* it, John. I don't know if we have a chance or not...." She began to cry in frustration. "But we damn sure don't if you won't tell me the truth."

"I know you mean that. I know how you hate disloyalty — and the next day I wracked my brain, but the truth is, I honestly *don't* remember anything after I got her to her room...and laid her on her bed." He was miserable, but he was telling the truth: he really couldn't remember.

Carol was still crying, but in her frustration was desperately grasping for a way to believe John and keep her self-respect. "I know this is crazy, but this question is more important to me than you will ever know. Were your clothes wrinkled — or were there any signs on them? Surely you remember that?" She knew she was being obsessive and that this had happened over five years ago, but she could not quiet the fear she felt.

He tried to remember, but the whole time after he put Claudette on the bed was a blank screen in his mind. He knew how proud and unforgiving Carol was when it came to disloyalty. Many friends had been excised for even minor infractions. She was a lot like her dad in that way — not that he could blame her this time, knowing how much she'd feared this very thing — and the fact that he was so drunk he couldn't remember something this important to her seemed like a bald-faced lie.

He finally just shook his head, and said sadly, "I'm sorry."

Carol was beginning to feel sick at her stomach from the drinking. She ached to cry but was wound in the mummy-tight bindings of her unspoken childhood fear. So instead she looked at John silently, and motioned him out.

When the door closed, she threw herself on the bed, buried her face in a pillow, and felt the bed begin to whirl, her mother's haunted face the day her father left suddenly before her. She jerked herself up on the side of the bed, and then her tears came.

19

Time Out for Repairs

~~~~~~~~~~~

The trip home from Paris was one of the worst experiences of John's life. Carol said nothing. They took off for Dallas at 9:00 a.m. The movie showing was an old one, "My Big Fat Greek Wedding." John asked for two headsets without thinking. Carol ignored hers. He saw people laughing around him, and thought, "This must be a funny movie." But he was too numb to follow the plot.

After lunch, he slept fitfully and had a frightening dream. In a dark room at night a beautiful woman was standing beside his bed. She obviously wanted to make love to him, but he knew he shouldn't. She unbuttoned her blouse, and suddenly, the lights went on and a loud voice was talking to him in French. He jumped in his seat and woke in a cold sweat. The flight attendant was repeating the information about going through customs. "Use the white card to list everything you are declaring. If you have any questions, push the flight attendant call button."

He thought, "My God, maybe I did sleep with Claudette and blocked it out because it would be such a crappy thing for me to do to Carol." He turned to Carol and started to tell her he'd like to talk to her, but she wasn't interested. Finally, he wrote her a note: "We need to talk about what we're going to do when we get home. Maybe we can use the five-minute sharing times to keep from fighting."

She looked at the note for a long time and then wrote back.

"We have a two-hour layover in Dallas. Maybe we could try it in the Admirals Club after we get through customs. But *no slick attempts* to *talk* me into *staying!*"

He felt hot anger redden his face. He was *not* trying to do *anything* slick, but she sure knew how to push his buttons. Finally, he nodded his agreement.

~~~~~

"No thanks. We'll just have a couple of Diet Cokes," John said to the bartender at the Admirals Club.

"I'll have a glass of Merlot," Carol said over John's shoulder.

The bartender raised his eyebrow, looking back and forth between them. "Will that be one Diet Coke then?" John glanced at her, but remembered they needed to talk. So he said evenly to the bartender, "That's right, you heard the lady." But to himself he said, "Steady boy, you don't need to trigger a grand exit now."

She insisted that he go first with his five minutes. He said, "Dr. M. told us that when people start to succeed in achieving their dreams all kinds of personal issues can come up to sabotage them. I think that's what's happening to us. What are your plans? Wil's coming home in a few days and we need to get through this."

Shaking her head, Carol pointed to the timer, and said, "Stick with sharing your stuff."

John calmed his anger and then talked about the business to try to keep the sharing going. In a calm, everyday voice, he began, "Everything is set to begin the acquisitions for the partnership as soon as the contracts are okay and the checks clear. We've already got our debts paid, and some capital in the bank. And we've got three deals lined up whereby we'll own a minor interest in a shopping mall in Denver, a small strip center in Vail, and the building of three all-weather storage facilities in Denver for a group out of Austin, Texas. We'll furnish the sites and build the buildings, but we'll also participate in the management with the principal by hiring the on-site managers and sharing the income. These guys are really hot. They have a 95 percent success ratio in the seventy-five facilities they've already built in Austin, Atlanta, Miami, and Nashville." Then, more enthusiastically, he said, "With the money Arthur's already got committed, we have the financial leverage to jump to a whole new level!

"I know you've got our books set up to process deals like this, and I need to know how involved you are going to be in the business when we get home." He looked directly at her and said, "Frankly, I'm not sure how this business could make it without you."

She nodded her understanding of what he was saying, but pointed to the timer and said, "You have another minute."

Instantly, John was angry again. He knew Carol was protecting herself from a free-for-all argument about her decision to back away, but it felt like she was controlling him with a time-wire around his neck. He continued evenly, "I know you are angry with me and don't trust me, but for God's sake, don't toss this marriage. We're *good* together, in business and — at home."

"Okay, time's up," she said quietly. Sniffing back her emotions, she handed the timer to him. He looked at her for a few seconds, and then set the timer for five minutes.

She tried to tell him what she'd heard him say, but she stopped in the middle of her recounting and said, "John, I hear you saying that you want me to stay in the business and keep being your partner."

He looked straight at her and aware she'd left out any reference to their marriage, he nodded slowly.

She continued, "I agree that the work we've done together in setting up the business to make the dream a reality is remarkable. But I'm surprised you want me to work that closely with you, even though we may... not be living together."

He looked out the window at an American passenger jet backing away from its gate, the glare from its silver nose blinding him for an instant. His stomach knotted, hearing her say out loud that she was processing what he was telling her in light of their not living together. But he kept listening and nodded his understanding of what she'd said.

"I don't know; I don't want to ruin the business. And I've cut the cord to Dad just as you have, so I can't run home. But everything is so confusing for me right now. After overcoming a lifetime hidden terror of being deserted, I finally trusted you on this trip, but now I feel like I did as a child — betrayed, scared to death. Since you didn't tell me about your meeting with Claudette, how could I ever trust you again? I can't believe you didn't know how deep this fear goes with me. I feel like I have to leave while I have the courage." Her face had metamorphosed into that of a little girl who'd lost her way home. She looked very sad and frightened.

John knew her reaction to break up the marriage without trying to work things out was not rational, and certainly not practical for either of them. He wanted to take her in his arms and tell her everything would be okay, but felt he couldn't since he was the problem in her eyes. Finally he said, "Why don't you call Dr. M. and find out if he'll see you?"

"We've just spent a *lot* of money going to Switzerland. We can't afford that. Besides, he's more your friend than mine. You'd get all his attention."

"Come on," he said quietly, "you know that's not true. He loves you too, and besides..." he paused and thought about what he was going to say, "...you can go without me. That way you can get time without me taking up your air space with him."

"You'd do that?"

"Sure, I want you to get whatever help you need, and I want to do this dream with you. But I want you to be happy as a person more than that. I can't help you decide what to do about me. And he's the best I know."

She looked at John for several seconds. This didn't fit the case she was building against him, but she was wary. Finally, she nodded.

John stood up. "Do you want me to call him, or would you rather?"

She looked tired, but giving him a hard look he'd never seen before, she said, "I'll do it. You're a little sneaky to trust right now," and she added with a definite nod, "and don't read my going to Switzerland wrong, my mind is pretty well made up about leaving."

20

Beginning the Guided Tour
through the Engine Room

Carol heard the car pull into the driveway. She ran to the front door, opened it and almost ran into Wil, who had just turned toward the house after saying good-bye to his friend, Abe.

"Wil! You're home!" She hugged his neck and realized that he was taller than John, and very muscular. "And you've grown!" She stepped back and looked him up and down.

He grinned, "It's good to be home, Mom, and you've gotten so tiny: You look like a college cheerleader." He looked over her shoulder, with a gaze she recognized.

Her expression changed. "He's not home yet. He works late a lot now."

Wil looked down at his mother, studying her face. "What's the matter? Has something gone wrong with the business?"

"Oh, no. It's going great. It's just . . . well, put your things in your old room while I fix you something to eat. Have you had lunch? How about a beer?"

"Whoa, slow down! Had lunch in the Phoenix airport between planes." He picked up his two bags and stopped on the bottom step. "And I still don't drink."

"Of course. I'm sorry. I'm a little rattled. Well, get comfortable and come back down. There's a lot to tell you."

Ten minutes later Wil was back downstairs in the den, lying on the black leather couch like he used to, watching the big TV, except now his legs hung over the armrest from the knees down. He couldn't believe he'd grown that much, until he remembered that since his freshman year in high school, he hadn't felt comfortable enough at home to relax that way.

Carol came in from the kitchen and nodded toward the stairs. "Do you have everything you need up there?"

"Yeah, everything's great. I really appreciate Dad letting me board with you a few days. He always told me his father said, "Once a man leaves home, he comes back when he's *invited*." I need to save some money till I start working and," Wil grinned, "the food is a lot better here than the YMCA."

Carol smiled wistfully and thought, "He's so much like his dad."

"What's the matter? You look tired. You okay?"

"Well, they sure taught you how to talk to a woman at Stanford. 'You look tired' is not a good opening line."

He kept looking at her, obviously concerned.

"Well, we might as well get it over with. You've got to know soon anyway."

"What?"

"It's about your father." And before she could stop herself, she was telling him about John getting drunk and spending the night with Claudette Fontaine.

She concluded, "The cock and bull story about the Fontaine's annual trip to Glion was crazy enough, but what hurt the most is that he claims when he carried her up and put her in her bed, he can't remember whether he slept with her or not. And he expects me to believe that! Wil, you should see that woman. She is one of the most beautiful women I have ever seen. And your father says he can't remember whether or not he had sex with her." She began to cry, "He's gone crazy. Does he think I'm some dumb little girl he can tell a thing like that to and I'll believe it? What kind of cowardice is that!"

Wil was sitting forward on the couch now, obviously upset. "Damn, what a stupid thing to do! Dad's got some serious problems with self-centeredness. I know I do too, but I'm so angry at him I could beat the crud out of him." Wil stopped, thinking, "But it's just not *like* Dad to make up that romantic story about the widow coming back to Glion."

"You're *missing* the *point*. Your father admitted he got drunk with this woman, but claimed at the end of the evening in her bedroom he couldn't *remember* whether he slept with her. You're a man — could he have 'forgotten' he had sex with her?"

"I think Dad did a dumb thing and maybe an immoral thing, but I've heard dozens of stories about that kind of 'forgetting' in A.A. They're called 'blackouts.' When some people drink too much, they 'black out' and honestly *can't* remember what happened. My roommate at the treatment center, years ago, was a very powerful man. He actually killed a man who attacked him in a bar. He hit the man so hard he broke his neck. He didn't remember it at all, even though the police arrested him while he was still at the bar and would have charged him with murder-one. But several people at the same table saw it all and attested to the fact that the man who was killed had attacked my roommate from behind first, and tried to kill him. My friend just reached over his shoulder, grabbed the other guy by the collar and brought his huge fist from the table to meet the face being drawn over his shoulder. Later he *didn't even remember* being attacked because he was in a blackout. The witness of the other people at his table got him released. But he could have gotten a death sentence and *never even remembered being attacked.*"

Carol looked hard at Wil. "Are you serious?"

"Do you remember when I was fifteen and got busted for getting drunk and taking your car to Dallas with a bag of marijuana in the front seat?"

"Of course I do."

"And the next morning I tried to tell Dad I didn't remember taking the car, and he hit me and knocked me down in the garage. Remember?"

"Yes, that was awful."

"Well, I was in a blackout too — I *didn't* remember. It's a little ironic that Dad may have ruined his life just like I did, by having his first blackout when he was with the woman that night."

"I'm so sorry about what we did to you. We didn't know."

"Hey don't worry, Mom, nobody forced me to get drunk."

Just then they heard the key in the front door, and then, "Is Wil here yet?"

The Denver airport was bustling, and the line to the baggage check counter was long for the American flight to Paris and Geneva via Dallas. Carol had finally gotten checked in and turned to walk toward her gate.

"Think it over," Wil said as he picked up her plane ticket and baggage check tickets and tipped the porter. "I know it must be devastating to find out about Dad having an emotional runaway with a beautiful woman just as you were finally willing to trust him. It was a dumb — stupid — thing for him to do. But it may have been. . . . "

"You're right about that," she interrupted, as she put her driver's license back in her purse. "Don't try to excuse him! You've never even been married. You can't possibly understand the shock of having someone you trust completely suddenly turn on you." Wil winced as she turned away.

They walked in silence toward the long line waiting to go through the metal detector. The loud conversation of the airport crowd was punctuated with gate announcements and passenger warnings about unattended luggage.

As they were approaching the point where only ticketed passengers could continue, Wil handed Carol her carry-on bag and said, "I know I've never had a wife turn on me and destroy a lifetime of trust, but . . . when I broke Dad's trust — got drunk and stole your car — at fifteen, he knocked me down and walked away — wouldn't even listen to me — rejected me completely — after being my idol and best friend all my life. I'm not saying he didn't have a right to his feelings about me, but I trusted him completely, and he walked away from me!" Then added a little sarcastically, "But by walking away, he missed a good chance to grow up and find out who he really was!"

Anger flashed in Carol's eyes as she stepped out of the line and dragged Wil by the arm with her. "And you're saying I'm immature, and if I don't stay with your father, I may not have a chance to grow up and find out who I am?"

He didn't say anything, and she continued, "Do you think just because you've been through a treatment center you can say that your father and I aren't grown up and in touch with our dysfunctional behavior?"

Wil looked at his mother and quietly set an emotional boundary between them as he answered thoughtfully. "Well, that *is* what treatment centers do — help people discover their true priorities, as well as the hidden character problems that keep them from becoming who they really are. That's why you and Dad sent me there — to grow up."

"Good Lord, you've turned into a preacher!" Carol said. "Let me tell you something, young man: I'm your mother and I knew you when you had dirty diapers. And if you think I'm going all the way to Switzerland because *I'm* immature, then you didn't hear me when I told you about *your father's dumb behavior!* And," she added in a low, tense voice, as she stepped quickly toward the x-ray machine, "if I decide to *leave* that adulterous bas . . . that adulterer, it will be an adult, reasonable choice — and *not* because *I'm* immature! Do you *understand* that?"

Wil looked at her back as she turned away and stepped haughtily through the metal detector. He raised his eyebrows and said softly to himself, "Yes ma'am."

As the cog train clanked to a stop at Glion, Carol was pleased to see Celeste waiting to greet her and remembered what a charming young woman she was. "It's good to see you again, Madame Martin. Dr. Magie was here, but he had to unexpectedly leave to meet an emergency patient. He said he is looking forward to seeing you this evening at seven."

On the walk to the hotel, Carol asked her about school and her family, and listened to her animated replies. "You know, Madame Martin, I have been accepted to be a foreign exchange student in the United States for my senior year abroad."

"Oh, I'd like to hear about that. Where are you going?"

Before Celeste could answer, they arrived at the hotel and François came to the door looking at his watch pointedly, and then at Celeste.

Carol said, "Hello, François, I'm so sorry if I made Celeste late. It was my fault."

"Ah, Madame Martin, it is nothing." He turned on his heels and disappeared.

"Thank you," Celeste whispered to Carol. Then, just before she disappeared, she whispered over her shoulder, "I do not yet know where I will go in the United States, but they said they'll tell me this week."

Dr. M. was quiet after Carol recounted what had happened between John and her. She wept when she told him about the wonder of their time of closeness after being in Glion together, but she completely broke down when she told about seeing Claudette in Paris and realizing she was in love with John. "Before I even met her I knew! I was almost overwhelmed — with fear — and jealousy — and then anger. Those feelings were so powerful, the only peace I could get was deciding I *have* to *leave* John." She paused and looked pleadingly at Dr. M. and said, "Am I insane? This jealousy feels like some kind of giant green monster inside me that can destroy me if I can't get it back in its cage."

Dr. M. nodded, and then stared into the fireplace for almost a minute. "This is what I hear you saying." And he repeated almost exactly what she had said.

Carol relaxed in her chair and sighed deeply. "That's the first time I've felt understood since this all began. But what can I do? I'm so confused, and I feel so unattractive, worthless."

"Think back in your childhood. What's the first time you can remember having those kinds of feelings? What was going on?"

Carol looked up in a corner of the room. "I don't *ever* remember feeling good about myself. From the time I was a little girl I hid my mistakes, and constructed a personality I thought people would like. By the time I got married, I was so busy being sweet, pretty, and clever and making good grades that I didn't know who I really was. I even hid that I was a serious student of English literature, and an omnivorous reader."

"How did that make you feel, trying to be what you thought everyone wanted you to be?"

"Tired. Very tired, and scared. I had to cover up any mistakes or failures. And the strange thing is I demanded that people I dated be perfect. Of course, they couldn't be, but I guess focusing on their mistakes took the spotlight off mine — or I thought it did. It's a wonder anyone ever wanted to marry me."

"But John did."

"Yes, he really did. I thought it was mostly hormones — why else would anyone want me? But after we were married, I realized he'd been raised by a mother who was a world-class critic of other people's behavior — but instead of hiding his real self the way I did, John just let those criticisms roll off his back. I think maybe the thing that attracted me most to him was that he recognized his abilities and actually had confidence that he could do what he wanted to, what he set out to do.

But when he seemed to be succeeding too much, I'd switch on my critical 'picking' just to let him know he wasn't perfect. Instead of getting angry, he'd just laugh and hold me and say, 'You're not going to run me off. And I'm not going to be perfect, so you might as well relax.' "

"What did you do?"

"I married him as fast as I could, before he graduated."

"And how did you arrange that?"

She frowned. "I don't really remember exactly."

Dr. M. nodded, and waited.

"That's not true, I do remember. But I can't tell you."

They sat in silence until he looked at his watch and said, "Well, our time—"

Carol interrupted him, talking fast, "I got very sexual with him, more uninhibited than I'd ever thought about being—before marriage."

"And you believe that was why he married you?"

She nodded vigorously. "Why else?"

"When John first told me about you, he mentioned that you were beautiful, but talked a lot more about the fact that you are creative, want to help people, and have a keen mind, and are very loyal and caring toward him, Wil and even your father. And he also said that you have a 'great business head,' and have been wonderful about budgeting and handling money since college."

"Really?" she said, looking surprised. "John said those things?"

Dr. M. nodded and then looked at the clock and said he could see her the following day at 4:00 p.m. "In the meantime, I'd like you to take an 8 x 11 pad and draw a line down the middle of the page. On one side, list all the positive character traits, habits, and other positive things you can think of about John. On the other side, list the negative traits, habits, etc., and bring the list with you when we meet tomorrow."

"Shall I do the lists in ten minutes?" Carol asked tongue-in-cheek.

"That would be good," Dr. Magie said, looking up at her over the rims of his reading glasses.

21

Evicting Ancient Father Feelings

Seeing Dr. M. smile when he opened the door made her feel safe and almost sane again. "Good afternoon, Carol. I'm looking forward to our session. Did you get some rest after you were here last evening?"

"No, I didn't. When I went to bed my thoughts were tumbling over each other like a thousand wasps caught in a clothes dryer. And they were stinging each other."

He smiled at the image. "That sounds harrowing."

"It was. When I'd think about leaving John and getting out of all this pain, I'd feel great relief and readiness to leave. Then thoughts of the wonderful things John said to you about me would surface — about my being smart, capable, and having a good business head, as well as being beautiful — and the thought of leaving would weaken. Finally, at about 3:00 a.m., I was exhausted, but I got up and turned on the light, and did what you asked me to do before this session. It was more difficult than I'd thought — to say good things about John or the marriage."

"Oh? How about listing the bad things?"

"That wasn't what I expected either." She handed him the page with the parallel columns listing the positive and negative things about John and their marriage (see the following page).

After the doctor had looked at Carol's lists, he asked, "What struck you as strange about the negative list?"

Carol laughed, "First, I want you to know that I was determined to be totally honest. But right away, when I had to make the positive list I felt great resistance in listing positive traits about John. But when I got into it, I listed some great things — in spite of not wanting to. But on the other hand, I could hardly wait to get to the 'bad' list, because I still had a lot of anger in my stomach and was anxious to reveal the unbearable facts about John and our painful marriage."

"And what happened then?"

"It was the strangest thing. Although I was ready to divorce John to be relieved of the painful anger and unquenchable jealousy, there were only three bad things I could think of. And only one of them was awful. But — and this is the mystery I want you to solve — the disloyal behavior, the main source of my complaint, outweighs the entire list

---

TRAITS ABOUT JOHN

Positive Traits	*Negative Traits*
Is normally sincere, kind, generous, good looking	Hard Headed
Wants to be a good father (but doesn't have a clue as how to be)	Won't (doesn't know how to) tell Wil he's sorry about hitting him and rejecting him for several years after he got busted for drinking, drug possession, and reckless driving at age fourteen
Good provider	
Excellent work ethic	
Plans well (thanks to Dr. M.) and is relentless in staying with something until it's done right	Was immoral and disloyal to me with C.F.
Intelligent and good with people	
Is honest (in business)	
Good communicator and persuasive salesman	
Is fair with his employees and partners	
Has a great reputation in financial community in Denver	

---

of positive qualities that almost any woman would be happy with in a husband, qualities that describe a marriage worth fighting for." Carol looked at her mentor, "What's going on? This is not sane thinking! And yet, I can't change it! Help!"

"Carol, when I told you positive things John said about you, you were surprised, and it is no wonder. You had been talking as if you think he only married you for your 'looks' and 'good sex.'"

Carol agreed. "Yes."

"When a couple is having trouble in their marriage," Dr. Magie continued, "They almost always begin to project their own worst fears, or their own secret bad behavior onto their partner — usually things that they have feared since childhood. In your case the fears could be about feeling deserted by your father because you believed yourself to be worthless and not attractive. However, it could be that you unconsciously attributed John's deceitful behavior to the "shame" hidden for years, about the sexual techniques you used to "trap" him with. In other words, your immediate and intense reaction may have been the fear of being deserted because you really weren't attractive and the fear that he might have found someone who was more beautiful and better at sex.

"This sort of mental scenario, when activated, can be very difficult to dislodge. If the partner denies the accusations, then he or she is 'lying,' because the offended party's fear is so deeply entrenched. And in a strange way, even the suspected behavior can seem more true or dreadful than the truth."

Carol listened attentively. "But Dr. M., I'm not jealous all the time. My deep sense that John was guilty *triggered* the jealousy."

"Yes, I understand what you are saying, but when you came here yesterday, you stated 'The Green Monster is so strong that I'm terrified that it will destroy my life if I can't get it back in its cage.' That sounds like you have a hiding place inside where you keep your jealousy under lock and key. But this time, the jealous feeling was so strong, you couldn't — can't — overpower it by mental effort. So leaving appears to be the only alternative."

Carol nodded slowly. "Dr. M., I tried to call John last night and couldn't reach him. When I hung up, I plummeted into fantasies and anger about Claudette and John. I finally called Cindy, his secretary, at home and found that he had flown to Dallas on a business trip. But I was still afraid, Dr. M. The fear that accompanies those fantasies drops on me like a hot wet blanket, threatening to smother me if I don't get out of our marriage." She looked up at Dr. M. and continued, "These are not just feelings. I have physical symptoms — my stomach cramps and I perspire all over. And I couldn't get to sleep all night."

"Dr. M., I thought I was past those powerful feelings. Is there anything we could do that would help me?"

Dr. M. started to speak, but Carol interrupted, "What I mean is, last week I realized that some of my insecurity and jealousy is due to my father's putting me down and giving me the message that I'm not smart and had better marry a strong intelligent man, "before the good ones are all gone." And later, this week, I tied that together with my shame about using sex to get John to marry me — and that therefore my jealousy and strong fears are that John might have met someone prettier and smarter than I am, and better...in bed. But just realizing where the feelings came from doesn't get rid of them for me. And after a sleepless night last night, I'm afraid I'll never be okay about this problem."

Dr. Magie waited until he felt she had said everything she needed to. Then he said, "Carol, can you recall the first time you experienced these intense feelings — perhaps when you were a child?"

After looking down at the hearth, Carol said, "When my father announced he was leaving my mother and me, and came to pick up his clothes, I had just gotten home from school and was having some milk and cookies in the kitchen. I heard my mother shouting at my father, "Get out of this house and go with your whore — and don't you *ever* come back!" I'd heard them fight before, but never like that.

He shouted, "Don't worry, there's nothing here worth coming back to," and slammed the door and left. I ran to my room sobbing, and my whole body was shaking with the same feelings of terror and shame I've been having lately — because I thought daddy meant *I* wasn't worth his coming back to see, and that I'd never see him again. How could I still have such overpowering feelings about things that happened so long ago?"

Dr. Magie replied, "When a parent or caregiver is in denial about his or her own feelings and doesn't deal with them, that adult often unconsciously 'dumps' those feelings of anger and fear in to the life of a child, and that child unwittingly carries the feelings for the adult even though the feelings are inappropriate and larger than normal. So," Dr. M. said quietly, "you're saying this irrational fear and drive to leave were first about your father, his emotional abuse of you, his desertion of you and your mother when you were a child."

Carol nodded and wept quietly into a tissue. Carol was dumbfounded and she asked, "If I'm carrying my father's feelings of fear and shame, how can I get rid of them?"

Dr. M. waited and then said, "Carol, if you would like to evict those strong feelings that are obviously still alive in you, we can go back to your childhood in what is called a guided regression."

"What's that?"

"You'll close your eyes and I'll ask you some questions to guide you back to the situation in your childhood when the abuse took place. I'll ask my nurse, whom you've met, to come in the room with us as a witness — this is customary since we are dealing with strong abuse issues from your past, some of which may come out of denial and be focused on me. This process can be frustrating, but also can release one from life long baffling and fearful, attitudes, and painful feelings, that are being projected inappropriately onto people in the present, causing a great deal of pain and confusion.

Carol nodded. "I'd like very much to do that. I am sick and tired of being controlled by these feelings, and I can't continue going for my dreams or even staying with John until I can overcome them. But I'm afraid. Is there any chance that I'll get stuck in my childhood and not be able to come back? And how will I know what to do? I'll be all alone."

"No," Dr. M. said, "you won't be alone. I will be with you at your side through the whole experience, and my nurse, Mme. Francis Dubois — you've met Nurse Francis — will come in to be with us. Any time you are too uncomfortable, you can tell me and we'll come back to the present."

Carol sighed deeply, "Okay, let's do it."

Dr. Magie nodded reassuringly as he got up to call his nurse. When she came in, although she had met Nurse Francis, Carol looked uncertain. Dr. M. explained, "It's always customary for a nurse to be present when doing this sort of regression." Carol nodded her assent.

"All right," Dr. M. began, "I have put an empty chair facing you a few feet in front of you, and I will continue sitting next to you. Now, close your eyes and relax. Picture yourself flowing back through the years to your childhood, to a specific time when you heard your father tell you that you were not good enough. He is sitting in the chair a few feet from you. Can you see him?"

"Yes."

"What's he doing?"

"He's talking to me. I must be about four or five, and I'm afraid of him."

"What is he doing and saying?"

"He's sort of sneering and saying, 'You're not smart enough to be a writer. You're a girl. You're supposed to learn how to clean house — and have babies."

In a little-girl voice, Carol said, "But, Daddy, I don't know how to have babies." In her adult voice, Carol continued, "I'm feeling very sad and hopeless and I can feel tears coming.

"Now he's throwing his head back and laughing and looking at me like I was the dumbest creature that ever breathed. 'Don't worry, your husband will show you how to have babies. He's in charge of that department. You just do what he says.'"

Dr. M. said quietly, "Carol, how do you feel about what he said to you about your not being smart enough to do anything except clean house and have babies, and that your husband will tell you how and when you'll do that?"

"I'm really angry about what he said, and I'm also afraid that he might be right and that I'm not smart enough, not good enough to do anything except be a dumb, cute, seductive housewife."

"Carol, do you know that this anger and fear of not being enough were passed onto you and dumped into your life because *he* was not being responsible and dealing with these feelings of fear, anger, and insecurity in his own life?"

Carol nodded and then described to Dr. M. two other occasions in her childhood, one being the time when she overheard her father and her mother shouting at each other as he was leaving the house and deserting her and her mother for another woman. The other occasion was ten years later when her mother almost had to beg her father for some financial help because of an illness she had that required a maid. By the time Carol relived these three excruciating experiences, she was exhausted.

Then Dr. M. said, "Would you like to give back to your father the anger and fear you've been carrying for him?"

Her eyes still closed, Carol nodded vigorously, but said quietly, "But I don't know how, and I'm afraid of him."

"Don't worry. Two of us are right here with you, Carol," Dr. M. said. "We will not let him hurt you." Nurse Francis touched Carol's shoulder and said "yes." Carol sighed and said, "What do I do?"

"You are going to tell your father how you feel about his behavior toward you and then tell him you are now giving these feelings back to him."

After a few seconds, her eyes still closed and her face still tight with fear, Carol said, "Dad, I'm really angry at you!" Her voice and feelings of anger grew stronger by the second as she continued getting louder and louder. "This is your shame you are dumping on me, your little girl. Well, I'm giving it back to you right now! Take your shame, your fears and your anger — I will not carry these feelings for you any longer! I give them back to you!"

Carol's stored uncoiling repressed anger replaced her fear. The anger was so fierce, so primal that it was frightening to hear. She stopped to catch her breath.

Dr. M. said, "Carol, keep your eyes closed and get in touch with those feelings of shame and anger and all the pain and fear they have caused you all these years. Now repeat what you said — with every ounce of energy you have."

And Carol did. She practically screamed the message, giving her carried fear and anger and shame back to her father. She was panting when she stopped.

Dr. M. asked, "Check your feelings; can you feel any more anger, fear, or shame left in you?"

"Well, yes some."

"Where is it located in your body?"

After a few seconds, "In my stomach."

"All right, I want you to repeat the confrontation — getting as angry as you can."

Eyes still closed, Carol confronted her father again, ending, "Take your shame, your fear, your anger back! I will *not* carry them any longer for you!"

This time when she stopped, she felt the anger in her chest, and the next time in her throat, and finally on the tip of her tongue. Although she was sweating and her voice had become hoarse, Dr. Magie directed, "One more time, Carol. Let's get this done."

Carol nodded as she wiped a strand of wet hair off her forehead. Then she began once more and this time experienced the anger and felt rage she had never known she was capable of, ending with "I will *not* carry these things for you any longer. I give them *back to you!*" When she stopped, she was breathing heavily, and her blouse was stuck to her back with perspiration.

"Where is your anger now, on your tongue still?"

"No sir," she almost croaked definitely. "Not a trace left."

"All right," Dr. M. answered, "you have given him back his own anger, fear and shame that he poured into your young life by not facing these same feelings in himself and not being responsible for them in his life. You are now free from his feelings. You may open your eyes."

Carol, still sweating but beginning to breathe more normally, grinned and raised her fist. "Yes!" she said, raising it to the ceiling. Then she snatched a tissue from the box beside her and mopped her face saying, "Whew!"

Dr. M. and Nurse Francis were smiling from ear to ear. After a few minutes of mopping and blowing her nose, Carol asked, "But what if those strong feelings come back, focused on John, the way they have recently?"

"You can stop whatever you are doing any time you feel that 'too-strong' anger, fear or shame. Close your eyes, picture in your mind as you did here your father trying to shame you. You can say silently, 'No, Father, *take* your anger, or shame or fear. I've given it back to you. *It's yours!*' And as you learn to do this more and more quickly, you will be amazed at how your inner wisdom will cheer you on, and you can even imagine her voice joining with yours — to help free you."

"This is *amazing*, Dr. M. I feel lighter, and in some way, freer than I've ever felt. Will I feel this way from now on?"

"I don't know, of course. People respond differently, but no one can experience such intense feelings all the time."

Carol looked at her mentor, "What do we do now?"

Dr. M. says, "Tomorrow we will start a practical approach to some simple ways to locate positive character traits that you have repressed because of your sense of being unworthy. You can begin to retrain your mind to find good things about yourself to replace these irrational negative feelings you've been carrying for so many years. These new truths may sound bland after your experience today, but they can let you experience some calmer alternatives to your compulsive anger and fear of desertion. You'll have some failures of course and some appropriate feelings of anger and fear, but just remind yourself that you have given those *out-sized carried* feelings back to your father."

"Can I take Wil or John through this process?"

"No, definitely not! You need to have a therapist trained in this technique to walk you through such a powerful process, and a nurse present.

You have gotten in touch with and released some very strong feelings today, Carol, and you've done a fine and courageous piece of work about your feelings carried forward from childhood. Do you have any questions?"

Carol was quiet for several seconds. "Dr. M. it's clear to me now that inside I've secretly felt worthless and inadequate for so long and tried to hide these feelings with makeup, wardrobe and being a sharp critical fault finder! I am afraid I might not even have any authentic positive character traits."

"It's not unusual to feel that way, Carol, but you've been carrying other people's fears and other feelings and burying your own positive traits — just like you buried your dreams — because you didn't feel like you deserved to accomplish any of the important dreams that you discovered. And you were programmed to fear *you* didn't have the ability to achieve them."

Carol thought about what had just happened. Then she said, "Before we go on, Dr. M., I have a question: Is this kind of discovery and change part of everyone's process of awakening and achieving their dreams?"

Dr. M. shook his head and smiled, "No, not everyone who achieve their dreams goes through what you've just done; not many in fact, although, most people who commit seriously to achieving their dreams run into some repressed basic human problems in their personal lives and their relationships that could stop them from achieving their life dream — if they don't face them. So the dream achieving process can become a sort of self-diagnosing path to personal transformation as well as success for some people. But each person will have her own blocks to discover and deal with."

Carol thought a moment, and then she asked, "Are you serious about there being a practical way I can discover what buried positive traits I may have?"

Dr. M. sighed his familiar sigh. "We'll see," he said. "Let's start tomorrow to search for your hidden character assets."

22

You've Got to Excavate the Positive

The sunrise burnished the lake far below the hotel balcony. Occasional shafts of light falling through a moving bank of billowing gray clouds created a quicksilver surface that glided across the purple-black depths of Lake Geneva.

Taking in the beauty of the lake, Carol inhaled the rich coffee scent rising from her steaming cup. "God, if you are real — and you must be, thank you for all this, and for the light that's breaking into *my* darkness. Please show me — tell me — what I need to know and to do."

Dr. Magie greeted her at his house that evening, "You look like you've had a good day, Carol."

"Oh yes, I got a wonderful night's sleep and all day I've seen beautiful things that I've ignored since I've been here."

"Wonderful, it's good to see you smiling again."

"Thank you. Whatever's next, I'm grateful to be thinking positively this evening."

"Good timing. That's what we're going to do this session — look for positive traits that have been invisible to you, traits you have that you've denied because of your shame and the interjected idea that you are worthless. You couldn't afford to see these positive traits before. They contradicted who you thought you were."

Carol scrunched her face like a skeptical little girl, "That sounds crazy. You mean that because my shame was reinforced so consistently when I was a child, I *kept myself* from seeing good things about me?"

Dr. M. shrugged and nodded. "It does sound crazy, but it's true for many people. No one knows what percent, but it seems half the people in the world believe at some level that they are worthless and unconsciously keep doing things to protect themselves from demonstrating they are worthless by projecting an image that says 'Oh, I couldn't do that, or be that, ever.' At the same time they dismiss compliments and also the awareness of the importance of positive things they do achieve or earn. The other half of the world seems to act as if they think they are superior, already great, exaggerating the compliments and achievements that come to them and denying or brushing off any negative experiences or criticism. They even contradict and reject the people who try to help them, since they believe they can or should do things by themselves. This cocky, grandiose second group is a lot harder to counsel.

Of course, there are many people who see and acknowledge their positive achievements and don't exaggerate either the positive or negative traits. But most people who come for therapy are either denying their positive traits or exaggerating them."

"Sounds a little like my life, and my father's. According to what you're saying, I guess I'm the sick one, and positive people like John are doing better. I always feel 'less than' other people except some who are obvious failures; and paradoxically think I'm a *lot better* than they are."

Dr. M. smiled, "No, Carol, both groups have insecurity and fear of not being enough, but their responses to those feelings are different. Some people repress their positive qualities and 'claim' their negative ones. You've indicated that you do that. To get help, such a person has to be shown that the source of the exaggerated shame is not his or her inherent self. The source is usually a parent or a caregiver who constantly told the child he or she was inadequate. Many children accept the messages from these shaming voices as being the truth about the way they are. When that happens, the child concludes that these negative or fearful feelings are his or her own authentic emotions."

"And you think that's what I did?" Carol half stated, half asked.

The doctor responded, "That's what you described to me when I asked you to tell me about your childhood, which is why I took you back to the painful situations and let you experience your father shaming you. When you visualized your father sitting in a chair in this room, you re-experienced and faced these situations where some of your abuse took place, and took that opportunity to give those feelings back to him."

"So that accounts for feeling like I had new eyes that could see things in a new way this morning?"

"That could well be. You were seeing things more as they actually are and not through someone else's evaluations. And there is another response that can occur when a child comes to believe he or she is worthless due to introjecting another's negativity and shaming feelings. The child is convinced that the negative characteristics must truly be his or hers, because after all the shaming parent is the largest authority in the child's life. If a child rebels and says 'No, those things are not true. I am smart and pretty,' the shaming becomes more intense. To keep from being punished or accused of being insane, the child surrenders his or her own positive self-awareness at some level. From then on that child may unconsciously deny or represses any positive traits he or she experiences that contradict the powerful parent's interjected shaming voices. That's when the voice of inner wisdom either disappears, or supports the child's strongest need — to *hide* any *good* characteristics that would cause the feared rejection from the child's 'higher power,' the shaming parent."

"Is that why I've always been uneasy when people compliment me — when I've always longed to be affirmed?"

"Give me a recent example of feeling uneasy when you've received a compliment you really wanted to believe?"

"That's easy. John became very affirming several times on our second honeymoon trip as he pointed out some positive character traits I didn't know I had. I was almost embarrassed. I didn't know whether they were real or not. I didn't think he was lying, but since no one close to me ever said such positive things about me to my face before, I didn't know how to tell if they were true. It's as if there might be a positive side of my life hidden from me that other people get glimpses of."

The old doctor nodded. "What you're saying makes a great deal of sense, Carol. Carl Jung postulated that everyone has an unconscious shadow side besides the seemingly dominant conscious personality. For Jung, this half conscious-half unconscious phenomenon meant that all people have traits and desires that they may not be aware of having. Today many people have the mistaken idea that their shadow side contains all the evil, dysfunctional things that they have repressed, so they are afraid to explore it as we're doing. But your shadow side can also include all kinds of positive, good things about yourself that you are not aware of. For instance, you, Carol, may have some strong traits like assertiveness, standing up for your rights with your father, the ability to confront unpleasant situations. The masculine-dominated culture in which you were raised saw those traits as inappropriate for a woman. Because of this, you may be in denial about your overtly strong traits, totally unconscious of having these and many other positive traits that the women in your family were not 'supposed to' have. It's beneficial to find and develop some of these buried positive traits, since they may be important assets aiding you to achieve your dreams."

Carol realized that, if what Dr. Magie was saying was true, then she might never fulfill her dream of being a writer unless she could get in touch with and recover some of the positive characteristics that could let her believe in herself. "Okay, Dr. M. I'm ready. What do I do?"

Smiling, Dr. M. said in an exaggerated mysterious voice, "Today we are going to begin to search for and uncover some of your lost positive traits."

"Sounds like we're going on some kind of magical Easter egg hunt," Carol chuckled.

Dr. M. smiled, "That's not a bad way to put it, Carol. What I'm going to show you is a simple way some people have found helpful in unearthing some of their positive character traits that for whatever reason are buried or hidden in their unconscious. As you discovered, even when someone points these positive traits out as John did, it can be difficult to accept them as being real. Therefore, I am going to let *you* decide if the positive traits you discover are real."

"Many people have done the exercise that I'm about to describe to you. Although some have been successful in making this search for positive traits alone, many find it much more effective to work within a group setting. We are dealing with material in our lives that has been unnoticed, discounted, or dormant. The dominant characteristic of denied material is that we cannot see it accurately in ourselves, but often we can see the same or similar traits clearly in others.

"Therapists have known about this phenomenon with regard to discovering *negative* traits for years. But what I'm telling you now is that you may also be able to discover some of your denied *positive* traits or behaviors by doing the exercise I will describe. It might be interesting for you and your women's 'go-for-your-dreams' group to do the following exercise together, since all people who are serious about achieving their dreams need to recover all the positive traits they can.

Carol thought, "You can say that again!"

"Although it seems as if it would be natural to point out positive traits in the lives of loved ones, people close to us may see these positive traits in our behaviors, but they often are reluctant to tell us about positive things they see. When Mrs. Magie and I were first married, it was difficult for me to affirm her about her intellectual abilities. My fear was that she might think she was smarter or better than I, which I already suspected. So I felt that pointing out her positive traits might diminish her regard for me." He chuckled. "I know that is not exactly mature thinking, I'm just telling you that's the way it was.

"But today I am going to help you look for positive traits in yourself. The exercise I'm going to describe for you gives you 'permission' to let your mind's eye, your practical inner wisdom, see in other people's positive attitudes and behaviors some truth about your own buried characteristics and behavior."

23

Locating Buried Personal Assets

———✳✳✳—✳✳✳—✳✳✳———

"First, Carol, for an entire day, write in a notebook the behaviors of people you contact that trigger a strong *positive* reaction in you. For example, you might go to the bank to take care of a discrepancy on your monthly statement, and although you are irritated that the bank made an error on your account, you are particularly impressed with the quiet, direct way the customer service agent listens carefully and then speaks to you calmly and positively in the face of your anger. If there is nothing about the encounter that was particularly outstanding to you, record nothing.

"We're not talking about noticing basic physical beauty of form, because such aspects are beyond anyone's control. Write about positive *actions* or *attitudes* of people you encounter, the ways they *behave* that elicit a strong, positive reaction from you, and perhaps causes you to say to yourself, 'I'd like to respond like that.' Your list may also include peoples' social habits, such as thoughtful courtesies, making you feel welcome, loved and so forth.

"In other words, if you have a friend who says, 'Good morning. How are you?' in a way that leaves you feeling cared for, or more valued and alive all day, make a note of it. Or you meet or hear about somebody who has a lot of tenacity in doing a difficult or unpleasant job, and you really admire their relentless pursuit of their goals. Note that. You may or may not be jealous that the person has that trait, but the point is that you really *admire* what that person does and have unusually positive feelings about it. Or perhaps you see someone taking a substantial risk to act with great integrity, like being honest about a mistake they made in not quoting a hidden cost in the price of an expensive insurance policy you bought from them, which admission could cause you to cancel the sale. You may really admire their courage in taking that risk and realize you would like to admit your mistakes that quickly, too.

"Write these things in your notebook, describe what the person says or does and how he or she says or does it. At the end of the day you will have the beginning of a list of descriptions of specific positive behaviors and attitudes you have personally observed. If this process stimulates you, keep gathering positive behaviors for several days. Many of these

141

behaviors you collect will relate to you in some way that you may not understand at first, but I believe that your inner wisdom wants you to succeed and alerts you to positive behaviors that relate to you.

"At the end of the day, rewrite the list of behaviors that got your attention, in order of their importance to you. Then destroy the first list.

"Spend ten minutes a day during the next week — looking at the list of attractive positive traits and behaviors recorded in your notebook. Read the list. Revisualize your experience. Reflect on the possibility that these may be character traits that are hidden inside your unconscious mind, a part of your shadow side, just waiting to come alive and light up your experience and relationships. See if you can perceive inside yourself a desire to be the kind of person who practices each of these behaviors. Perhaps you've been afraid to express them because no one ever taught you how, or it may have been that such behaviors did not have value for your parents or caregivers, and they ridiculed you for expressing them.

"Study your list and try on the idea that the same or similar positive traits or habits are waiting in your unconscious to be awakened, called out of hiding — as your dreams were. Your inner wisdom has selected the particular traits you responded to because *those* traits may already be part of who you already are.

"For instance, you might want to say 'hello' to more people you don't know well and become the kind of person who is more friendly and outgoing, but you're afraid to do that because people might misunderstand, thinking you're being insincere, flirting, manipulating, or using them in some other way. When your inner wisdom helps you recognize that you would like to behave in a certain way, you may be able to see one or two ways in which you already have the underlying characteristic. You may also realize that you are afraid to express this behavior more openly because the interjected shaming voices of parents warn you not to risk it.

"Third, after checking with your inner wisdom about whether or not these are traits you'd really like to be able to express, share the first behavior on your reordered list with your dream group or someone supportive, like John. Describe where and how you noticed it. And for the next week, *practice that behavior* in some real-life situation *every day.*

"Fourth, and finally, in the meeting after you practiced the behavior for a week, tell your fellow adventurer or group what you did, how you felt doing it, and what responses your new behavior drew.

Carol was thoughtful, "I have a lot of resistance to doing this experiment. Frankly, it seems shallow and obvious, and the behaviors not that important."

"I know, Carol, but what you are fighting may be your cognitive education that tells you that change doesn't take place through intuitive knowledge that doesn't require study, follow or conform to accepted theories of education or cognition. The facts are that the locked doors of significant behavioral change often swing on very small hinges — small behaviors — and what we are doing is to find these frozen hinges and oiling them by faith in our perceptions and the willingness to trust our intuitions and learn to discover and integrate positive behaviors by trying them before you know if they are natural parts of you. But though this approach is simple, it is *not* easy."

Dr. Magie laughed and shook his head as he continued, "Getting in touch with my positive characteristics was much more difficult for me than my negative ones. I remember my mother telling me, 'Don't ever tell people good things about yourself. They'll think you're boasting.' Consequently, I learned to repress, to push out of sight the positive things about myself. I wanted to believe them, but it just didn't feel right for me to do so. It's no wonder I didn't have much confidence in the fact that I could actualize my dreams and be like other people whom I admired. The negative voices inside me would say, 'You're not really good enough, intelligent enough, strong enough, courageous or caring enough. You're selfish. You'd be foolish to try that.'

"This happened to me for so many years that even as an adult — a caring, physician and a competent therapist — I could not see some of my best qualities. But because of this experiment the positive behaviors of other people affected me so definitely I was finally convinced that they were already parts of me, undeveloped and dormant. Consequently, I had a head start as I tried to actualize such positive characteristics and behaviors. My wife and the people in our goal-accomplishing adventure group confirmed that I'd been in denial about the fact that I already had several of these positive traits. After that, those behaviors became more natural."

"Excuse me for interrupting," Carol broke in, "but how important is it to discover your buried assets in order to have a good life and reach your dreams?

Dr. Magie smiled and shook his head. "It's not necessary for everyone who succeeds to do this exercise. Some people have little interest in this inner part of the journey to their dreams. They may think this process is simplistic because it is so simple and direct, or they may be convinced that they are already in touch with their positive traits. But my experience and that of other people who have been out of touch with their positive traits has been that the adventure to accomplish life goals is much easier and more rewarding when we discover and consciously develop our positive relational traits. Life seems much richer for me because I enjoy the process of self-discovery and personal growth. And now part of the richness of the dream actualizing adventure for me is sharing these discoveries and behaviors with others along the way."

"With people like me?" Carol said, smiling broadly.

"Yes, Carol, people like you."

"This process you're describing," Carol mused thoughtfully, "is another way to change my own behaviors or attitudes in a remarkably short time. And it really does seem too simple — naïve in fact — to be important. Why do these simple exercises work, Dr. M.?"

Dr. Magie cocked his head and looked down for a few seconds, before replying. "Carol, all the exercises I've taught you and John have one thing in common: they can be assimilated and the results evaluated directly, intuitively, without having to learn a complicated theoretical basis. That is, you don't have to use cognitive processes, historical precedents, or certain theories. For example, in the search for positive traits exercise, you can tell *immediately* without any analysis whether or not the behavior you are witnessing is important to you. Also, when you report that behavior to your group, they can tell instantly, without having to reason it out, whether or not you exercise the same trait."

"Are there any other exercises you've tried that a group might do to stimulate the discovery of positive traits? I'll need all the help I can get. Actually, I feel fear when I think about doing *this* exercise alone. And a cautious inner voice is telling me right now, 'Carol, this stuff is so superficial, how can it help?' I'm all confused. What's going on?"

"Who does that voice sound like, Carol?"

Carol thought for a moment and then shook her head. "Good grief, my father, of course."

"That's why it is really important to find someone else or a group to go on this adventure with you. Before long, if you are being honest with them, they can tell intuitively what you are really like — even if they cannot analyze how they know. And their understanding and acceptance of you can help to deal with unwanted interference from your past."

Carol thought a few seconds. "I'm almost sure my women's group will want to do this," she said.

Dr. M. thought a moment. "Since you asked, there is another small exercise that can be helpful to supplement other ways of gaining self-awareness in a short time. After a group develops a safe, supportive atmosphere, you can ask others in the group if they would be willing to experiment to help each other verify the search for positive traits. If they are willing, suggest that each member tell one or two positive traits they see in each other member of the group. Try to give specific examples. If you go first, one person after another around the circle will express one or two positive traits they experience your having. Anyone who is uneasy can pass.

"Examples might include 'You are a very friendly person. You asked about where I came to Denver from and welcomed me when I first came into this group.' Or, 'you have a lot of integrity. Several times you corrected something you described when you realized it wasn't exactly the way you had described it.' Specific examples should be given when possible. There is a chance that the group members may choose not to try this experiment, and it is usually not productive to try to talk a group or an individual into doing something like this. However, one such session was so moving to Mrs. Magie and me that we wept when group members listed positive things they saw in our behaviors and attitudes. Some people may be afraid either that they really don't have anything good that the others could point to, or that others might not be able to think of anything positive to say about them. Let the group know that if anyone feels uncomfortable or afraid of asking for such feedback, that person can pass and not participate. But for those who do participate, hearing people they know say aloud simple, positive traits can give them a *strong* additional motivation to change their behavior in order to express a particular attractive, but formerly ignored, character asset."

"But, Dr. M., be honest" Carol said, "isn't the first exercise you discussed just wishful thinking? Just because I *like* something *someone else does,* surely that doesn't mean that I *have* that trait."

"That's exactly what the exercises are about," Dr. M. replied, "finding out if such positive behaviors are inherent in us and not just wishful thinking. I know it sounds strange, but think about it. Of all the positive behaviors you could be strongly attracted to, why would you choose — with some assurance — the particular ones *you* respond to and write down on your list? It doesn't really matter whether you chose these traits because you were once loved by people who had them, or whether you were not loved by people who had the traits, and you longed to be loved by them. The fact is that somehow these particular positive traits got planted in the archives of your inner wisdom as being important to you. It's as if some of them have been waiting for you to bring them out into the sunlight of consciousness so they can flower, and the chances of those discovered traits or behaviors growing and blossoming under *these* circumstances are many times greater than if you tried to change to a behavior you selected from a printed list in a psychological manual, a behavior to which you did not feel strongly attracted.

"This is very similar to having an aptitude. Having a high aptitude to do a certain thing is no guarantee that you will be great at it. Rather, it means that if you choose to try to do that for which you have a strong aptitude, your *chances of succeeding are far greater* than they would be for someone who tried to do the same things but did not have strong aptitude in that area. So I'm saying that when you are strongly drawn to a social behavior, *that* behavior may be easier for you to develop than one to which you are not strongly attracted, but feel you should be.

"Of course there are many exceptions to any explanation of human behavior. It can be true that you simply like something you see someone else doing because it's positive or pleasing, and that doesn't mean that behavior is something you need to discover in yourself and actualize. The point here is that most often the behaviors or traits we respond strongly to in others are about us in some way."

"Dr. M., this whole line of thinking is very new to me. Again and again you have showed me ways to look for things in places and in perspectives I never would have imagined. And I'm eager to take these exercises home and try them with the group of women who have come to mean so much to me."

"The Dream Team?" Dr. Magie asked smiling.

Carol nodded. "But it's only few days until the time for me to go home and there's a nagging question that keeps coming up in my mind. Something that just doesn't make sense about what you've taught me. There's something inside me that sometimes seems to compel me to make sudden decisions that are destructive to my happiness. It's almost as if a part of me comes alive in certain situations and overrides my otherwise reasonable judgement — and before I know it, I've said or done something that sabotages my relationships or the achievement of my goals."

"Yes, we can take a look at the problem of having a hidden motivator. And I think we are at a good place to do it. We'll start in the morning."

EXERCISE SEVEN
Locating Buried Character Assets

1. For one entire day, note and describe in writing positive things you saw people doing that day that you really admired or were unusually affected by (e.g., being friendly, disciplined, acting with integrity, courage, courtesy, etc.).

2. At the end of the day, rewrite the behaviors you noticed in the order of their importance or attractiveness to you. If the process stimulates your interest, keep gathering behaviors for several days.

3. Each evening for the next week read the descriptions over, and reflect on how these positive behaviors and attitudes already may be part of you, waiting to be called forward and owned. Imagine yourself doing those behaviors. Make notes about your feelings as you imagine this.

4. With your partner or in your group meeting, share the first behavior on your list and how you feel about it. Ask if this behavior is something that seems natural for you. During the following week, practice that behavior every day. Note what happens and your reactions.

5. At your next meeting, tell you partner or the group what you did, how you felt, and how people responded to your new behavior.

6. You can try this experiment with any of the other positive behaviors you would really like to be parts of your ongoing life. Our experience indicated that a new habit can often be established by practicing it for thirty days. You may want to choose one or more behaviors and continue to practice them.

24

Business on the Fast Track

—————

"Carol!" John was surprised by her call. She'd been in Glion for over a week and this was the first time he'd heard from her.

"How are you and Wil getting along?"

John laughed, "With each other?"

"Yes."

"Ms. Martin, you have spawned a remarkable son. If the strong, silent type hadn't already been invented, they'd have to do it for Wil. He makes Clint Eastwood seem like a late-night disk jockey. He's respectful, but in the time you've been gone, he's said about ten words — like 'please pass the butter.' Barbara probably talks to him more than I do while she's making dinner and cleaning house."

"Do *you* talk to him a lot?"

He laughed, "I guess I'm not much better."

"How's he doing at the office?"

"He's a natural — just like he was in foot . . . sports. He brings a notebook to every meeting and takes copious notes. And when he asks questions, they're the right questions. He has the highest aptitude for this kind of business I've ever seen."

"Have you told him that?"

"Are you kidding? He's just beginning. This is boot camp. The message from me is 'more, more, faster, faster!'"

Carol realized she was on the verge of giving some wifely advice, so she decided to change the subject. "Well, what's he doing for a social life?"

"You mean girls? Well, he's gone most nights."

"What's he do?"

"How would I know? He doesn't tell me anything about his personal life. Why don't you ask him? You want me to have him call you?"

"No," she paused. "Actually I'm not doing much better than you are about getting information from him."

"Oh?"

"We had a little argument at the Denver airport. John, I called because I plan to stay another week if Dr. M. can work me in. He's really helping me, and I think we're getting into some things that are crucial to my — our — future."

John was disappointed and a little angry, but he did notice she said *our* future. He had hoped that by this time she'd be ready to come home and work things out — get their life on track again. He'd felt he could convince her he wanted to be married to her, not anyone else. And it wasn't just him — the company needed her back, too. Wil was doing a good job handling the daily and monthly financial records, but now substantial amounts of committed funds were coming in, and John needed Carol's help in determining the cash flow needs and reserve. He didn't have control over Carol and they both knew it. He figured the call was probably her way of checking to see if he still considered her a part of the business.

"Sure, Honey, but hurry home as soon as it's right. I really need you. And say hello to Dr. M."

"Okay, and . . . thanks for your support, John." The line went dead.

John was starting upstairs to bed when the telephone rang again. He ran to get it. "Carol?"

"Carol? You drinking, John?" Arthur's voice sounded amused.

"What are you doing calling at this time of night, Arthur? Did you stumble into another bunch of solvent wannabe-investors with foreign accents?"

"Yes and no. I got that e-mail you sent before the trip to Europe, about the numbers on controlled-temperature storage facilities and how you wanted to set up another limited partnership to build and manage fifty new facilities with a hundred units each."

"What e-mail?"

"You know, your message to Bill and me last week." While Arthur continued talking, John recovered the e-mail on his laptop, which was turned on:

CONFIDENTIAL

Arthur:

Here's a rough possibility for the future. Estimated figures only — ballpark. This is only for you and Bill only, but this is one of the hot real estate investment developments across the country. Lots of interest.

Proposal to build and manage twenty new upscale private storage facilities, each with two hundred storage units. Costs: Building cost per unit (including land costs) $50 per square foot x 150 square feet = $7,500 per unit = $1,500,000

Total investment for twenty facilities @ $1,500,000 = $30,000,000

Estimated payout: Complete facility and lease spaces. Sell entire project to corporation. Average sales price of six such two-hundred-unit facilities during last twenty-four months $50,000,000 or a $20,000,000 profit for average two years investment. (Adjusted for size, etc.)

John

"Arthur, you didn't *show* that to anyone, did you?

"Well, yes, actually I did. I sent a copy to all of our investors in the Martin Industries LP #1."

"No! Arthur, we're not *ready* to take on something that big right now. It will be a couple of years minimum before we're big enough to move comfortably on that, considering the other prospects we're already developing for the first partnership.

"Well, at least you haven't got anyone signed up. Just e-mail them back, Arthur. Tell them our plans have changed and that project has been temporarily put on the back burner until the second half of next year."

"Gosh, John, it's not quite that simple. After your sterling performance at the George V, my telephone rang off the hook. It seems that although a lot of Europeans don't like us Americans, suddenly investments in the U.S. are the hottest thing going. The problem and the opportunity exists because Europeans don't know who they can *trust* to invest within the U.S. after all the Enron and other scandals, and because of an accident of history or the hand of God, the mantel of trust has fallen on me and you— us!"

"What are you talking about, Arthur?"

"Well, because of my getting these guys in and out of the 'Dot Com' cloak-and-dagger-show at just the right times they trust me, and because your friend, Bill Castle, was with me on that one they trust him, too."

"Bill? What does he have to do with this?"

"He was my silent partner, and was also an honest witness about what I'd done for him. You may not know this, but I made Bill about $100 million in three years. And back then when we were celebrating with our new — and much richer — English and French friends, all Bill could talk about was this young American he was mentoring who was actually brilliant *and* honest. That's why it was so easy to sell Martin Partnership #1. And now all the circumstances are aligned to create an intense market demand to invest with John Martin of Denver, Colorado, U.S.A."

"You're drunk, Arthur!"

"That's true, but that doesn't make what I'm saying a lie! Although I realize now, I may have overstepped a little by sending your confidential memo to your cheering backers letting them in first on a new proposal."

"Damn it, Arthur! What else have you done?"

"Are you going to be in town next weekend?"

"You mean a week from tomorrow? Why?"

"Because Bill has invited a planeload of these happy investors to his ranch near Vail to play, and to hear an informal sneak preview of your brilliant new plan. He's totally enthusiastic. He'd already invited some of them to come ski. When we talked about your e-mail, he remembered Carol's on a trip, so he offered to furnish all the technical support to get brochures printed, etc."

"Arthur, you've got these people coming in *eight* days. With all I've got going, I can't put together anything credible in a week!"

"That's fine. We've told them you aren't ready to go public with this proposal — you're just going to throw together a few pages of rough data and would like to get their feedback. John, these guys have never been treated this way by big-time financial people. The idea that you want to get down with them informally *doubled* the attendance! What do you think about that?"

"I think you'd better call them and say something's come up for me and I can't make that meeting."

"You can't do this? What's come up?"

"Sanity, Arthur. Sanity. This is too fast."

"Listen, I know how you must feel, but the truth is, four of our investors have been researching just the kind of storage facility you're talking about, and they think it's even better than you do. They believe a version of it will go in several European cities. So if your preliminary numbers check out, they'll be responsible for $40 million — $10 million each when you get ready to do it. This deal will hand you three million up front, plus it'll fund and build your whole organization for five years!"

"It's too much, too fast, Arthur."

"You told me you had a dream to build a successful real estate business. Well, here it is, on a Colorado silver platter."

Realizing he hadn't looked at his dream list in a while, John paused to consider Arthur's proposal. Resting the phone on his shoulder, he looked at his 3 x 5 card dream list and saw this jump-start was in the right direction in several ways, and with careful planning, it was a perfect piece of the dream. This presentation would not be a commitment, only a preview of coming attractions. He'd have to do a fast action plan with the team to get a polished presentation ready. But with Bill's people at his disposal, that wouldn't be all that hard. He already had gateway data from a couple of accounting consultants, and had studied the project for months. He'd call his real estate research friend at Colorado U. and pay him a big bonus to put together a team of MBA grad students to get the data and organize it simply for the meeting. They could also get pictures of possible locations and completed projects from Internet periodicals. Since Bill already had his neck out with his guests, he knew he could get him to fund this instant overtime project, whatever the cost.

"Are you still on the line?"

John put the phone back to his ear. "Yeah, I'm here. Was there anything else?

"You'll do it then?"

"Yeah, we'll put a little something together for the meeting as an example of the kinds of things we can do. If that's all, I've got to get to bed — early morning tomorrow."

"Only one other thing, John. The four $10 million investors from Paris are coming and they want very much to see you privately sometime during their stay.

"Who are they?"

"The CEO Banker from London, he's the bell cow for all the young Turks there, the corporate attorney for Fontaine Industries and old Oscar, the last Fontaine heir on the Board, and the new chair — you remember meeting her in Paris — Claudette Fontaine."

25

Why Would My Inner Wisdom Sabotage My Own Deepest Desires?

―――――

"Good morning, Carol. Did you sleep well?"

"No. I felt like I wanted to run away to the British Virgin Islands and not leave a forwarding address. Have you ever felt like that?"

"Yes," Dr. Magie chuckled. "I have sometimes. For me it's the island of Majorca in the Mediterranean."

Carol sighed with relief and then announced, "We've been talking for more than a week now, and I think I'm finally beginning to understand why I've felt so much pressure from my inner wisdom to walk away from a marriage of twenty-eight years. I couldn't believe the force of the drive to leave John. What he did in getting drunk with a beautiful woman and being intimate with her is a serious matter. But my reaction to leave without investigation was not rational. I can see that John is a good husband who made a couple of bad and possibly immoral decisions while drinking. But my fear was off the chart. So my problem is that this urge to leave does not feel like an irrational response. It was an inner voice that told me to leave. It *sounded like* the same wise voice that told me about my dreams and helped me share them with John, and I thought I could trust it. But now, I'm confused. Why it would tell me to leave my marriage if that weren't the best thing for me to do?"

"Carol, what you heard could have been the interjected voice of your father — if getting out was what he would have done to avoid his feelings. But it could also under certain conditions have been your inner wisdom."

"How?"

"Well, I told you that when a living problem arises, your inner wisdom's job is to sift through the library of all your experiences and assemble a collection of truths, strategies, and solutions to the problem you're facing. Remember, the material stored in each person's inner library pertains to *that person's* personality type and dominant goals."

"But doesn't the inner wisdom have any morality or sense of balance?"

"Don't forget that inner wisdom is only a hypothetical construct to help us understand an invisible, but recognizable part of the mind that processes information in certain ways for us. It acts like a sort of librarian/guide to help us meet our basic needs and accomplish our dreams and specific goals, whatever they are. It's not programmed to be good or bad. It's only a functionary concept to help us fulfill our deepest purposes and desires at any given time. The inner wisdom also tries to warn us and help us escape if our *fear* becomes the dominant motivating purpose, because the thing feared threatens a deeper value we have, even if that motivating is unconscious to us.

"The problem I hear you expressing Carol is this: Since your deepest conscious desire is to stay in your marriage and to build a loving and safe relationship with John, why did your inner wisdom advise you, with such force, to *leave* the relationship — thus going *against* your deepest desire to stay?"

"That's my question all right."

Dr. M. looked at Carol with great compassion. "When you and John got in touch with your dreams, you knew deeply and intuitively that they were appropriate for you. And when you committed to them, you got the energy and guidance to begin checking and implementing your dreams on the basis of that intuitive trust in their validity for you. John started the new business, and you started relating to him on a more intimate level of trust — first by helping him in the business, then by investigating your own dreams of becoming a writer, and finally by taking the second honeymoon trip — with remarkable results, according to your reports. And your inner wisdom seemed to be guiding you both."

"That's right," Carol interrupted, "but I'm confused about why my inner wisdom turned on me and suggested I leave the relationship. It doesn't make sense. Do you mean my strongest value changed?"

"No, I didn't say it changed. I said it was *revealed* to be different than you had always thought. Your conscious focus and dreams from your list were to trust John, be more open and intimate, and be a writer. Your inner wisdom responded and helped. But the revelation of John's encounter with Claudette Fontaine — and your conviction that she was in love with him, triggered a *deeper* motivation than your goals, a jealousy that was somehow connected to the fear of being deserted and abandoned. When your inner wisdom received that message of fear from you and perceived it as your most important goal, your desire to avoid this most feared consequence was stronger than your drive to stay and work things out. At that moment, imagine that you heard your inner wisdom reasoning, 'All right, given the intense pain and fear and jealousy coming from this stronger motivation — avoiding the pain of desertion — divorce is the most practical solution.'"

"You call that wisdom? Advising someone to leave a marriage and business? If what you're telling me is true, then saving our marriage is hopeless. I'm terrified to put my fear of being deserted as a lower priority than to work things out. What would I do if I take the chance and John rejects me anyway? But how can I tell my inner wisdom it's getting the wrong signal about what my highest value is? I really love John and I want to stay in our marriage."

"Remember the inner wisdom is guided by whatever your most important value or motivation *actually is* at any given time, not by what you *think* it is. Because the inner wisdom is connected to our unconscious hopes, dreams and need for security, it doesn't often make mistakes about what's truly most important to us — even if we're in denial about it. Most people I've known have, at times, thought their highest value was one thing, only to discover — to their horror — that under pressure *another* value was *much* stronger."

"How could that happen? Couldn't they remember what was most important to them?"

"That's what makes it so difficult to be an effective counselor or spiritual advisor. Everyone — from leaders of nations to husbands and wives — hides their true values from others and sometimes *from themselves* until under pressure, they do things that sabotage their avowed highest principals and character traits. I remember first discovering this paradoxical phenomenon one morning when I was a child having breakfast with my mother — who saw herself as a scrupulously honest person — and taught me to be that way too. The telephone rang; it was a call from an acquaintance inviting her to a party the following week. I heard Mother say to the woman, 'Oh thank you, I'd love to come, but next Thursday afternoon I have to take Charles to the doctor for his checkup.' When she hung up, I was confused. I said, 'Mother, you took me for my checkup yesterday.' She looked slightly flustered, but said in an irritated voice, 'Well, its too late to call back now.' Thinking back on that moment years later, I realized my mother's highest value was not always absolute honesty. Sometimes it was more important to lie in order to hide a truth that might get her rejected socially — the truth that she did not want to go to her friend's party."

"Wait," Carol interrupted, "that was just a white lie. You said professional politicians and medical people can deceive themselves by having a hidden but powerful motivation."

Dr. Magie scratched his head behind his left ear and then replied, "All right, let's take a successful psychiatrist with a perfect ethical/moral record of performance with patients. This highly trained professional honestly believes his greatest motivation is to be moral, and have integrity and good boundaries with his patients. His purpose is to free them from their childhood wounds and resulting adult issues. But his secret, hidden from himself, is that he has a wound concerning his own sexuality that causes him to want very strongly to have an illicit sexual relationship. This secret motivation is very powerful, but it has been repressed by this intelligent, capable and moral man. So the psychiatrist is not aware of the strength of his desire. But there comes a time when things are not going well in his personal life, his financial investments, and perhaps with his wife and children. The doctor has not been sleeping well. His practice goes on as usual until one day a patient comes who is very attractive sexually to the doctor. Ordinarily he would merely notice that she was attractive and go on with the consultation, since the ethics of the medical professional clearly forbid having sex with a patient. Even though the psychiatrist's personal morals agree completely with his professional ethics, he enters into an illicit sexual liaison with the woman who came to consult him. The doctor knows he's doing something that's totally against his morality but seems to be both drawn to and driven to have the affair. The doctor's inner wisdom may first object, but then switch and help him figure out ingenious ways for the liaison to continue undetected, all of which are in conflict with the psychiatrist's conscious and sincere commitment to the highest medical ethics.

This is a clear case of an intelligent, ethical, highly skilled person being 'compelled' by an unseen central motivator to have an illicit sexual affair that is in a given set of circumstances stronger than his honest conscious commitment to his moral principles. This unconscious motivator could cause him to ruin his relationships and his vocation.

But this surprising surfacing of a strong denied motivator is not just about sex. 'Honest' people can cheat on their taxes, embezzle funds from a corporation, or even a church after a lifetime of ethical behavior. The newspapers are filled with front-page accounts of these baffling and destructive moral earthquakes happening in the lives of respected teachers, ordained religious ministers, or the president of a nation. People are often surprised at how many times such departures from the stated ethics of otherwise moral men and women take place, and the perpetrator is often honestly baffled that he would do something so contrary to his most deeply held conscious values, like cheat to become famous, wealthy or get elected.

I'm suggesting that the cleverness and resources of inner wisdom are always at the service of one's strongest core values at any given moment. I'm saying that the psychiatrist's stronger hidden desire was actually succeeding when he acted out sexually. Many of the professionals I've counseled who've broken their moral codes and vows this way are surprised and horrified. They say and apparently believe things like, 'I was just not myself when I did that — even when the affair or embezzling lasted for months or even years. Because they were in denial about their hidden motivation, a wound that motivated them to act out and sabotage their entire professional career.

"What I'm saying is that our *actual decisions and behavior* reveal what our strongest values and goals truly are, *not* our public statements or even our sincere conscious intentions. And the inner wisdom always becomes the servant and guide to actualize and accomplish our deepest goals even if we are not conscious of what they are."

Carol thought about what Dr. M. had said and then said quietly, "So you're saying if we're not aware that we may have a strong, hidden motivator that's counter-productive to our conscious values and goals, we could sabotage our relationships or our life's work if an opportunity arose to protect or actualize our hidden goal?"

The wise old physician sat quietly, letting her digest what she had said.

"Oh, dear God! That's what I'm about to do — sabotage my marriage, and the financial freedom that would allow me to be creative and continue learning to write! And because I'm afraid to face what caused my original fear of rejection and desertion, I was ready to give up all that to avoid the pain of working through what's happening between John and me now." She paused. "I guess my question is whether I'm ready to risk discovering what my unconscious motives are so I can reconcile with John, and grow up and reach my dreams." Her eyes filled with tears. "You know what Wil's parting comment to me at the Denver airport was? He said, 'Maybe this is an opportunity for you and Dad both to find out who you really are.'"

Her look of amazement at her son's wisdom quickly gave way to a smile that was both proud and teasing, "That boy has his mother's intelligence!"

They both laughed, knowing she had decided to stay and try to work things out with John. As they walked to the door, she stopped and asked, "How do I begin to find out who I really am — and change? What is it that fuels my fear and jealousy? I feel like we're getting close to the secret thing that motivates my whole life."

Carol turned to her mentor like a frightened little girl. "Dr. M., can I really change at that level?"

"Some people can, when they want to change enough, and since you've already faced your father's abuse, I think you're one of those. We'll begin in the morning, but we'll have to finish later. We just got some bad news. I have to go with Mrs. Magie. Her sister is having cancer surgery in Paris day after tomorrow."

"Oh, I'm sorry — about Mrs. Magie's sister. I'd thought we had another week scheduled. But I certainly understand. Well maybe I can surprise John by coming home early."

26

The Search for the Hidden Motivator That Can Bushwhack Our Goals — and Lives

―*mm―mm―mm*―

Carol woke up at 5:30 a.m. and was the first guest in the dining room.

"Bon jour, Madame Martin," François said smiling.

"Bon jour, François, am I too early for coffee?"

"No, of course, not," he said, gesturing and leading her toward a table by the picture window. "I'll have some for you in three minutes."

Just before they arrived at the table for two, however, François seemed to change his mind and seated Carol one table to the left of the one he had originally selected. It was a little thing, but it struck Carol as strange. Her stomach tightened as if in danger, and suddenly, she was alert.

Once Carol was seated with the white linen napkin in her lap and François had brought her coffee and rolls, he nodded and turned to go.

"François?"

"Oui, Madame?" he said, turning back toward her.

Carol nodded toward the next table that he had passed by and asked calmly, "I know it was several years ago, but was that the table Mr. Martin shared with Madame Fontaine when he was here he first time?"

Carol had her answer in François' alarmed look. She said soothingly, "He told me all about it, the death of her husband and about their annual trip to Glion to drink the wine. So sad about her loss. We had dinner with her and her cousin in Paris on the way home from our last trip. They're lovely people."

François nodded gravely, *"Oui, Madame. "* He started to turn away.

"François."

"Oui, Madame?"

Mr. Martin said that Madame Fontaine became ill that night and that you actually picked her up and carried her upstairs to her room." (Why am I lying to him?)

"Oh no, Madame. She was not feeling well, but no one carried her to her room. She was perfectly able to walk by herself," he added.

Carol was almost overcome with shame and said to herself, "Why in heaven's name did you do that? You stupid twit! You should have known he wouldn't tell you — and you lied!"

Once seated in the big leather chair in the study, Dr. M. sat opposite her and waited quietly, until finally she said, "I've been thinking a lot about what we discussed yesterday, especially your belief that whatever is the most important value to each person at a given time — the most crucial possession, relationship, desire or fear tied to that person's sense of identity — can be the motivational key to that person's seemingly uncharacteristic and often self defeating behavior, even if the person is not aware of the dominance of that motivation. You said this motivator when triggered by certain circumstances can subvert and shape information and guidance furnished by our inner wisdom 'librarian' to the end of achieving or acquiring the fulfillment of our deepest motivation or purpose, whether we are *conscious* of that purpose or not. Have I got it?"

Dr. Magie heard a hard edge to Carol's words that he hadn't experienced before. "Basically," he replied slowly, "that's what I meant to say."

Carol nodded and continued, "If this is true, then before a person can change her life in any significant and comprehensive way, it's essential that she discover what value, goal or motivator is at the center of her life and is most important to her. Otherwise, every time her conscious values, plans or circumstances are significantly different from this central value, she'll be vulnerable to experiencing confusing stress and indecision, and may behave inappropriately. She may do or say things that are contradictory to her conscious best interests. And the inner wisdom will support the strongest part of her. The conscious, reasonable side may want to do the rational, socially appropriate thing that proceeds from her consciously accepted values and ways of responding. But when a situation comes along that triggers her unconscious agenda, she may do something seemingly self-defeating, irrational or even unethical and wonder why." Carol paused and then said, "Is that right? Do I have it?"

Dr. Magie nodded, amazed that she'd put that together in the midst of her stress.

She continued, "The symptoms of my secret central purpose or agenda are unreasonable jealousy and fear of desertion. I spent most of last night trying to see what the deeper source of my hidden motivation might be. I tried to discount your theory. I scoffed at it and said to myself, 'What is so important to me that I would become a scheming, irrational, dishonest person? What? I don't even know.'" Carol slapped her hands on the leather chair arms with a smack. She was angry and frustrated. "I *hate* not knowing what's driving me nuts...." She began to weep and reached for a tissue from the box beside her chair.

After several minutes, she was calm and limp. Staring into the fire, she continued, "This morning at breakfast, I got undeniable proof that there's something important inside me leading me to do dishonest things that are against my conscious desire to save our marriage and face myself. And I made a fool of myself." She told him about lying to François and trying to pump him to give her some scrap of information she could use to condemn John.

"Is that what you want to do, leave John?"

"No," she said forcefully, "I'm ready to get on with tracking down what it is that's more important to me than my marriage. What triggers my monumental jealousy and causes my inner wisdom to push me toward destroying the very relationship that in my sane moments I want to keep and heal?"

Dr. Magie waited and then said, "Carol, I think we educated people may be true masters of deceit in our personal lives, for we even deceive ourselves. We wear masks of success, happiness, adequacy, and integrity so much that we convince ourselves we are who we project ourselves to be. Consequently, thinking we have it all together, we are without the basic prerequisites for deep transformational change: inner integrity and humility. When we're confronted by others with even small deceptions or inconsistencies in our behavior, we react with denial, anger, fear, lies and self-justification. Only later do we sense these reactions were inappropriately strong. The ensuing arguments lead us to back away from the person who noticed our imperfection, and we're likely to wind up feeling alienated from ourselves because we don't understand what we are protecting or the strong need to justify behavior that is irrational even to us."

"This fear of being discovered as wrong or different from who we present ourselves to be is sometimes a consequence of trying to protect our unconscious hidden central motivation when it's not compatible with the life we're projecting to others. And I believe this dissonance leads to anxiety, anger, lack of intimacy, loneliness and fear that people will discover 'who we really are' — which we don't even know."

"Wait," Carol said, "What's an example of someone having an inappropriately strong reaction to having a mistake or fault pointed out?"

Dr. Magie thought a few seconds and then said, "Do you remember telling me that when as a child you challenged something your father said, perhaps even about something of little consequence, he became enraged, and shamed or punished you?"

Carol nodded, "Yes, and you're right. His behavior was the far edge of inappropriate. I didn't see it then, but I do now."

"I've spoken to dozens of individuals and groups about their inner lives, and their feedback has convinced me that people everywhere are crying out in the privacy of their own hearts for a way to become free from powerful, but denied inner motivations that sometimes activate and are out of their control."

Carol's eyes were riveted on Magie, "Since we're so afraid to face ourselves on this level, what can give us the courage to confront and expose what we've spent a lifetime hiding, even from ourselves?"

The old physician replied, "The most significant difficulty in identifying a hidden motivator is that although it is hidden from us, it feels like it must be something unacceptable and yet also deeply tied to our security. So we won't even look for it, much less voluntarily *change* it, unless we sense we're about to lose something we're not willing to live without, like a primary relationship or our vocation, health or sanity. The decision to face one's denial and look inside for what we fear will be an unacceptable part of our lives, may come when one finds another person who appears to understand this separation, chaos and the agony of a divided self, someone who cares enough just to listen, without judgement or trying to change our reality. Often, we don't even listen to our own families and friends like this — without interrupting or trying to change them. The lack of an understanding ear can lead people to do bizarre things they ordinarily would not do, for example, I think the unfulfilled need to be heard and understood without judgment is one of the greatest causes of marital infidelity. Sometimes an affair is not so much about sex as it is about being heard and understood by someone who knows your weaknesses and listens without condemning. This loneliness and sense of shame from battling out-of-character behavior can be so great that some people will trade their bodies, all that is important to them for the sense of being accepted as they are. Others will destroy what they hold dear to avoid being exposed and revealed as inadequate."

Carol asked, "Tell me again, what would make a person willing to look inside herself for the hidden motivator of her dysfunctional or uncharacteristic behavior?"

"As I said, the combination of being in extreme confusion and misery and finding a safe person who hears you and also is willing to share his or her own experience of separation and loneliness. These things are often the keys to being willing to look at your hidden motivator. In some cases, the desire to achieve an all-important goal may motivate one to change if the secret motivator seems to be threatening the achievement of the goal."

"Yes," Carol said quietly. "All of that is precisely where I am with you right now. But how do I proceed from here?"

"In my own life, I was so afraid of what I might find out about myself that I backed off again and again from getting help to discover my hidden motivator. I used any excuse I could come up with to avoid this discovery. Finally my mentor, Walter Mueller, confronted me with what I was doing."

Carol suddenly remembered that she'd forgotten to change her plane reservations from the coming week to in the next morning. She interrupted, "I'm so sorry, but could we take a break?" I need to make an important call I forgot about."

"Of course," he chuckled, "I'll get us some coffee."

Carol was irritated, "What are you laughing at? Did I say something amusing?"

"Yes," he said, and disappeared.

Returning in a few minutes with their coffee, he could see she was angry, but merely asked pleasantly, "Did your call go through all right?"

She looked at him coldly. "What's going on here? I've been completely open with you and let you into places no one else has ever been. But when you laughed at me just before I made the call to the airport, I realized what I've been feeling for the past week or ten days. You're stalking me emotionally somehow, trying to get me to go somewhere I don't want to go. I feel like you are a relentless bird-dog, and I'm tired of it."

He wasn't smiling now; he was listening closely to her accusation. He thought a few seconds and then said simply, "Is there more?"

She relaxed a little and continued, "I've been getting the feeling you think I'm not much of a person, and you're about to prove it by ferreting out the fact that my hidden central motivator is superficial or not acceptable."

After waiting to make sure Carol was finished, Dr. Magie said, "Thank you for telling me what you're thinking and feeling. You're saying you think I've been stalking you as a hunting dog tracks its quarry, and you're angry about that. Also, you believe I don't esteem you as being an adequate person, and I'm about to demonstrate my lack of respect by uncovering your denied motivating purpose, demonstrating that you are unacceptable. Yes?"

"Yes, pretty much."

"I can see how you would feel those things, and thinking I'm stalking you has to be painful, as open as you've been with me about your thoughts and feelings. I feel sad about that."

After a period of silence, she said, "Well, aren't you going to tell me what you're really thinking? You could start by telling me what was so amusing about my suddenly remembering to call the airline to change my reservations."

"Carol, I've always respected you as a person, but never more than just now when you were willing to risk our relationship to confront me with your perceptions about what I've been thinking and doing. I was amused at your suddenly interrupting our session because I had just indicated that we were now going to focus specifically on finding your hidden primary motivating value. I had told you that at this point in my own search I kept dodging and using anything possible with my mentor to avoid going on with the process. So I laughed because after you appeared to be focused on what we were doing, suddenly your inner wisdom helped you recall something that allowed you to stop focusing on the process we'd just begun. I recalled doing virtually the same thing at this point in my own journey, and I remembered that my mentor had confronted me with the fact that my interruption was an unconscious tactic, a ploy, to protect my hidden primary motivator from being discovered."

Carol moved to the front of her chair as she blurted, "Well, that's *not* true of me! If I hadn't called when I did, I might not have been able to get a reservation in the morning — a situation you caused by shortening our scheduled time together. And you're making my being responsible look like I was evading finding the truth about myself!"

Dr. Magie was sitting quietly, thinking about what was happening, when Carol stood abruptly and announced, "I can see we're not communicating well. I realize you're under pressure to get ready to leave with Mrs. Magie this afternoon. I don't want to be a hindrance to you — or her — any longer."

Dr. Magie was still listening. Finally he said, "What would you like to do?"

She was all business, "It's obvious our process has broken down. Since I've decided to go back to Denver and try to work through things with John, I'm going to leave you now to get ready for your trip. I'm going to pack and then take a long hike up the mountain to think through what I've learned. Tomorrow I'll fly home and surprise John, and begin our reconciliation by being *very* loving." She looked at Dr. Magie, almost daring him to challenge her decision.

He stood and said gently, "My love and prayers are with you both. If you and John would like to stay in touch or proceed on the journey we've begun, let me know. I care a great deal for each of you and am grateful that our lives have intersected."

Carol suddenly felt bereft, realizing that Dr. Magie was acknowledging and confirming her right to the freedom from him that she said she wanted. Turning at the front door and asked hesitantly, "How long will you be away with Mrs. Magie, in case something unforeseen comes up?"

"Actually we're not sure until we see how Mrs. Magie's sister responds to treatment. I'm due in Boston in three weeks for some lectures, but if her sister stabilizes in time, we plan to come early for some rest and relaxation. Would you like me to contact you when we get to Boston?"

"Oh, yes." Relieved that she hadn't alienated him by her behavior, she added, "And ... thank you ... for everything." Suddenly, she crossed quickly to him and gave him a hug. Then she was gone.

27

Being Playful — with Fire

The next morning after breakfast, Carol was checking out at the front desk when Celeste came in the side door, breathless from running to catch her before she left.

"Hello, Celeste."

"Good morning, Mrs. Martin," Celeste said, "I have such wonderful news!"

"What?"

"Although the family in Utah had to cancel the invitation for me to come for my year abroad, another family has requested that I stay with them — and their school has a ski team too — and they live in Denver, Colorado!" Celeste's eyes were shining with happiness.

"That's wonderful news, Celeste. What's the name of the family that requested you?"

"Mr. and Mrs. William Castle; and they say that you told them about me. I had almost given up after the Utah family had to cancel. This is like a miracle from God! Thank, you."

"That's wonderful, Celeste! The Castles are some of our closest friends." Carol had to think a few seconds before she remembered telling Fran about Celeste being a champion downhill skier in Montreux, and that she wanted to be an exchange student in the U.S. Since the Castles were all fanatical skiers and their children's prep school team was highly rated in competition, Carol wasn't surprised that Fran had written the request for Celeste to stay with them, not knowing she'd already been accepted in Utah.

"It'll be so nice to have you in Denver. When will you come?"

"Next week, if possible, because school starts the following week."

Carol looked at the clock behind the front desk. "Call us when you get settled in Denver." Smiling, she handed Celeste a card and gave her a hug.

"Darn it, Wil, you're too smart to act arrogant around the people in the company. We're building a remarkable team, and there *aren't* going to be any prima donnas. Are you listening?"

Wil nodded his head about a quarter of an inch. He looked relaxed in his sweat suit and running shoes.

"I can't *hear* you!" John said cocking his head. He was at his wits' end for the hundredth time since Carol had been gone.

"Yes sir," Wil said evenly, "I'm listening."

"Well, what have you got to say about your attitude? You're 6′3″ and built like an NFL linebacker, and when you scowl impatiently at people, it scares the hell out of them. You look like you're going to throw them out a window."

"I'm not being arrogant," Wil answered evenly, obviously angry at this father's accusations. "It's just that I've been studying every aspect of the company's operations, and some of these people don't know what they're doing, and they're not being honest with you. They're covering up their mistakes and trying to look good instead of doing the grunt work to learn the business."

John started for the kitchen to get a beer, saying over his shoulder, "People who are willing to do the grunt work don't quit the team when the going gets a little rough."

Wil said, "It's interesting that you'd wait until the night before I go back to school for eight weeks to mention your evaluation of my work attitude — when I won't be able to do anything about it."

"Why are you going back to school now?"

"Dad, I told you my major professor is dying and asked me to help him get his research in order so someone else can continue it. I talked to you about this last week." His teeth clenched, and his fists knotted as he got up and walked outside. John had gone for the jugular in referring to his quitting the high school football team and sabotaging his athletic career by wild partying. "God, he plays rough," he thought, as he stretched his legs on the front porch and tightened the laces of his running shoes. Then he started running toward the shopping center in the moonlight. He said to himself, "What's the matter with him? I've worked my butt off for him, put in some serious checks and balances to allow the company to have better control of finances, and I've developed a system for getting new people familiar with his unorthodox ten-minute planning and evaluation systems. And he's never even mentioned anything good I've done. He must really hate my guts."

He pulled out his cell phone and called his AA sponsor. In a few seconds he heard the familiar gravelly voice, "Al here."

"Any chance you're going to an eight o'clock meeting?"

"Yeah, need a ride?"

"Either a ride or a drink. I'm about a block away from the Gateway complex — can you pick me up there?"

The noise level at the Metropolitan Club was always higher on Fridays. Arthur and John were finishing lunch.

"So did you tell Carol about the partners' meeting tonight?" Arthur asked. "We'd sure like to have her here to help Fran entertain them at dinner."

"No, she's still in Switzerland — not scheduled to come home till next week. Besides, the last party you and Bill cooked up for the partners in Paris wasn't exactly wonderful for her. I'll tell her all about the latest developments when she gets home."

"Sorry, John, well Claudette and Oscar Fontaine have requested some private time with you tonight after dinner. They want to discuss the possibility of joining Martin Industries, the Castles and me in the whole storage company project including plans for starting a European branch, possibly another $20 million investment.

"Tell them we'll send them the information when we've got all the loose ends buttoned down on the U.S. venture. We can talk then."

Arthur played with his fork, pushing a small roll back and forth on the linen tablecloth like a hockey player about to make a shot. Then he looked up. "I already told them I'd bring them by your house after the meeting for a night cap and perhaps a little time to get acquainted. These two have checked out the world economy, and their financial consultants have told them the rest of the world is either in such chaos or high risk that the U.S. is still the best place to invest and preserve capital. And the Fontaine group has been very pleased with the quality of your investments for the first partnership. And for some reason Claudette Fontaine believes in you and your future."

John cocked his head and squinted at Arthur to see if he was serious. "I appreciate your enthusiasm, and I agree it'll be an important development. But I want you to really hear me. We're not going to make any *commitments* at this time. If you forget, I'll contradict you publicly. Part of the system I've learned is always to have integrity with investors. Is that clear?"

Arthur nodded.

Then John said in a normal tone, "Yeah, I know that the Fontaines believe in us. And they're good people. Although Oscar looks like an old pit bull, I think he's just an experienced Frenchman who's making sure his little cousin doesn't get had by some money-grabbing Yankee materialists. He's probably got good instincts about that," John added, looking pointedly at Arthur, as he continued, "We're not exactly running away from their advances."

"Well, if he's worried about us 'overpursuing' them, you're bound to be making him feel real safe! For God's sake, you leave every time they come into a room!" Arthur didn't know about his relationship with Claudette, or that Carol was in Switzerland because of it, and John wasn't about to tell him.

"Whatever you're doing, it's working," Arthur said heartily, "The lady is more persistent every time you back off and Oscar is reassured that you aren't trying to exploit them. I can tell he's more relaxed. Since you're not going to dance with her and she'll have her chaperone along, couldn't they just stop by for a few minutes after the party?"

Carol hadn't called again, and John had to admit that kind of financial participation by one of the largest companies in the world would be invaluable. Besides, what could happen with Claudette if Oscar and Arthur were there? "Okay, bring them by, but *don't* let this go past *1:00 a.m.* I've got a busy schedule tomorrow."

—*mm*—

Carol had slept on the first half of the fight from Paris, but when the plane finally touched down on American soil at the Dallas/Ft. Worth airport, the passengers applauded and she woke up abruptly. As the flight took off again for Denver, she felt a wave of fear, would John think her surprise was stupid?

She felt as if she were sneaking into Denver to have an affair with John. She'd decided to give their marriage her best effort — and she was going to begin by romancing him and making love so passionately that whatever Claudette had done would pale in comparison. Carol had never before had the courage not to call ahead and let him know exactly when she was coming in, especially something as unusual as arriving several days early. John didn't like surprises. But now an hour before landing in Denver, it was too late to worry about that, she looked at her watch, stood and got the light hanging bag out of the overhead compartment. She was about to change into a knockout red dress with a white silk scarf she'd carried on board.

Carol realized now that although much of her fear and anger had been the result of her relationship with her father, she had no doubt that the scarier issue might be her uncontrollable and nameless hidden motivator. In any case, she felt angry about John's hiding the meeting with Claudette Fontaine — even if it was only a peccadillo. Carol said to herself, "If we do work through that incident there will have to be a clear 'no contact rule' with Claudette until I've had more experience dealing with my jealousy and carried feelings." In the meantime, she was glad Claudette lived across the ocean.

The American flight attendant was working her way down the aisle asking, "May I get you anything else?" When her turn came, Carol responded, "Yes, thank you. I'll have a martini on the rocks — very dry, please."

28

Till Death Us Do Part

~~~~~~

The dinner that evening at the Castles' mountain home was spectacular. Bill's parents had owned a ranch half an hour into the mountains west of Denver, and they died, Bill and Fran had a new house built by one of Frank Lloyd Wright's most gifted students. Straddling the big Thompson River at the end of a canyon, there were large bedroom wings on each side of the river and a huge glass-walled "great hall" ballroom spanned the roaring white waters twenty-five hundred feet below. From the porch of the great hall, one could look downstream at the sun setting among the giant pines at the valley's end, a mile below the house.

The guests from France and England were entranced, and when at the end of dinner, Arthur spoke of this being an authentic time of adventure for him with his associates and friends, the Castles and the Martins, he reiterated the financial opportunities they were uncovering in creative real estate ventures. "And now the time is coming," Arthur said quietly, "when we can open these new real estate opportunities to investors; and we've decided to give this brief preview of the kinds of opportunities we see to our European friends who have invested with Martin Industries' initial limited partnership. Tonight John has agreed to preview an idea that we've been investigating. John . . ." He moved from the mike to welcome John. The group was fascinated with John's PowerPoint presentation. After he finished, Arthur returned. "Because of the size and variety of potentially lucrative opportunities we are discovering, we've decided to form and manage a series of limited partnerships that can move quickly and generate faster and larger returns. This way, we can evaluate deals much more quickly, meaning we can make decisions to take advantage of opportunities spawned by sudden changes that are going on around us."

One of the French investors asked, "Do you have an example of capitalizing on a sudden opportunity?"

"A good question." Arthur thought a moment, "Some months ago, John got a call from a large national corporation that had just acquired a smaller commercial real estate investment company in a merger. The purchaser's problem was that the acquired company turned out to have the deed to a large, expensive tract of land, a deed that had a development clause requiring that a shopping center be commenced almost immediately on the property or the deed would revert to the original owner. This time requirement had slipped through the cracks in the merger. And doing the necessary investigation to commence construction within the contractual time limit seemed impossible. As a last-minute desperation move, the acquiring company — that was now holding the deed — offered John a large percentage of the entire shopping center project if he could check the deal out and stake out the construction site by midnight two days after the date of their call. John, would you describe the way you approached evaluating this project?"

John stood again. "Ordinarily we would not consider trying to evaluate such a large project in that time frame. But we do have a procedure for making fast evaluations. The problem we faced was to investigate and coordinate a number of aspects of the project at lightning speed — including getting a top-flight attorney to check the title directly from the county records; evaluating the proposed shopping center in terms of location, traffic flow, existing contracts or contacts with tenants after completion, other shopping competition in the area, cost of construction; and nailing down the insurance and subcontractor — all in two days.

"Our acquisitions team met for eight hours that night, designing a plan in less than an hour that included everything we needed to know before we could make an educated bet on the success of the project. Then, in that same preliminary meeting, every part of the plan was assigned specifically to someone on the team to check or oversee. That night and the next morning, each team coordinator hired independent surveyors, analysts, and subcontractors they knew to work on an emergency contract basis until all items were being investigated. The contract people were offered a high premium bonus tied to making the deadline. And everyone involved committed to work around the clock to get his or her part of the checking done in thirty hours. Three of us received and assimilated information, and created a best estimate evaluation sheet by plugging in the figures as they came in, realizing that exact numbers could be assessed later. We allowed for a 25 percent margin of error for underestimating costs and cut the estimated income figures by 30 percent in figuring the total cost, income and pay out of the investment."

Arthur stepped up and said, "John okayed the plans at 10:30 p.m. the second day. The surveyors and site crews who were standing by broke ground at 11:45 p.m., saving the purchase contract for the land and earning John's investors half interest in what has the potential to be a $30 million project. They evaluated this prospect in thirty hours."

Arthur let that fact sink in, and then said, "Not many prospects come along which are that dramatic, but our new company's agility is based on incredible commitment and ability from John's group and the planning techniques he has developed to determine what needs to be done within a very short time frame."

The group applauded spontaneously.

Arthur asked if there were any further questions.

Oscar Fontaine raised his forefinger, "How can you be certain of the outcome when all is done so quickly?"

John smiled, "Monsieur Fontaine, one is never 100 percent sure that any project will be profitable. But I learned from a very wise man how a group of people with experience can come up with an evaluation plan in as fast as ten to twenty minutes." Fontaine looked skeptical. John said, "I, too, had a lot of trouble believing this approach to active planning would work in such a short time. But since we began using this method to screen every prospect, we can handle a larger influx of new opportunities precisely because we can eliminate impractical deals quickly. We would not usually assume such large risk on such short notice; however," and John smiled, "I happened to be familiar with that area of Denver, lest you think we're magicians — or insane."

The group laughed appreciatively at John's candor, and the dinner ended on a convivial note.

John lit a cheery fire in the fireplace, as Arthur pointed out to Oscar and Claudette the striking moonlit mountain view through the large living room window of the Martin's home, but then Arthur took Oscar out in the back yard, leaving Claudette and John alone. John could feel an eerie electricity in the room, as if their meeting in Glion had been only a week before. She was an amazing woman. He had forgotten how beautiful she was.

"Well, my friend, John Martin, how are things with you?"

John hesitated and then calmly began his practiced words, "Claudette, you are a beautiful, intelligent, desirable woman." John's words were honest but neither encouraging nor shaming as he continued. "But I'm happily married and certainly did not intend to lead you on that night in Glion."

"Lead me on?"

"Encourage you to think that I was being more than a friend."

At that moment Carol tiptoed in the front door and was about to enter the living room, when she saw Claudette and John sitting together. She recoiled and froze against the wall, Claudette's reply was as clear as a bell in her ears.

"I know you care for me. That night in Glion you undressed me and slipped my white silk robe on me. And I cannot tell you how moved I was when I woke the next morning, knowing you had done these things." Claudette laughed a wonderful lover's laugh. "Then I saw the tiny silver vase with the beautiful rose you had put on my bedside table. Where you got the rose at that time of evening, I can't imagine. But," she said, looking directly into John's eyes, "that was the most sensitive and romantic thing that has ever happened to me. Can one call that merely friendship?"

John was about to object, when Carol stepped into the room.

"Surprise!" she said to John, "I got a chance to come home early!" She whirled around like a model. "Look at the sexy red dress I got for you in Geneva!" And then pretending to notice Claudette for the first time, she said with remarkable composure, "Why, Claudette Fontaine! How in the world did you find your way here, all the way from Paris?" She glanced around the room at the cozy fire and the two half empty glasses, "No ropes or chains. I assume you arrived under your own power, perhaps in the rented Mercedes in the driveway?" Carol was a little tipsy from the drinks on the plane. Her breath was coming fast and her words were tight and unreal. "Now, the only question is, did she surprise you too, John, or did you invite her?"

While John was trying to think of what to say, Carol walked over to the small antique letter writing desk and opened the upper right-hand drawer, where she kept the small 32-caliber revolver her father had given her and taught her to shoot when she was twelve. Carol sighed deeply and reached for the gun.

"Carol!"

Carol's hand dropped into the drawer as she whipped her head around. A beaming Arthur Bennet came through the patio door toward her with outstretched arms, followed by Oscar Fontaine. She released the gun and closed the drawer in a single motion.

"Hello Arthur," she exclaimed in shock as she responded to his bear hug. Noticing his formal dress, she asked calmly, "How was the party?"

"We missed you. John said you wouldn't be back till next week." He turned to John, "You rascal, you were going to surprise us!"

John shrugged slightly, as Carol said, "John didn't know I was coming. I was going to surprise him, too, but my flight didn't get in early enough."

John squinted at her, but didn't say anything, still poised to rush her if she had taken the gun from the drawer.

After a few moments of pleasantries, the guests began to leave. Calmly, in an almost matter-of-fact way, Carol drew Claudette aside and said, "Sorry about my grand entrance, but as you can tell, there's almost nothing I wouldn't do to keep my man."

Claudette looked directly at Carol as the men left the house and said with equal poise, "I can't fault you for that. He's the best I've ever...known."

Carol watched them leave. It was not going to be easy to stop and process what had just happened, but she was on a mission: come home to her husband. Asking John if he would please bring her luggage, she went up to get ready for bed.

She had never been so wild and free, as she loved John that night.

The next morning when John woke, he felt warm and peaceful all over. Before he opened his eyes, he reached across the bed, but Carol was gone. The bedside clock said 7:15. He sat up and called "Carol!" but no answer. Then he saw the note pinned to her satin pillow:

> John,
>
> Save my place! I've gone to a special all-day meeting of the Dream Team. Will be back by six. We can catch up then.
>
> Carol

John was sitting at the dining room table looking over the list of calls Barbara had handed him when Carol pulled in the driveway at 6:15. He looked up, searching for the safest thing to say to this strange new wife who'd seemingly just come home from the Land of Oz. He said, "How was your meeting?"

"Great, we've all become even closer friends. I called them from Glion when I realized I could come home early — and agreed to come to the meeting today. Since you didn't know I was coming, I knew you wouldn't have anything planned for me — and you looked so peaceful and happy this morning, I couldn't bear to wake you."

He raised his eyebrows, waiting for — he didn't know what — then said, "Well, how are you? How did the time with Dr. M. go?"

She leaned back in her chair, and mused, "Life changing, I think. Dr. M. is one wise old man."

"Tell me about it."

She told him Dr. M. had said when a person's emotional responses are incredibly strong, it's often because that person is carrying undealt-with feelings of a parent or guardian.

She then described how Dr. M.'s leading her back into her childhood and helped her reexperience her father's emotional abuse and his desertion of her and her mother. She hadn't planned to tell John about the session during which she gave her carried feelings back to her father, but since he was listening intently and empathizing with her, she told him anyway.

John had never heard of "carried" feelings, much less that way of dealing with them. He hadn't even known that it was possible that a child could introject an abuser's feelings — of fear, anger and jealousy — and the child could subsequently experience and express the feelings as if they were her own.

She continued, "All this is to say that I realized my feelings of jealousy, anger and fear of desertion were so big, because a large part of them were my father's feelings that he had unknowingly dumped into my life by not facing them himself. She paused, and then said, "But Dr. M. also told me about another reason people mess up their lives without knowing why they are doing it."

John was suddenly alert, braced for her to tell him something he was doing wrong. But she continued, "He said many people have a hidden — unconscious — motivation that causes them to try to control people or situations without knowing why they are doing it."

"What are you saying?"

She replied uneasily, "You know, like when you get angry and can't get along with Wil, and you tell me, 'I don't know why I can't get along with that boy.' Anyway, whatever the hidden motivator is, it often causes us to be confused and do things that are inappropriate or out of proportion — like my irrational outbursts when I'm jealous."

John started to interrupt, but Carol waved him off and continued, "I was determined to have this talk with you about the hidden motivator idea and about my carried feelings when I got home, before the subject of Claudette could come up.

That way you would understand why my jealousy of Claudette was so uncontrollably strong. But when I walked in last night and saw the two of you alone together, I lost it again." She paused, "You know, I might have shot one or both of you if Arthur hadn't come on stage when he did."

"I know. I knew what was in that drawer." He looked at her to see if she wanted to say anything about that. When she didn't comment, he said, "That's amazing stuff about carried feelings. Thanks for sharing it. But — what happened to you after Arthur and Oscar came in? You were scary-calm. Knowing you, and knowing the gun was in the drawer, I couldn't believe how quickly you pulled out of your . . ." John paused, searching for the appropriate words, "pulled out of your jealousy attack and became a perfect hostess."

"My backing off wasn't a consequence of seeing you with Claudette. When I saw Arthur and then Oscar, I knew you'd had some sort of meeting with the investors. And knowing Arthur, I figured he dangled you in front of the Fontaines as a way to reel them in for future projects. That's when I remembered what I'd just learned from Dr. M. about how to deal with 'too huge' feelings when they arise now. Behind my calm face, I was saying silently to my dad, 'This is your anger. Those are your murderous feelings. I give them back to you! Get them out of my life.'"

"And did they leave?" he asked, incredulously.

"Not completely, but enough that I could handle my own jealous feelings and let my social training take over. Of course, hearing Claudette's description of your night with her in Glion from her perspective was hardly encouraging, but," she added quickly, "I don't want to go there now."

"But how in the *world* were you able to go upstairs and make love the way you did — after what you'd heard and done? You were amazing!" He whistled and shook his head.

Carol smiled. She was a little embarrassed by his whistle, but secretly pleased, as scenes of herself in action flashed across the screen of her memory. She said, "My loving you that way was not totally romantic. If you *ever did* remember the last part of the evening in Glion and recalled that you slept with her, I just wanted you to know that I'm as good, or better, than she is."

John was just about to respond when their private line began to ring. Carol picked up the receiver and, putting her hand over the mouth piece, said to John, "I'm not finished with you about Claudette — and I can tell you she's not nearly finished with you either, so don't think we've settled this issue."

"Hello," then, "who's calling, please?" Her face broke into a big smile, "Dr. M.! Where are you? Can you come see us before you have to start lecturing? Yes, yes, that will be great! Anytime you can. We're anxious to see you. Is Mrs. Magie with you? Oh, I'm sorry she can't come now, but we'll look forward to seeing her when she can join you. How is her sister doing? Well, that's good news. Would you like our travel people to make your reservations? Okay, e-mail or call when you get the exact day and time. I can't wait to see you!"

When she hung up, she was radiant. "He's in Boston, and next week he's coming here for a few days! Hope that's okay."

"Sure, we'll take him whenever we can get him."

29

Unmasking the Inner Wisdom

John was particularly excited about Dr. Magie's coming to visit Denver. He had been thinking about the underlying meanings of the various processes and perspectives their old friend had given them. But driving to the airport to meet Dr. M.'s flight, John realized that he really wanted to talk about some unexpected inner conflicts and some different kinds of questions that had come up: "What is success, beyond the numbers and the attention it's bringing? How much success is enough? And most of all, who am I now, and what's happened to my relationship with Wil?" Though this was a social visit, he hoped they might still have time together to discuss some of the unrest he was experiencing.

Carol was excited too, but for different reasons. Reflecting on her recent counseling sessions in Glion, she realized how much her outlook had changed. Instead of attacking John, or running away to some illusory place to hide from the pain of his apparent involvement with Claudette, and from her own possible failure to reconcile with him, she was defending her territory like a tiger. With her new sense of self-worth, Carol had also increased insight about her own motivations, character issues and assets. But she was eager to ask Dr. Magie to help her identify her hidden motivator that evidently jumped in at unexpected times and sabotaged her attempts to reconcile with John.

As they both waited in the baggage claim area, John said, "I feel like a kid meeting his sports hero."

"Me too!"

When they looked up and saw Dr. Magie stepping onto the down escalator out of the "passenger only" restricted area, John was surprised at how short he was. Charles Magie was such a giant in his mind that John thought of him as being much taller than his five feet, ten inches.

When Dr. M. saw them, he waved enthusiastically. They waved back and mouthed, "Welcome!" Carol spontaneously blew him a kiss.

While waiting for their guest's luggage, they asked about Mrs. Magie's sister. "The surgery was not as severe as the doctors had originally feared. The cancer was totally contained and removed in the operation, but Mrs. Magie is going to stay for a few days, to visit and make sure her sister doesn't have a reaction to the medications. I hope she'll join

174

me in a week or ten days. In the meantime, I'm glad we could have this visit together. How are things going with you two?"

John reported how the business was progressing and how fortunate they had been to find several incredible opportunities for the partnership.

"What about the storage unit plan you described in your e-mail?" Dr. Magie asked. "That sounds like a certain success. I wish we had a small facility in Glion. As more tourists come, the local people benefit. So they buy more things for themselves and their homes. Being a thrifty people who don't throw anything away, we are becoming pack rats with no place to store the old things." Dr. Magie stopped and smiled as he continued, "Just like any civilized people."

John started to launch into his plan to proceed nationwide, but caught Carol's eye as she pointed to her watch, and realized it was late. Dr. M. was no doubt exhausted from his trip.

Picking up Dr. M.'s bag, John said, "Let's talk about this later. If you're up for it, we're planning a little sightseeing trip tomorrow, and on the way we may get a chance to drive by the first storage facility we bought to evaluate how they really work."

The following day John and Carol took Dr. Magie on a day trip to Boulder. He was delighted with the city at the base of the Rocky Mountains, and as they drove by the University of Colorado, John explained, "Several of the graduate faculty also consult with Martin Industries, researching and teaching us about areas of opportunity we are considering."

Then they drove into the mountains to Estes Park and on up to a lookout point at the Rocky Mountain's 'Continental Divide.' "Look," said Dr. M. "What are those Asian children doing?"

"They're feeding peanuts to the ground squirrels that live among the boulders on the other side of the stone retaining wall. That's been going on for as long as I can remember." As they watched together, John savored the special moment they shared as friends. On the way home, they stopped on the outskirts of Denver to tour the storage facility John had mentioned the night before.

When they arrived home that evening, they enjoyed a delicious mountain trout dinner Barbara had prepared, after which they settled in the family room for a visit. The crackling fire in the fireplace reflected on the heavy walnut beams and the polished tile floor, creating a quiet, intimate ambience.

"Dr. M.," John said, "some questions have been coming up in my mind about some personal difficulties I'm running into along with all the success and acclaim that have come to me — us — as we focused on the dreams you helped us discover."

"Would you like to talk about that now?"

"Yeah, I thought I was this intelligent, rational, hard working American male who could build a successful business and do the work it would take to have a happy and loving family. The business part is true, but I feel like I'm batting close to zero on the happy loving family part. The problems surface when I'm dealing with Wil in particular. An irrational and certainly self-defeating compulsion comes over me to make sure he does things right. I can hear myself becoming supercritical. From my perspective I'm just trying to help him — but something about our personal encounters drives him up the wall, something about — my attitude?

"When we first met, you described how accessing our inner wisdom can help us make sound decisions, as it selects facts, experiences, strategies and other data for us from 'storage' that will help us to achieve our goals. And largely that has been true — except when I have these mystifying and painful experiences with Wil. I just don't understand the intensity of our conflict. Do many men you've dealt with have problems of this depth communicating with their grown children?"

"Your relationship with Wil sounds very painful. And the answer to your question is yes; successful men often have this kind of conflict with their grown sons. Although part of it is very irrational, the conflict is very important. In fact, Paul Tournier said that the way this problem between a son and his father is resolved may be the most significant event in the son's development. Your relationship with Wil may relate to your dream achieving adventure. Do you remember when you and I first spoke of life dreaming, I asked you to choose an overall condition or state you would like to attain through achieving your dreams?"

"Yeah," John said, "mine was peace of mind."

"I had you choose an overall goal because in the process of succeeding to achieve their specifically listed goals — especially vocational goals — many people lose track of their overall life goal and become very unhappy or anxious. Sometimes they're brought up short by relationship conflicts or emotional pressure like you and Carol and you and Wil have experienced. Although the problems don't seem to relate to their goals, the facts are that just as they are succeeding wonderfully they may realize they have not achieved their overall life goal of happiness or, in your case, peace of mind. And when this happens, they may become mystified to discover that they feel compelled or coerced from within to do things in their relationships that are destructive to their overall goal."

"Yeah, that's exactly where I am," John said. "Everything is ahead of schedule about achieving our dreams, but something is wrong inside me that pops up unexpectedly in my relationship with Wil — and sometimes Carol. And I can't get a handle on whatever it is that causes this compulsive and self-defeating behavior, but it is driving me nuts.

"Dr. M., do you have any ideas about where this compulsion might come from? It's getting so bad that I'm afraid I'll drive him away for good."

"The answer to your question is 'no' and 'yes.' I don't know the specific source of that behavior in your life, but I have counseled a number of men who have discovered a strong hidden and compulsive motivation to control certain people or areas of their lives."

"What did these people discover their hidden motivators were?"

"Although the specific reasons for this baffling compulsion to control were different, there were some common elements."

"Common elements?"

"Yes, usually a long forgotten childhood trauma or emotional wound in the life of the controlling father caused by his own parents' thoughtless or abusive behavior."

"For example?"

Dr. M pursed his lips. "Well, one patient said that he couldn't remember his father ever teaching him to do anything — from tying his shoes to shaking hands with people he met — or telling him that he loved him, or expressing any emotion in his presence, except anger. Because a father's responsibility is to provide a secure and nurturing relationship for his children and give them love a guidance in the skills of living, the father's failure to do these things created a childhood wound in the sense that this patient had grown up insecure and hiding his feelings — just as his father had. The son pushed his own fears and insecurities into his unconscious like a giant beach ball. Although the grown son was no longer conscious of his father's neglect, the son's need to conceal his own feelings and keep the beach ball of his fear out of sight, led this boy as a man, to try to control anyone who threatened to reveal that he was not adequate, especially family members. And when anyone pointed out a mistake or threatened to reveal this man's ineptitude, a very exaggerated anger exploded out of nowhere to control the person who threatened him.

"This kind of explosive, inappropriate anger may emerge like the surfacing of a submerged beach ball — suddenly and unexpectedly — with a good bit of force, and hurt someone. This inappropriate and controlling behavior is often surprising and baffling to the one who has repressed the hurt, fear or need for love beneath the faceless hidden motivation to control."

John leaned back in the leather chair, "That's very interesting, but my childhood was nothing like your example."

Carol looked at John sharply, obviously surprised by his response.

Dr. M. continued to answer John's question. "As I was telling Carol when she was in Glion recently, since this deep motivating purpose is unconscious, our behavior stemming from it is often confusing and frightening. So whatever its source, you may have a strong hidden motivating purpose pertaining to Carol or Wil that causes you to do or say things that contradict and supersede achieving your conscious dreams. This contradictory behavior — like your being compelled to try to control Wil — could trigger the conflict, stress and guilt you spoke of.

Carol, who had been listening carefully, said, "Dr. M., are you saying that the process of discovering and achieving our goals can actually lead us to see a *deep personal issue* inside us, a hidden conflict that no amount of success can resolve? A problem that must be resolved before we can realize the freedom of our *overall* life goal of happiness, in my case or peace of mind in John's?"

Dr. Magie looked at Carol, "Yes, Carol, that's what I'm saying."

Carol was excited, "On the plane from Switzerland, I thought about our last session in Glion when my anger shot to the surface like a beach ball I'd been holding under water. I was angry that you suggested that I sabotaged our counseling session and came home early — because you were about to help me discover what my hidden motivator actually is — and I was afraid to look. Your process was threatening to reveal my secret hidden motivator. Now, I think I see what you meant, and you were right on target."

Dr. Magie said, "Thank you, Carol. That was probably hard to admit, and I appreciate you're doing so."

"If that's true," Carol continued, "it's very important for John and me to discover what our hidden motivating purposes are because the repressed motivator can wreak havoc in our family relationships and sabotage both our success goals *and* our overall goal of happiness."

"That could happen."

"Well, I'd like to find out now, before I ruin my life by not knowing what's controlling it. Would you like to do that, too, John?"

"I'm not sure what you're talking about, or that I need to do it — my decisions are mostly sound."

Carol glowered at him, "Yeah, you sure are able to make good, sound decisions, like jeopardizing our marriage by getting blind drunk with a stranger, carrying her to her hotel room, putting her to bed, and not even being able to remember if you had sex with her." Carol took a deep breath and then continued more calmly, "If I hadn't been with Dr. M. for days, talking about how this might work, I'd be skeptical too. But if you care about our marriage, I hope you'll stay and be open to finding out how we're almost hard-wired for all this confusing drama and conflict in our lives."

John didn't look happy, but he was curious, and he also realized that his own recent problems with Wil might be about a hidden motivator of some kind. So he said, "Okay, tell us how we can discover the powerful hidden purpose that we keep defending against discovery, this loose cannon causing trouble in our family."

After listening carefully to the interchange between Carol and John, Dr. Magie said, "You're both asking me to lead you through the process for uncovering the controlling hidden value or commitment of your life that you may not be aware of. Have I got it?"

"That's right."

"First, I want to say that the hidden controlling motivator is only another intuitive model to help picture a painful, invisible experience, and that some people may not have such a source of internal conflict. The process I'm going to take you through to try to locate your hidden central value or motivating purpose is another method, like the ten-minute dream search, that seems to be much too simple to really get at one of the most well-defended areas many people keep locked in denial for their entire lives. And like the other processes and exercises to which I have introduced you, this one does not work for everyone."

"Okay," John said, "let's get it done."

30

Facing and Confronting
the Hidden Controller

Dr. Magie hesitated. "I am carefully considering whether to take you two through this process of discovering the hidden controller of your inner wisdom's agenda."

"Why?" John asked.

"Because of the virtually universal experience of denial, couples tend to argue defensively about each other's hidden central agendas. Let's say, we have a father who thinks his wife constantly tries to control their daughter. If he confronts her about her controlling their daughter, and she is in denial about that behavior, she will often snap back in anger, "I am *not* trying to control her. I'm only trying to help." And she really believes she is only helping, even though everyone who sees her in action thinks she *is* controlling and is in denial about it. In her own mind, her inner wisdom imparts countless rationalizations supporting the position that her actions are appropriate, or even necessary for her daughter's well-being. If someone outside the family confronts her, her inner wisdom may even tell her, 'This person who is accusing you isn't on the same wavelength that you are. Just back away from him; He obviously doesn't understand you.' So unless you understand how denial can affect the acceptance of a hidden motive, you can have some painful arguments, and you two have recently been involved in one."

Carol acknowledged, "Thank you for explaining, Dr. M. I can see why you'd hesitate. I guess I already gave you a taste of that rejection the last morning in Glion. I hope you'll go ahead and do this for us."

"All right, then, let's give it a try. You two will each need paper and a pencil. Let's meet back here in, say . . ."

"Ten minutes?" Carol laughed.

"Yep," added John, slapping his knees. "That should be just about right."

They returned on time with paper, pencils and steaming cups of hot chocolate. Resting his elbows on his knees, Dr. Magie leaned forward to look each of them in the eye. "In a moment," he said gently, "I'm going to ask you to look inside your own lives. First, try to be as honest as you possibly can. You do not have to tell me or each other what you discover. This privacy will help you honestly consider what I'm asking you to do as well as reduce the tendency to deny any unwelcome truths you may find. Second, be very specific with yourself about what you discover.

"Now, to begin, look into your memory and ask yourself the question, 'what is the most important thing in the world that has motivated my actions?' The temptation is to answer with something general like 'my dreams,' 'my family,' 'my work,' 'success,' or 'the American way of life.' Or something abstract like "truth," or "honor." These can ordinarily be eliminated because they would not need to be repressed motivators; they are all conventionally accepted values and dreams.

"Another way to think about this that may help you focus on what might more nearly be your hidden purpose is this: 'What is it that you find yourself thinking about again and again, when your mind is not engaged with work or a specific activity?' People have reported such things as a spouse, a child, being great at one's vocation, being considered brilliant, clever, or socially sophisticated. Some said their recurring thoughts when they were alone were about sex, or beauty — or lack of these. Others mentioned their own problems as the recurring focus: jealousy, how people are treating them or relating to them, or fears of financial failure, or of not being enough, of rejection.

"I'm not suggesting that any of these recurring thoughts are evil, but whatever the thought, it can be like the beach ball you mentioned a few moments ago, Carol. When a beach ball is held under water in the center of your mind it is under pressure. You push it out of sight — repress it, dismiss it, and get busy with the work of the day. But when you're alone, it comes back up again and again — sometimes with a lot of energy — over the months and years, to sit in the middle of the pool of your attention."

"This time you have only *five* minutes. Write all the recurring thoughts that fit the criteria I gave you. If you are not sure whether to include something, write the thought anyway. Keep writing and trying to remember your unprompted recurring thoughts, in the past as well as the present, until five minutes are up. Go!"

When the five minutes were up, John asked, "Couldn't these more or less compulsive thoughts — for example — the recurring thoughts of a parent about a child, simply indicate normal parental love for the child? Constant thoughts about one's business, aren't they part of a legitimate drive for success?"

"Of course they could be," Dr. Magie replied. "But whatever the source of thought, the fact that one thinks about it again and again without some immediate outside stimulus means that beneath that thought could be a deeper desire, fear, or compulsion that has an unusual amount of power in it. When we began the dream listing process years ago, John, you brought up the same question about the unspectac- ular dreams you listed. And my response about their possible relevance is the same: 'Why did those dreams you listed come to mind, and not other dreams?' And of all the recurring thoughts from your life, why would these surface? So assume for the time being that these recurring thoughts are significant."

"Next I want you to do two things. First: take the list of recurring thoughts you've made and reorder them in terms of their intensity or importance. Don't spend a lot of time analyzing. Just go by your first impression when you look the list over. Which were most intense, or frequent, and which less? Second: when you are finished reordering the thoughts, see if you can cluster any of them together as part of the same single deeper desire, fear, or need for security, etc. Go!"

When they had finished reordering their lists of recurring thoughts and trying to group them according to similar underlying needs, fears, or desires, John and Carol were quiet. Neither wanted to reveal their lists right away. Dr. Magie broke the silence. "I made a new list while you were making yours. I recalled twelve recurring thoughts that were predominant at different times in my life. Five were different from each other: Being a good athlete; trying to be a sharp student, trying to be an outstanding debater, thinking about sex and girls, and wondering about God. The other seven recurring thoughts were all reflective of a single, deep insecurity about not being enough: thoughts about being popular or not, of not being invited, fear of failing a examination, fear of being revealed as a coward by having to wrestle or box in school, fear of looking or being inadequate in social situations with wealthy or "high society" power people, fear of marrying the wrong woman, fear of women's anger, fear of not being successful as a physician. These were all manifestations of a deep fear of failure and being rejected.

"I asked you to reexamine your lists, because whatever thoughts keeps recurring in your mind are possibly related to an unconscious, non-negotiable purpose or relationship the hiding of which is a power- ful hidden motivator that causes certain choices and behaviors in your life designed to cover up your hidden secret motivating fear or desire.

"In my case you can see that the recurring thoughts that surfaced in the five minutes of our game reveal a person almost obsessed with feelings of inadequacy which is my hidden motivator that jumped into action at every challenge to my need to my hard earned appearance of adequacy. Throughout my life I have been a compulsive overachiever to avoid the shame of being revealed as not enough. I have earned several degrees, written numerous articles and books and worked incessantly to succeed. I have paid a tremendous price not to be revealed as inade- quate. I have built much of my life working to belie my insecurity — my hidden, but highly motivating purpose."

Carol and John continued to be silent. Neither could believe that this humble, vulnerable man had spent a lifetime hiding all the things he had just revealed to them.

Finally Carol said, "Thank you for sharing those things, Dr. M. Your doing that helps me to see why I've denied my hidden motivator. I had not realized how different my conscious presentation of myself is from my inner core fear, and why I have been so jealous and touchy whenever anyone accused me of being wrong or inadequate about almost anything.

"But if this unconscious hiding of our secret purpose is almost universal, as you seem to imply, why can't we all just face it and get help with it? Good Lord, you've shown more courage than any person I've ever known in being free enough to reveal your hidden purpose to us. Why is this such a big deal? Even some of the people I know who profess to be very religious and trusting seem to be afraid of being revealed as inadequate. Are they as unaware of their hidden motivator as the rest of us?

Dr. Magie hesitated a few seconds. "Of course, I don't know about your friends, but perhaps the reason most of us who are religious people don't want to discover and own this repressed hot spot of our inner life is that the thing we are hiding is what we worship, our real god."

"Worship?" Carol and John exclaimed almost in unison.

"Well, what is a god if not the object of our most intense focus that determines and reshapes our priorities and behavior, or what we *obey* without question?"

"Exactly how does our hidden fear play itself out as our god?" John said intently.

"Well, an obvious example of a hidden fear becoming a person's god might be in the experience of an addict or alcoholic. Every alcoholic has a hidden god at an operational level, and that god is alcohol. An alcoholic's recurring thoughts involve drinking much of the time. His or her inner wisdom works night and day to figure out ingenious ways to hide how much he or she drinks or even the fact that he or she has had a drink. When an alcoholic wants a drink but has no money to buy alcohol, he or she will obey the urge, his god, even to the extent of sacrificing almost anything or anyone he knows or prostituting himself or herself in some way to get the money. An alcoholic may even steal the family's Christmas money, or savings set-aside for the children's future. So alcohol appears to be the alcoholic's god, though he or she may deny that hotly. But a closer examination usually reveals that the hidden motivator behind the drinking is fear. When an alcoholic is unwilling to face his or her hidden inner fear and resolve it, the pain gets so bad that he or she drinks to medicate or alleviate the pain.

"So the god we obey may be a substance like alcohol, or as in my case, an attachment to success, but either covers up our fear of inadequacy.

In short, anything that controls your behavior and determines how you spend your time and what you do with your life is what you obey, and therefore, is in a practical, operational sense, your god."

John said, bristling, "Are you saying Carol and I are addicts of some sort?"

"No, and I'm not implying that it's wrong to love a spouse, child, or vocation to compensate for one's inadequacies, or take an occasional drink. I am saying that it's spiritually dysfunctional to love any of these things more *than anything.*"

"Why?" John said.

"Because, you unconsciously make that child, or whatever the object of your devotion is, your god. You make the child or object responsible for your happiness and fulfillment. And when a parent makes his or her child or spouse responsible for his or her happiness or sense of self-worth in this way, the pressure on that person is tremendous. No one can fulfill that god assignment for someone else. If the child is healthy and fortunate, he or she will sense the parent's expectations — for the child to fulfill the parent's hidden purpose — are too much, out of reach or inappropriate. In order to survive, such a child either has to try to escape the parent's control to become who he or she was made to be, or go along with this impossible assignment and never live his or her own life. The strong resistance the child must exert toward the parent in order to escape can break the parent's heart, creating a great deal of baffling conflict and tension in the lives of both the child and the parent, because the parent is not conscious of what he or she is doing to the child. Because of denial, the parent thinks he or she is controlling the child for the child's benefit. And the same would be true of a spouse. Making one's spouse responsible for one's happiness puts tremendous pressure on that person, and a strain on that relationship."

"Wait a minute! Wait just one minute!" John exploded. "Let's say you're right, and we discover that compensating for some fear of failure, or insecurity is a hidden motivator. Let's say this thing we discover controls our inner wisdom's selection of content and the direction of our behavior in some baffling and compulsive ways. Since whatever we find is so deeply entrenched, like an addiction, what if we can't dislodge it and replace it with our best conscious efforts, values and purposes? How can we possibly change, if we've already tried to change our behavior, but can't?"

"John, you don't exactly beat around the bush. That's the great question that every valid therapeutic method has asked and tried to answer. All the healing models are variations of helping people to do three things: To discover what keeps them from being free to be or do what they truly want to be or do and then helping them find the courage to face and own the consequences of their controlling behavior, and then finally, helping them discover the possible decisions or actions that can lead to changes, and freedom from the compulsion to put a person or behavior in a god-like position. Have I understood your question?"

John nodded slowly without smiling and then asked skeptically, "Okay, let's assume that Carol and I have examined our recurring thoughts throughout our lives. And each of us has said that we are ready to face our hidden motivators and change them. But because they are so entrenched, we discover that we don't have the power to change them. What do we do now?"

EXERCISE EIGHT
Locating and Confronting a Hidden Motivating Controller

The rationale of doing this exercise is that whatever keeps showing up in your mind as 'recurring and intense' may be related to a hidden but powerful motivator that shapes some of your important choices, behaviors and ways of presenting yourself through the programming of your inner wisdom. If you are doing this exercise with another person or a group, you do not need to tell your leader or anyone else what you uncover so, try to be very *honest* and *specific* with yourself about what you discover.

1. With blank paper and a pencil with an eraser, find a private place to think and write.

2. Look into your inner life and ask yourself the question: "What is it that I find myself thinking about again and again, when my mind is not engaged with work or a specific activity?"

   a. Remember that conventionally accepted values and dreams are what come to mind immediately, because there's no need to hide them. But these are not the hidden motivators for which you are looking.

   b. Look beyond these immediate thoughts to find hidden ones, if you have any. Ask yourself, "What is it that I find myself thinking about again and again when my mind is not engaged with work or a specific activity?" (Some examples are: thinking about your spouse, child, vocation, being considered a brilliant person, socially sophisticated, or a great spiritual person, sex, beauty, etc., or fears of not "being enough.") Whatever thoughts come back again and again to sit in the center stage of your attention when you are alone may be symptoms of a deeper issue.

3. Set an alarm for five minutes from now. During this time write all the recurring thoughts (like the above) that you have had at different times in your life — especially those that recur without an external stimulus being present. List even the childhood thoughts you can

remember (e.g., Do people like me? Will I be invited? Did I have strong resentments, fears, or thoughts about masturbation, etc.?) If you are not sure some of your thoughts are appropriate to list, write them anyway. No one will see the items on this list, unless you choose to reveal them. Keep writing until the alarm goes off.

4. Renumber the list of recurring thoughts in terms of the strength of their intensity or importance to you. Go by your first impression

5. Rewrite the list in the new order and throw away the original list.

6. Study the list for three to five minutes to see if any of the recurring thoughts can be clustered together as manifestations of the same deeper desire, fear, or need for security.

Not everyone who does this exercise discovers a hidden motivating purpose or fear. But if you do find something you believe to be interfering with your conscious dreams, goals, way of giving and receiving love, or the freedom to risk being who you want to be, the next few chapters describe how Carol and John dealt with what they discovered by doing this exercise.

31

Is There Any Help Out There?
A Probe

―――――――――

"Your question John was, 'What if you realize that you have a conflicting self-defeating agenda because of a hidden motivation, but discover also that you're powerless to change or dislodge that fear or purpose?' The only solution I know is to find and cultivate a sense of security and strength beyond yourself, a sense of safety and goodness *more powerful* than your hidden inner motivation or purpose. This security from beyond yourself must be powerful and accessible enough to support you in the attempt to expel the fear, or false security, from the center of your life."

"And where," John asked with exaggerated pleasantness, "might we find security which is so powerful it can rid us of our secret fears and compulsions?"

"Most people I've counseled seem to try one of four things to get this security. One person thinks, 'If I get enough education, I'll be rid of my insecurity and the unreal aspects of my thinking.' Another may strive for professional acclamation, thinking, 'If I get enough approval from the right people, I won't be fearful or defensive.' Still another may focus on acquiring great wealth, or political or social status, thinking, 'With enough money or power I will feel secure and can be real about who I am.' And finally one might work hard to develop and preserve physical beauty.

"Whatever security source one seeks, the unconscious hope is to gain the strength to jettison or de-fang the motivating source of our self-defeating efforts to be more or different than we are. We need the courage, strength and honesty to love and trust, without which we are doomed to a life of being controlled by our secret fears.

"As a young man," Dr. Magie said pensively, "I succeeded in a fairly substantial way in three of those areas, but none of these 'securities' did the job for me. I was still touchy, controlling and anxious about my performance, fending off any slights or accusations that appeared to cast doubt on my unconscious disguise. This was a very stressful time for me."

Carol broke in, "We've already had enough success and made enough money so I know that those things will never give me the security to face the hidden inner purpose dominating my life. What did you finally do that brought you from the frantic running toward success back to Glion and the loving, self-acceptance you've found?"

"What did I do when all the compensatory attempts to dislodge my central secret agenda failed?" He chuckled, "Well, being who I am, I began an intense intellectual search for a solution."

"What did you find?"

Dr. Magie shook his head, remembering, "In the complex academic and medical thickets in which I lived, I wanted a complex, intellectually respectable answer. Instead, my mentor, Walter Mueller, helped me find a simple but terribly difficult solution which was the last thing I was looking for.

"After telling me his own story of intellectual searching as a young man, he said he realized his unconscious motivating problem was 'control,' the need to control people, events, and outcomes in his own and others' lives so he would feel superior in some way. Walter reread the works of his scientific and philosophical heroes and even visited with some of them. He was astounded to learn how difficult it was for them to deal with their own needs to control. Since control was the underlying problem that had crippled their relationships and kept them from the freedom they sought, several of them told Walter that their search and experiences led them to seek a power greater than themselves — God. After talking to Paul Tournier and Carl Jung, Walter came to realize what faith in God meant to these men and that it was the only way on the horizon for him to become free from his own deepest compulsions and complexes.

"Walter said to me, 'As strange as may sound, Charles, I found a doorway to personal and psychological freedom from the excessive need to be in control. The doorway was opened by an attempt to surrender my whole life to God — as the only source of power large enough to dislodge my deeply entrenched self-centered fears and insecurity that led to my compulsion to control.'

"I remember being extremely disappointed to hear what Walter said he had discovered. But I couldn't deny his life had changed, significantly. He wasn't the same anal-retentive bookworm I had known in school. So I asked him to tell me how our common intellectual heroes had changed his mind because, as I told him, "I don't understand God, and I'm not at all sure I even believe in God."

"I won't bore you with the long account, except to say that he told me, 'The paradox, Charles, is that evidently one can only find this sort of truth *experientially.*' Then he laughed. 'It's a little like marriage. You can get a Ph.D. in marriage and think you know about marriage. But six months after your wedding you realize that you knew very little about marriage, in fact I concluded that to know anything significant about marriage, you have to be married.' And evidently, one can only learn what surrendering to God means by surrendering to God. 'The good news,' he said to me, 'is that you can begin to grasp the healing process of surrender, on a of experimental basis.' "

"Experimental?" John asked.

"After many weeks of discussions, study and conversations with Walter and other people I respected, I noticed a change in my attitude. I did have the certitude I had been seeking, but rather an attitude of willingness — willingness to make an experiment of faith. One evening when I was alone I found myself saying, 'God, I don't know if you are real, and I really don't want you or anyone to control my life. But I know that controlling my life and my family, trying to be more than I am is my basic problem, and it's crippling my relationships, so I surrender as much of myself as I honestly can to as much of you as I understand — which isn't a lot. And I give you permission to teach me what's real about you in any way you can.' "

"And that was the beginning of healing for me."

When Dr. Magie finished his account, Carol was weeping, though she didn't know why, but John was obviously disgusted. Having kept silent during Dr. Magie's story as long as he could, he ignored Carol's response, and said scornfully, "That doesn't make sense. You're a medical doctor, a scientist, a recognized expert in certain aspects of human behavior, and yet you are asking me to believe there is a God out there that is personal and wants to interact with me? That God will guide me in some real way through my inner wisdom? I mean you must have read Freud's attack on the whole spiritual hypothesis, that believing in God is all about wish fulfillment. When people say that God is like a super-powerful and loving father and that God presides over a moral universe, Freud says those people are only projecting their own deepest wishes!"

Dr. Magie responded calmly, "I did study Freud's books and papers rather thoroughly as a young man, and I believed what he was saying, in effect, that faith in God is illusory and of no real substance. But over the years, quite a number of sensitive, intelligent people have come to my office for counseling, people who I considered to have an authentic faith. And their faith, their surrender to God, had a manifestly significant effect on their physical and emotional health. It gave them integrity in facing the fear of their painful issues. It inspired their creativity. It enabled them to relate honestly and lovingly to people around them, and finally, to face emotional crises with serenity.

"So the conclusion I finally reached about the existence of God was, if all peoples in all times have expressed a longing for a moral, loving, parent-like God, it could be because there is a moral, loving, parent-like God who can fulfill these longings.

"Of course, the nature and the object of their faith commitment were crucial. In other words, my patients' faith in God gave them courage and power to change their lives in a *healthy* direction. They would say things like, 'I can risk failing and being wrong for the first time because if I fail or am proven wrong, I have security outside the place of failure, a safe place to go in relationship to God and other people.' Some have said, 'The more I trust God, the more I'm able to relate honestly with people, since I believe God accepts me in failure or success.'"

John shot back, "You're saying the reason all people experience a hunger for God and a moral universe that makes sense is that God and morality are actually at the heart of the human experience? Is there any real evidence for such a belief?"

"All the hungers we're born with can be satisfied by something in the world. Hunger can be satisfied with food, thirst with water, sexual drive with sexual relations. What satisfies every one of these hungers is available somewhere in the human experience, and each hunger has its particular purpose in keeping the human race going. No one thinks our hunger for food, sex and water are merely parts of a wish-fulfillment complex we picked up in our families of origin. So I agree with Freud that all peoples all over the world have expressed some sort of desire to be accepted by, or even to worship a father or mother-like God. But if that's true, and if people have been transformed in positive directions by responding to such a God, it makes just as much sense to say there is a God who satisfies our hunger for God as it does to say God is a projection of our need for a parent-like God derived from the fact that no one ever had a perfect parent."

"Look," John said, voice rising, "I respect you more than anyone I've ever known, but if what you're saying is true, how could any thinking person prove that reality — the existence of God — enough to surrender his life to God the way you did?"

"The first time you came to Glion, did you believe that in ten minutes you could uncover your dreams and discover what you want to do for the rest of your life?"

"You know I didn't."

"Do you believe it now?"

"Yes."

"Did you find rational, cognitive argument in a book by a scientist like Freud?"

John shook his head.

"Why, then, did you commit to enter such an irrational, unproven process?"

"I entered your process and discovered it was true because I trusted you enough to try your crazy ten-minute dream discovery process and got in touch with my unconscious dreams."

"That's right. Was that a scientific thing to do?"

John shook his head.

Dr. Magie said in his caring way, "You're speaking as a scientist might. But in this case, you're in the wrong branch of science. You're trying to prove the reality of God through an abstract theory I'm suggesting that the only way people have found to prove to their satisfaction that God is real and powerful enough to help them change their deepest motivations is through their experience. As a Christian, I took the reality of God as a hypothesis and set out to 'prove it' by trying the ways of living and relating suggested in the biblical record.

All this talk of surrendering made John restless, since the biases of his particular educational experience equated God with naïveté, and surrender with defeat and failure — and certainly *not* a healthy life of freedom and the release of usable personal power to solve difficult problems.

Noticing his discomfort Dr. Magie said, "This idea of surrendering to God is especially difficult to discuss, because the surrender process is another intuitive experience that seems irrational — like the ten-minute dream discovery process." He paused a moment. "Didn't you tell me you played football in college?"

"Yes."

"Did you have a good coach?"

"Oh yeah, he was an all-America quarterback at a Big Ten university, and his win-loss record at our small school was 82 percent. Every kid in the state wanted to play for him!"

"Did he have any requirements for freshman coming into his program?"

"Lord, yes. Not a binding or picky set of rules — he just told the freshmen, 'If you want to play, you do whatever it takes to be in top physical condition, learn our offensive and defensive philosophy and specific formations.' Things like that. As a matter of fact, he concluded his talk to incoming freshmen by saying, 'You do everything I tell you to, including making your grades, and I'll help you become the best football player that's inside your skin.' And he did exactly that again and again for me and a good many others. When I signed up, I had no idea how hard it was to be on the team or how hard I would have to work to get there. Working with him, I changed completely. When I'd been in high school, I avoided things like mowing our lawn or emptying the trash or cleaning up my room before I went to school. Every morning I'd argue with Dad to let me sleep a little longer when he woke me up. But when I went out for that football team in college, under that coach, I quit being lazy overnight. I ran the stadium steps at 6:00 a.m., worked out with weights, and did miles of running all year long. And no one had to remind me to do any of these things."

Dr. Magie said, "I hadn't thought about it until now, but it sounds a little like you surrendered to your college coach, not really knowing in advance what that would mean — and got virtually your entire life at that time transformed."

John squinted his eyes and looked at Dr. Magie. Grudgingly he said, "I suppose."

"Why did you do it, give yourself to that coach, particularly when you had no idea how hard it would be or exactly what you'd have to do?"

"One part of it was what I'd heard about him on the radio and in the sports pages."

"Who recruited you?"

"The school sent out a couple of coaches who talked to me and my family, but the ones who really convinced me to enroll weren't the recruiters. It was the two boys I played ball with in high school who graduated the year before and came back to our school the next spring raving about the coach and the program."

"And when you surrendered — signed up — the changes began. That's the part surrender plays in transformational change. That's how surrender can lead to a new life focus and the courage to deal with our secret, self-defeating inner purpose."

John said, indignantly, "Are you saying that surrender to God will jerk the old secret agenda out like a bad tooth?"

"No. I don't think people can ever get completely rid of their fears or unhealthy, controlling behaviors, but the continual surrender of one's life to God will often give people the courage and power to face and control those hidden destructive, self-centered motivations we've been discussing. Over time, this surrendered living can reprogram our inner wisdom to be in accord with the purposes of a loving, generous God."

John shook his head, a sullen look on his face, until he finally said, "You're beginning to sound like a tent meeting revivalist. I believe you're sincere about your faith in God, and I appreciate the football analogy, but can you tell me about any really heavyweight thinkers, true intellectuals who've surrendered their entire lives to God? And if so, exactly what did they receive from God after they surrendered?"

32

Cracks in the Armor?

~~~~~~~~~~~~~~~~~~~~~~~

John looked at the alarm clock at 4:30. He'd slept only sporadically, and he'd had an unsettling dream about being assigned guard duty in hell to keep people from escaping. In the predawn darkness John stared up toward the ceiling, as Carol slept softly beside him. He had *seen* her sleep through most of the night, and that ticked him off for some reason, but his anger wasn't focused on Carol. He was angry at Dr. M. and his calm way of not being upset when John thought he should have been. He had been in a number of religious arguments in the past, but Dr. M. was so grounded in what he believed that it had been impossible to throw him off balance with John's standard questions.

John asked himself, "Why in the hell is this question of finding a security great enough to give a person the courage to face and deal with a secret hidden focus so loaded for me?"

He was afraid he knew the answer. He had discovered in the exercise to discover his hidden motivator that almost all his frustration, unhappiness and thoughts — when his mind was free — were focused on how his relationship with Wil was going. He knew he was probably too hard on Wil, but that was the way his own father had raised him — demanding the best and always raising the bar without much affirmation.

But John realized clearly that what he really wanted from Wil was his love and respect, so they could have the relationship he had always wanted with his own father, but never had. "But," he said to himself, "that desire is not a bad thing, just the normal response of a caring father." John had repressed his deep need for Wil to become what he wanted him to be that led to his irrational picky criticism. And since Wil was still new on the company payroll, John hadn't had to deal with the issue of turning loose when Wil succeeded by doing things on his own.

But the company was changing rapidly, and just this week Cindy had shown John an incredibly effective flow chart structure she had put into place during the past week. The new structure was already improving the company's efficiency in dealing with the rapidly increasing number of deals, people and requests for information that came thorough every day. The plan was simple but it gave John and his team immediate access to everything they needed to make decisions and move more quickly.

When Cindy explained to John how the new system was helping, he realized that Cindy was not just a smart and efficient executive secretary, but some kind of business genius. Virtually nothing would fall through the cracks — even if the company increased 100 percent a year — as long as the system was installed and monitored in every department with Cindy, in John's office updating the central switchboard. When he'd finished analyzing what Cindy had done, John had called her into his office at closing time the day before.

"Cindy, this exactly what we need right now to handle and assimilate the growth that's about to jump on us! I want you to walk me through this new structure and process as to how it works — step by step."

Cindy looked uncomfortable, but John insisted.

"About a month ago it was apparent that Martin Industries was beginning to wallow in a lot of unnecessary chaos. Although the financial and acquisition plans worked really well, combining so many new employees and prospects led to an enormous increase in calls, letters and e-mails requesting specific information. We started having a lot of confusion about procedures and job descriptions.

"I knew that many companies have gotten bogged down with a glut of unanswered inquiries and some had gone under because of not handling time-sensitive inquiries and deadlines fast enough.

"So after getting your approval to work on it, the blue procedure book you have in your hands was designed. Your and Carol's mission statement and goals for Martin Industries were copied on the first two pages with the understanding that everything in the operational plan would enable these purposes. Then we gathered and indexed the information, describing specifically the company's confidentiality procedures, ethical policies and procedures, and medical and retirement plans.

"At this point, you remember I wrote your and my understanding of every department's specific responsibilities in a letter to each department head over your signature. The department heads each talked this over with their staffs so that everything that particular department was responsible for on the acquisition, development and follow-up of new prospects was listed, including exactly who handled each aspect of the deals. Then each department head verified his or her understanding of the flow of information, money and steps in completing their part of each project as these things were to be handled by that particular department. This way, at any point in the development of projects, you and I would have the name and extension number of the person or persons dealing with any specific part of each deal.

Cindy continued her description of the plan to John. "You remember my showing you a draft of the letters going out and the revised and agreed to adjustments by the department heads. Without giving you any more details, what we wound up with was a book of general company procedures regarding personnel responsibility, with separate chapters for each department. The control page kept in each department was the letter signed by you as CEO and each department head stating in detail everything that department (and each person in it) is responsible for. This was accepted and initialed by each employee setting out who handled each kind of information or query that department dealt with.

"At the end of our project, the company had a complete book — the Blue Book — covering who specifically was responsible for everything that might flow through Martin Industries. And since each appropriate employee had seen and signed off on the plan and his or her responsibilities, there was no one way to pass the buck or claim one was not responsible for his or her assigned work."

John said, "This is amazing. How has it worked out in the concrete situations?"

Cindy replied, "If someone calls and wants to get information about the title to a tract of land we are going to build on for example, I, as your secretary, or my assistant, can just open the book to the table of contents or the department 'chapter' involved, and give the caller the name of the person responsible for legal and land title information. And in two minutes or less, the caller will be connected to the company expert on that specific information."

John had been elated as he remembered a number of partners and contractors had complained that it was getting more and more difficult to get important information from Martin Industries. Cindy stood, prepared to leave.

Smiling broadly, John said, "Sit down, Cindy, sit down." She hesitated but John nodded and motioned her to sit. "Cindy, this is a deceptively simple piece of work one person can oversee that will give us a rightly earned reputation for being the best communicating company around."

Cindy interrupted, "But I'd like to tell you something...."

John held up his hand to stop her. "Because of this work I'm doing something I've never before considered. I'm giving you a double promotion and an equivalent salary increase.

"Please, Mr. Martin, wait. I haven't been honest with you. It's true I did a lot of the work compiling the information that went into this plan and book. But the whole idea was Wil's. He swore me to secrecy about it being his idea because he saw the complexity and chaos we were facing in the company and felt if you knew he had come up with this idea so soon, you would — you might not see its real merits."

"My god, Cindy, why did you go along with such a stupid idea — as though I wouldn't see the value of this if I knew Wil had done it?"

Cindy pursed her lips and thought a few seconds. "Because I agreed with him. It's no secret that you've discounted his contributions in meetings since he got here. I really appreciate your affirmation of me, but I can't accept that promotion and raise."

John didn't hear the last sentence. Cindy had always been honest and direct as well as smart. And if she had seen him putting Wil down in front of the other executives, then it must be true.

John looked again at the green numbers on the alarm clock on his side of the bed: 4:50 a.m. "Damn," he thought, "it seems like an hour since 4:30." He threw his legs out of bed and stood up. He was filled with shame and anger — shame about what Cindy had told him concerning his putting Wil down, and anger at Dr. Magie because he himself was feeling out of control. He was going to catch Dr. M. early and have some clarifying conversation, whether Dr. M. liked it or not. "I'll beat Magie down stairs, fix the coffee to establish the fact that this is my house and my territory." John knew it wasn't a very mature way to think, but he couldn't seem to stop himself.

EXERCISE NINE
A Simple Organizational Communication Structure

This is a process for creating a communication system for companies or organizations with at least three or more departments. Using this system, any request for information can be routed to the department and specific employee responsible for that task or process a company (or other organization) performs in its operations.

1. Call a meeting (approximately two hours) for all department heads and departmental secretaries or equivalent.

2. Ask each department's representatives to list *everything* that department does within ten minutes. For example:

    Acquisitions Department
    - Attorneys
    - Abstracts
    - Title opinions
    - Bank drafts
    - Any critical date requirements pertaining to acquisitions
    - Future rentals, stock options or other payments to be made regarding acquired properties, etc.)

3. Next, alphabetize the list.

4. Put that department's alphabetized list of everything it is responsible for on a white board or PowerPoint slide so that the entire group can view it. During the next ten minutes, ask *all other* department heads and secretaries together to add anything else they have observed the department being considered has handled before.

5. After additions are alphabetized into the list, the combined list is turned in to the president or executive committee for later review with the department head of each department so that the final responsibility list can be discussed and negotiated.

6. After the final list has been approved and accepted by a department head, he or she will go over the list with members of the department, and each item will be assigned to and accepted by a person in the department. The final list will be written by the department head in a letter to the president of the company signed by the department head acknowledging accountability for all responsibilities on the list. On a copy of the letter retained by the department secretary, each member of that department will then initial his or her specific items of responsibility.

7. When every department has gone through the process, the president will have a book containing a copy of each department's alphabetized list. The president can decide who will monitor the list and pass the information to the designated person. In this way, anyone who calls or e-mails a request for information about any part of any project, activity, or function of the company, the president or person monitoring the list can refer appropriate calls or other requests to the specific person responsible in a matter of a few seconds.

8. Some advantages of this simple system are:

   a. Cuts confusion or disagreements about who is responsible for *everything* the company/organization does, since both management and all employees have initialed copies accepting each responsibility.

   b. Saves a great deal of time and guesswork when one department needs information about something handled by another department.

   c. Eliminates much buck-passing and excuses of employees saying, "I didn't realize that was my responsibility."

   d. Makes it possible for new employees or people getting promotions or job changes to determine their new responsibilities and the scope of their new departmental operations very quickly.

   e. Aids management in realistic budgeting and in evaluating workloads and departmental requests to hire additional employees.

Note: This is merely a rough, suggestive sketch and is not intended as an organizational template.

33

Some Surprise Witnesses Take the Stand

~~~

At the bottom of the stairway, John raised his hand to flip the light switch, but the lights were already on, there was a fire in the fireplace, and he could smell the hot coffee.

Dr. Magie looked up in surprise from a book he was reading in the big leather chair nearest the fireplace. "Good morning, John. How about a cup of coffee?"

John's stomach knotted. Irrationally, he wanted to tell the old man he could take the coffee and pour it up his own nose, and he almost said, "No, thanks." But he needed the coffee so much he just mumbled, "Thanks."

"Cream and sugar, right?"

"Not this morning — thanks."

Aware John was more than just a little upset, Dr. Magie waited a few seconds in silence, and then he went back to reading his book.

John asked himself, "How can I let him know what's bothering me?" to which his inner voice answered, "How about just telling him the truth? That will have the additional advantage of being honest!"

That *really* made John mad, but he broke the silence. "I'm not at all happy about how condescending you have been to me with my questions, particularly about God. You hesitate before taking the conversation in a spiritual direction, as if I wouldn't be intelligent enough to understand."

Dr. Magie looked genuinely surprised, "Is there more about that?"

"Well, for one thing, I asked you about what 'surrender' meant to you, and when I didn't accept your first attempt to explain, you set me up by asking about my football coach and how I was recruited at eighteen years old."

"So you're upset because I didn't answer your questions in a respectful way. Is that right?"

"Yeah, that's it."

Dr. Magie waited in silence until John blurted out, "Damn it, this is *my* house, Charles Magie. I'm a grown man, and I'm the host here. I realize you're a lot older than I am, but I'd appreciate your giving me the respect of being straight with me!"

Dr. Magie looked John directly in the eyes. "All right, John Martin," he responded, a hard edge in his voice. "You may be the host here, but you're acting like an adolescent right now! I love you and respect you very much, but no more nonsense, please. What's the problem? What is it you want to hear?"

"Well, you can begin by telling me about some *respectable* thinkers who became Christians *after* getting their education."

Dr. Magie thought a few seconds. Then the hard edge changed to a tone of excitement, and his eyes sparkled. "John, there are so many outstanding people in various fields who have become Christians and powerful thinkers, so many whose lives are passing through my mind, that it would take a long time for me to even list them! These men have some of the sharpest minds not only in the context of religion, but in the whole history of ideas around the world.

"One would certainly have to be Blaise Pascal, the seventeenth-century French mathematician, philosopher, and inventor. He was so bright that while in his twenties he invented the adding machine and the syringe, and co-developed the mathematical theory of probability. He created Pascal's Wager, suggesting that betting on the existence of God is rational, whether or not God exists. In fact Pascal was so brilliant that he wrote some of his essays and letters under a pseudonym because the intelligentsia wouldn't have believed such a young man could write so incisively about things like 'the mathematical and intuitive minds.' When Pascal became Christian, he developed into an amazing apologist for faith with integrity.[5] After his death, my philosophy professor said that a sheet of paper was discovered sewn in Pascal's coat, describing his experience of surrender to God. It said something like, 'Fire, fire, fire. Not the god of Plato and Aristotle, but the God of Moses, Elijah and Jesus.'

"C. S. Lewis was another outstanding scholar with an agile, creative mind. A confirmed atheist, he taught philosophy and English language literature at both Oxford and Cambridge. A brilliant skeptic, Lewis couldn't understand how thinking people could be Christian, and went through a terrible struggle for years against believing in God, especially surrendering to God. But after much searching and evaluation, there came a moment when he realized that knowing God could not be accomplished through cognitive, mental processes and he described one evening in his room when he sensed something like the steady, unrelenting approach of — I think he phrased it — 'him whom I earnestly desired not to meet.' Lewis said that what he feared had at last come upon him, and he gave in, and admitted that God was God, and knelt and prayed. Later he said that on that night he had been one of the most dejected and reluctant converts in all of England. He said he did not see then that the most shining and obvious thing was the divine humility that would accept converts even on such reluctant terms. Lewis went on to be perhaps the leading apologist for God in the twentieth century.[6]

"But, John, almost without exception most of the men and women I could tell you about experienced a real struggle of resisting God, and especially resisted the notion of surrendering to God."

"And what changed their minds?"

"Usually they met someone who had struggled as they were struggling against God, but who, following a surrender to God, were living an enhanced quality of life and had clarity of vision in all kinds of ways. These seekers became willing to surrender because of the authenticity and personal development they could see in the lives of people they knew to be brilliant scholars or leaders in other fields."

"For example — who is someone who examined a leader's surrendered life and became a Christian?"

Dr. Magie thought a few seconds and said, "The first one who comes to mind was a young teacher of rhetoric around the year 400 AD who later became a philosopher and Roman military commander in North Africa. He was inquiring about God with an outstanding church leader named Ambrose, bishop of Milan, who had been so impressive in faith that, when he converted to Christianity, he was ordained a deacon, a priest, and a bishop on the *same day*. Ambrose told this young teacher that he, Ambrose, was going through a very busy time, but he would be happy to talk to the young man about his faith as soon as he could. Not to be put off the young man came to the bishop's office just to sit and watch Ambrose for a period of days. In part because of what he saw and heard just watching Ambrose work, make decisions and love people as a Bishop, this young man went home, had a spiritual experience and surrendered his life to God, and St. Augustine, as we have come to know him, became one of the primary shapers of Western theological thought for the entire Christian Church since. He became the bishop of Hippo in North Africa, and through his writings was a leading opponent of the heretics of his time.[7]

"Okay, some people who were agnostic or atheistic scholars surrendered, but what did these scholars and other brilliant people *receive,* what did they actually get when they *surrendered* to God that they couldn't have gotten by *studying about* God?"

"A man named Martin Buber in the twentieth century helped many people see the difference between studying about God and a real interaction with God through surrender. He said what a person receives from God is not specific content, but what he called a 'Presence as power,' and when that contact with this Presence takes place, the person finds himself or herself 'bound in a relationship,' having no idea how that state was brought about. From then on this relationship with God as

Presence — as he put it — 'doesn't make life lighter, but makes it heavier — heavy with *meaning*' ' Nothing thereafter is meaningless,' said Buber. These intellectual giants tell us that the lifelong search for meaning can be both triggered and fulfilled in what Buber called an 'I-Thou relationship with God.' "[8]

John was silent and then said thoughtfully. "I had no idea that so many outstanding thinkers had sought and surrendered to God. But the biographical language you're using is so different from scientific jargon that it's hard for me to give it credence. Is that what you meant when you said we would have to enter 'the world of intuitive knowledge?' "

"That's right. The great psychiatrist, Carl Jung, said the truth about authentic religion is a 'revealed truth' rather than a reasoned philosophy. The ideas of faith are products of what Jung called a preconscious knowledge, a knowledge that slips beneath reason and creedal statements as expressed in words and reason by philosophy and science. Jung said this more basic preconscious knowledge always expresses itself in symbols."[9]

"Wait a minute," John said. "If the most important knowledge about God and religion is expressed in symbols, a lot of highly educated people aren't going to understand it. Isn't that a serious problem?"

"Yes, it is for the people who don't recognize the value of intuitive and symbolic knowledge. Jung went on to say that even if our intellect doesn't get these ideas, they still work, because our unconscious, and what we've been calling the inner wisdom, acknowledges the truth as coming from valid universal psychic facts. That's why faith is enough, if one has faith, and surrender puts one in the position of absorbing this kind of deep connection to reality directly."

Just then Carol came downstairs in her robe and slippers.

Dr. Magie stood and said, "Good morning, Carol. We started early since John has a meeting this morning. But we weren't leaving you out.

Just as John started to ask another question, Carol interrupted, "I've heard you two going at it for a time and it sounds like you've been on the stand for several hours." Carol walked over and poured herself some coffee. "Wouldn't you like to take a break?"

Dr. Magie smiled, "Sounds like a good idea to me. But let me take just a minute to finish answering the specific question John asked." He turned to John. "I heard you asking earlier, 'If we each have our own unique hidden motivator, fear, inadequacy, or way of defending ourselves, how would surrendering to God help with dislodging this entrenched hidden controlling purpose?' "

John said, "Close enough."

"Well, I'm not about to tell you how God might operate in your life. But my experience indicates that what each person receives from God as a result of a spiritual surrender seems to take the shape of *that person's particular need, problem, or agenda* — the unique issue about which the pain got so great that the person could not alleviate it with his or her greatest effort through education, power, wealth or physical beauty."

John stood up and stretched. "Dr. M., I love and respect you, and I appreciate your shedding light on the search for help and meaning that can lead some to surrender to God. I can't honestly make that surrender right now. I have some things I still think I'm supposed to handle. But if I ever do surrender, I suspect it will be because of your life and your friendship." John looked at his watch, "I'm sorry, but I have to get ready for a meeting at the office. I'll see you both at supper."

John gave Carol a hug and kiss on the way out, and shook hands with Dr. Magie and smiled.

mm

After breakfast, Carol and Dr. Magie sat in companionable silence, sipping coffee and looking out at the mountains in the bright, early morning sunlight. Carol said, "When you took us through the process to help find our hidden inner motivator, it became mountain-stream clear to me what is programming my inner wisdom to react so strongly with jealousy and anger at all kinds of things."

Dr. M. said, "Would you like to tell me about that?"

"What I think about all the time is me and my happiness, and my ideas of what's right for me and everyone around me. I'm evidently compelled to be right and the center, the queen of our house — and in groups that I can control by stealth. I hated discovering that, and I almost hated you for not talking me out of it. But now that I see myself better, I realize I'm still trying to get John to be totally mine. As crazy as that sounds, inside me it feels like 'owning' him as my husband is the right thing somehow. So when anything, even the success of our business looks like it's going to take him out of my control and being the source of his happiness, I change into a different person. My inner wisdom kicks in, and before I know it, I find a way either to work closer with him on the business so he won't drift away, or to criticize, pick and whine at him so he'll pay more attention to me. And my inordinate jealousy of Claudette is because she threatened to take control of John away — especially if she slept with him. Before you talked to us about our hidden motivators, I felt it was appropriate for me to be the center of everything and of everyone's life. When I wasn't, I didn't feel secure or happy. This secret motivating need to be the central in everyone's life has lurked behind just about every decision I've made.

"When I finally saw this, I was ashamed and really tried to change, but my resolution would last about ten minutes before I was rearranging everyone's chairs again. I simply could not give up this deep need I have to be the director of this show, and even understanding it doesn't change my need to be the center of attention."

"Thank you, Carol, for trusting me with that."

The cheery yellow flames of the morning fire in the fireplace danced along the rim of the pine logs. A few pine cone cracks of sound popped, and wisps of white smoke puffed up occasionally from half-hidden coals. After some moments of shared silence, Carol spoke, her voice like a vulnerable young girl's. "Will you help me surrender to God, Dr. M? I'm terrified to turn loose. A hundred fearful questions are buzzing around in my brain. 'Where will I have to go? What will I have to do? Will God take everyone I love away if I quit trying to control everything?' I'm really afraid."

Dr. Magie smiled lovingly at her. "I don't know what God will do in your life, Carol, but I'm smiling now because I had all the same fears when I came to this moment. As a doctor of medicine trained in Freud's methods and theories, I knew I was headed for a lot of rejection if it became known that I had surrendered to God. The very rejection I'd always feared would come true, but my awareness that I was 'not right' somehow, in spite of all the notoriety I was getting, and that I could not change or heal myself was so painful and such an ego insult that I finally had to surrender. And when I looked at the life of my mentor, Walter, and of my hero, Dr. Tournier, I was drawn forward into the surrender by their loving and courageous qualities — and their downright happiness.

"But, Carol, anyone who knows the nature and depth of this surrender to God and is not afraid to turn loose has not really understood what's involved. When a person chooses God as her higher power to save her from her wild ride toward self-destruction, she's dealing with primal change and primal fear on the way to a chance for a new life."

"Well, Dr. M. I'm miserable enough to risk it now. What do I have to do? I'm ready. Do I have to say something?"

"Carol, there is no right way to surrender. Every person who has been having a terrible physical or emotional struggle with another person knows when she quits fighting and surrenders in that human situation. Frederick Buechner, a man I respect a lot, described the moment of contact with God as not so much saying or believing this thing or that about God, but rather, he said in effect that we hear a voice, and then we start to go toward it without really knowing what to believe about the voice, or about ourselves, and yet we go. Buechner said, 'Faith is standing in the darkness, and a hand is there, and we take it.' "[10]

Carol said, "That's right, something like that is happening to me. I'm moving toward something that's calling me out of my darkness." Then she had a sudden thought and said, "But what about Jesus? Why are Christians so insistent in bringing Jesus into the picture?"

Dr. Magie didn't seem at all surprised at her question. He said quietly, "There are a number of reasons. For one thing, remember you have decided that you're ready to surrender your life to God. So, now, the nature and character of the God to whom you are going to surrender is very important. Is God a vindictive, sly, legalistic monster waiting to punish you for your sins if you surrender? Or loving, forgiving and honest, waiting to lead you to freedom and intimacy with God and people? There's no way to tell from studying nature.

"To provide an answer to the question 'What is God like?' a theory or theological formula wouldn't work either because both a Ph.D. and an uneducated drifter would need to be able to grasp the answer. For all kinds of people to get it, God needed to be presented in an intuitive symbolic form that could be grasped without complicated rational processes. We Christians say that Jesus is a living, walking-around, talking, loving, risking, one-man presentation of God in street clothes. Anyone who meets up with Jesus can know firsthand what the God is like, to whom they are asked to surrender. Any of us who can open ourselves enough to feel the pain of seeing beyond our denial, and see how we have put ourselves in the center where only God should be, can grasp the personality of God enough to make a decision to surrender.

But surrender doesn't mean joining a religious organization and becoming a valid member. Surrender means that you're willing to give up on believing in your own power to change what you cannot change, by surrendering, you become open to a new power, and a new life, a new way of seeing the world with God as the center. But the direct transmission of the intimacy and power of God to deal with our self-defeating hidden motivation, appears to come through our willingness to surrender to the Jesus-like God seen to be walking, caring, forgiving, and surrendering love. And as begin to live the life that results, we can discover that this power we received is strong enough to allow us to see, flush out and deal with our hidden motivator's agendas and the problems they have caused in our relationships. This process of learning to discover and change any behaviors and attitudes that block the continuing progress of surrendering can free us from the web of contradiction and denial which had us trapped. And my experience is that this very personal power is received as a person surrenders to God the controlling motivation that has replaced God in his or her life. The experienced reality of God's being with us, and the companionship of other people who have surrendered, provide the courage to risk our personal worlds falling apart leaving us alone — which is the threat our hidden motivator has held over our heads when someone threatened to reveal it.

Dr. Magie paused, and then concluded, "So it doesn't seem to matter much what you say, the important thing about surrendering is that you intend to surrender your life and your will to God."

Carol was silent, thinking about what she had heard. Instinctively bowing her head for a few seconds, she softly said,. "God, I surrender the motivating center of my life to you, my swollen insatiable self that works so hard to be in the center of everyone's life. Please help me begin to replace my convoluted, self-centered addiction to playing your role in my family's lives and trying to make sure everyone treats me as the queen. I surrender my life, my family, my jealousy and the future to you. Please help me to move out of the driver's seat and give you the wheels so you can take me where you want me to go. I'm really afraid, but I want to trust you with everything. Thank you."

Dr. Magie had spontaneously bowed his head as Carol did. When he looked up now, she was weeping quietly.

"Are you all right, Carol?" he asked gently.

Carol looked up at him as she dabbed her tears with a tissue. "Oh, *yes,*" she said, looking more relaxed than he'd ever seen her.

"I have no idea where this will take me, but I feel as if I don't have to be the beautiful wonder girl any more." She looked at their old friend, who was obviously tired but also happy.

"Thank you, Dr. M, for everything. What do I do now?"

"Nothing. Just relax — although thanking God is not a bad way to begin an intimate relationship with him. But the wonder of surrender is that you don't have to *do* anything to earn or keep the relationship. While I am here, if you'd like, we'll begin to look at a way to contact God on a regular, intimate basis, to get guidance."

Carol said, "I'd like that."

"This is not just a religion that wakes up on certain days and occasions, Carol; it's a new and intimate relationship with God that is always with you, whatever you're doing. And as you make space in your inner life by giving God permission to move into the citadel, the control room in your life, God will begin to help you deal with your hidden motivator that you have now unmasked — and reprogram your inner wisdom. You will find things you've always done will change, and some of the changes will seem to be the result of some sort of automatic transformation — the spontaneous changes of attitude or loving responses — that make some people feel they have been given a new life."

They sat together in silence for a few seconds, after which Carol looked up and said, "Thank you, God." Then she stood and moved over to hug Dr. Magie, saying, "And thank you, dear friend. I never would have known how to begin without you." Carol smiled as she spoke and then glanced up, "And you too, of course."

34

Discovering Denied
Personal Defects

John was up early the next morning. Though held up at the office until 10:00 p.m. the night before, he was sitting at the breakfast room table, coffee cup in hand, looking out the bay window at the mountain when Dr. Magie walked in at 6:30. As the older man paused to look at the white-capped Rockies in the clear early morning sunshine, John went to the kitchen and returned with a steaming cup of coffee in each hand.

"Hello, Dr. M."

"Good morning, John." He nodded at the mountain scene, "Beautiful, isn't it?"

"Yeah," John said. "I realized this morning I've had so much on my mind since we built this place that I've hardly seen the mountains out there." Then he held up one of the cups. "Coffee?"

"Yes, thank you."

"Last night I didn't sleep much, Dr. M. The talk about religion and God yesterday was very interesting, but somehow it really pulled my chain. I was shocked that you are so committed to God." John shook his head slightly, picked up his cup and looked out the window before he continued. "I know you wouldn't try to manipulate me, but I still I felt pressured to surrender my life to God, and I can see how defensive I must have sounded."

"Actually," Dr. Magie said, "other people have responded to me that way when I get excited about the way God has changed things in my life and in the lives of other frightened, controlling people like me — who've surrendered to God. I want the best for you so much that I'm passionate to show you what I've discovered. That, plus the fact that your negative history with religious people may have caused you to shut down when you experienced my enthusiasm. Of course, it could be that I was manipulating you and was in denial about it. But it doesn't feel that way to me.

John looked at Dr. Magie. He thought, "How did he do that? He responded to me without either putting me down or trying to smooth things over, and he showed me that he heard the strength of my resistance to talking about God with him — all in two sentences." Out loud he said, "Yes, you heard me." Then he was quiet and seemed to be thinking.

After about a minute, Dr. Magie said, "Is there more about that, John?"

"Yes," John said, and his words tumbled out, "I've got a real struggle going on inside me about what to do with you." John laughed, realizing how that sounded. "What I mean is, I love you like a father and I want to keep learning all I can from you. But now that I know how important God is to you, I'm afraid you'll hone in on changing me, and we won't be able to have a normal relationship."

"You're saying that because I've come out of the closet and told you I'm a Christian, you're afraid I'll keep sticking God into every conversation, and you'd hate that. Did I hear you right?"

John chuckled, "Yeah, I guess you did."

Dr. Magie smiled at his young friend, "Nothing's changed. We've known each other for years, and my relationship with you has never been about making you religious. I love you, too, and I don't think you'll have to worry about my dragging God into the conversation every five minutes. So far, since last night, you're the only one who's brought up religion." He stopped and frowned, "I certainly hope you won't foul up our relationship by continuing to bring up the subject of religion every five minutes — okay?"

John laughed. "Yeah, I think I can keep the lid on my God talk." He smiled affectionately at the older man.

"All right, good. Now, what else is on your mind this morning?"

Just then, Carol came, almost skipping down the stairs. "Hey, what are a couple of good looking timber wolves like you two doing desecrating the house of Little Red Riding Hood?"

Dr. Magie smiled.

John laughed, "Don't worry. She won't exterminate us if she gets her coffee soon."

After Carol had given John and Dr. Magie the task of setting the table, she fixed them a breakfast of pancakes, sausage and fresh strawberries. The smell of the sausage cooking and the sight of the snow-capped mountains whisked Dr. Magie back to his childhood for a few seconds.

After breakfast, John said thoughtfully, "Yesterday I wanted to talk about some negative reactions I've been getting from my employees, as well as my family. But the time went by, and then I didn't make it home until too late to talk."

Dr. Magie took a sip of coffee and kept listening as John continued, "I realize that since the negative reactions are coming from several *different* people, some of the problems have got to be about me. But I can't see what they are. So my question to you is: How can a person discover personal behavioral defects in his own life that he's not aware of —

defects that may ruin relationships and block the road to cooperative working and living?"

"What kind of negative reactions?" Dr. Magie asked.

"Well it's hard to get a handle on. They aren't overtly angry, but sometimes when I'm talking to them they don't look at me, and they don't seem particularly pleased when an article in some publication is very positive about me. They don't seem as enthusiastic about the company's success somehow. I can't figure out what's wrong."

Carol listened quietly and thoughtfully across the table. She and Dr. Magie both seemed to be thinking about something far away. Finally, Dr. M. answered, "At one point, when I had made a list of my dreams and began to realize them, something seemed to go wrong. I discovered this first in my family, when I noticed their silences and their slightly veiled sarcasm and anger directed at me. This development surprised me because I had always thought of myself as being such a sensitive, understanding man." Dr. Magie smiled, shook his head, and then continued, "I'd tried so hard to be a positive influence on other people, I couldn't imagine that I would try to control anyone. Later I realized the trouble began when I got some public attention because of my writing and lecturing all over the world, and I began to neglect my family. One day I overheard my wife talking to her sister over the telephone, 'When he gets home he expects us to give him standing ovations as he tells us about all the exciting things he saw and did' — things my family hadn't been invited to see and do. And when they didn't appear to be interested in what I was achieving — all for their benefit of course — Il tended to be short with them, to give advice about their lives, to straighten them out.

"One evening, my wife said, 'You know, Charles, you're getting to be just like your father!'

"I almost exploded! My father had emotionally deserted my mother and me as he received promotions and became successful, which had made me furious. At home he seemed distant and judgmental. For example, if I would interrupt his reading the newspaper when I was a boy, to ask him a question he would close the paper without putting it down, his finger keeping his place, and give me a look of disapproval, combined with an appearance of impatience and a kind of disgust, a look I took to mean, 'I can't imagine your wanting to ask another of your inane questions.' Then I'd become confused and forget what I had wanted to know.

"So when Mrs. Magie accused me of being like my father, I became almost irrationally angry, but even as I denied it, I knew she was right! Thinking back I saw I had unconsciously begun to use my father's impatient, shaming look with my children, and my family felt judged, controlled, and shamed by that look, just as I had. Finally, the increasing distance between my wife, my children and me spread to my office, and the pain became so great that I couldn't enjoy my work. I finally went for help."

John squinted at Dr. M., reliving some of the reactions he'd noticed at the office, and with Wil and Carol. Then he said, "Yeah, they seem to think I'm getting a superior attitude. And as I said, Wil acts like he thinks I'm a total controller. I can't *see* that I've changed that way, but . . . What did you do to find out what you were doing, besides your father 'look' that people were reacting to?"

"I went to my mentor, Walter, who had watched me develop and use the intuitive ten-minute technique. I told him I was realizing my dreams, but in the process I was having to reexamine my whole life because of the stupid ten-minute process. He smiled at me and said, 'Charles, I seem to remember something you told me when you taught me the dream discovering exercise. You said, 'Walter, one of the secrets you may discover after learning to tap your inner wisdom is that it gets tired of your making the same mistakes over and over. It starts sending you nudges and clues about character and behavioral faults that you need to be aware of and change in order to realize the dreams, as well as to be a happy, whole person.' "

Dr. M. shook his head, "I was not at all pleased with his turning my own advice back on me, but I realized that my inner wisdom was telling me to listen to the truth my family and employees — and now Walter — were telling me. And even though I was filled with a desire to justify myself — after all, I was working hard to provide for my family — I went home and meditated. And I remembered hearing about an approach to discovering one's own character defects. "I took this back to Walter and we worked through it."

At this point Dr. M. said, "Would you like for me to tell you the process Walter and I came up with for locating self-defeating habits and denied character defects?"

"Yes, I would."

"I would, too," Carol agreed, and she got up to bring pencils and paper. Dr. Magie pulled two small notebooks out of his brief case for Carol and John while she was gone.

"All right," he said. "We can't go through the entire exercise today because part of it involves your doing some research away from home for an entire day. But we can get started now, and I'll give you the rest of the exercise to do when you can.

"The idea of this exercise is to uncover the kinds of the negative and self-defeating habits and relational defects about which we are in denial, that are causing us pain in our relationships. First, take your pad and pencil with you for a full day, at home, in the office and any place else where you interact with people. Note all the things that irritate you about what other people do or say. For example, you may see somebody who is openly or subtly trying to correct you or change you, and you find yourself getting angry at that person. You may feel angry or frustrated when someone crowds in front of you in a grocery line or in traffic, or someone tries to control a business meeting. Or you may bristle and fume about someone not returning your calls, or not answering an e-mail or memo you sent asking for some information or advice. You may see someone using cowardly or deceptive manipulation with a spouse or child and feel anger or great uneasiness.

"As you encounter these behaviors and incidents, write them in your notebook. At the end of the day put them in the order of their apparent negative effect on you." Dr. Magie waited while John and Carol copied his instructions in their notebooks.

"When you have described what you observed people did that irritated you, take ten minutes to add other irritating behaviors of others you can recall throughout your life that disturb you. As a matter of fact, let's take ten minutes right now to list every recurring, irritating behavior of people at the office or at home that you can recall — from any time in your life. Even if something you recall seems too insignificant to list, write it down anyway. Any questions? Okay, go.

After ten minutes, Dr. Magie asked, "Any questions?"

Carol said, "This is really interesting. I found myself jumping on some behaviors, but on others, equally as irritating, an inner voice said, 'You shouldn't be angry about that.'"

"Who did that voice sound like?"

"My father," Carol said.

"Carol, don't pay any attention to voices that try to stop you from finding the truth about yourself."

John asked, "What kinds of things did you discover, Dr. M.?"

"My list contained things like..." Dr. M. stopped and looked in his brief case. Pulling out a file, he opened it. "Here's a copy of several lists I still go over occasionally. Some of the things I noted are: A man obviously tried to control the outcome of a planning committee meeting of which I was a part in our church. He ridiculed and squelched suggestions by others that differed from his agenda and I felt angry about that. Another behavior I listed was," and he read, "my wife asked me if I wanted to accept a social invitation we had received, but later when I wanted to discuss the invitation, it turned out that she had already accepted the invitation — before talking to me — and we were committed to go. Another irritating behavior was about my youngest child, who is full-grown and lives in Italy. She did not write and thank me for a nice birthday gift I sent." He looked up and John and Carol nodded.

"All right," Dr. Magie concluded, "When you finish listing and compiling all these irritating behaviors, sign your name at the bottom of the list.

"What?!" John exclaimed.

"Signing your name like that is a shock, but what you are doing is accepting your *willingness to face* your denied personal defects."

Dr. Magie resumed, "The rather incredible discovery Walter and I made was that the very things that irritated us most in many instances were dysfunctional behaviors and defects of our own, of which we were not conscious. So some of the traits you listed may be parts of your own shadow side which you have denied, even projected onto other people."

"Hey, Dr. M., this sounds more than a little far-fetched. Are you saying that everything I observe that irritates me significantly is somehow about *me?*"

Dr. M. responded. "At first, I doubted these behaviors I hated in others had anything to do with me at all. They seemed, in fact, to be the opposite of what I saw or believed myself to be."

Carol cut in. "How did you come to believe that the behaviors you didn't like — were angered by, in fact — were things you did yourself but were in denial about?"

Dr. Magie laughed. "Well, it wasn't easy, but because we realized that most people are in denial about their abusive or self-centered behavior, Walter and I decided to check *our own* behavior against the behaviors we found so obnoxious.

"Our plan was to take ten minutes to try to recall times we had been accused of behaviors similar to those that irritated us. We further decided to ask members of the men's group in which we participated if they could see any of these defects in us."

"What did you find out?" asked John.

"At first, I was relieved to discover that I couldn't think of any ways my behavior had been like the ones that irritated me. But Walter suggested that perhaps our own enacted version of the negative behavior would not always be done the *same way* we'd seen another person do it. In other words, though my behaviors were different, they might be more subtle attempts to *accomplish the same things* that I perceived others trying to accomplish with their controlling or abusive behavior. I did not believe this, but I reexamined the behaviors I listed in light of his suggestion, and when I did, I came to see that in my case this was true!"

Carol tapped her pencil on the notebook page. "Can you give us a specific example of a behavior in your life being different from, but like one of those you hated in someone else?"

"Certainly, Carol. Take the person I saw who angered me by the way he controlled the planning meeting at church. Even though this was a meeting of his peers, the leader's controlling manner was abusive and disrespectful, like an arrogant boss talking down to menial employees, as if they didn't have any good sense of their own. When I first studied that item on my list, I had exclaimed to Walter, 'I do not do that! I simply do *not* control like that man does!

" 'This is the test,' Walter proposed. 'If people get angry with us when we're trying to help them, chances are we're doing something else besides helping them — perhaps controlling, even though it may be unintentional. People don't usually get angry at someone who is authentically helping them in an appropriate manner.'

"Walter had smiled and said innocently, 'How *do* you control, Charles?'

"And then, suddenly I saw it. When I had offered to take my family to a large amusement park in France, nobody got angry, because I thought they might want a vacation. But then I recalled other times when I thought I was just helping my family members, that they did feel controlled, and said so. I said, laughing, 'Well, Walter, I seem to control in a very quiet, civilized way.'

"Walter nodded and suggested, 'Think about the way you lead meetings, what do you do?' And after a ten-minute study, I realized that I did the same thing as the man whose abusive behavior angered me, only my style was quite different.

Carol raised her eyebrows and listened carefully.

"In meetings, I am usually very respectful and straightforward, as opposed to being abusive and loud, but as I thought about this, I recalled that I have often planned and schemed ahead of time to get my way. I would sometimes contact the other people separately, beforehand, who were to attend the meeting and try to influence them individually, yes, manipulate them, to my way of thinking. By this tactic I tried to make sure I got my way, but I wanted it to appear that the decisions all came naturally from the group or as a result of some kind of vote in the meeting. I realized that this behavior, in fact, was at least as controlling as the person trying to control the meeting overtly, and my method was more deceitful, because I did the controlling behind the scenes rather than openly.

John commented, "Whew, that's heavy! What did you do to deal with that controlling when you discovered you were doing it?"

"Well, at first I was so shocked that I tried to tell myself that my kind of controlling was not as bad as the overt kind that abused people and shamed them. But finally I just admitted that I am a controller and confessed that to my family. I told them I didn't know if I could quit, but I was going to do my best. Then I surrendered my controlling to God."

John and Carol were silent for an embarrassingly long time. Then Carol changed the subject. "Dr. M., in my psychology class I was warned that it is a deluded counselor who tries to heal himself. Isn't what you are suggesting we try a little like that?"

Dr. Magie nodded, "Yes, I believe that, too — about the dangers of trying to heal oneself — when dealing with serious clinical symptoms. But I'm telling you about this intuitive ten-minute technique because it has really helped me and many others to locate and change some baffling, self-defeating behaviors in a very short time. And doing this exercise with a group, or at least another person, is very important in overcoming denial that keeps us from being able to face and confront personal defects. Group members can help each other enormously by giving feedback when it's requested, and sharing with the group about discoveries they may have made.

John said, "Is there anything else you can do to overcome the character problems that surface through this exercise?"

"Walter and I found that if we especially disliked the traits we discovered, it could be helpful to list each of the negative traits in a sentence. For instance, I might write, 'I am a subtle controller.' Then, in space just below each trait, write the opposite of the trait. For instance, underneath my statement about the man controlling the planning committee, I wrote, "I respect the right of others to have their opinions and live according to their own choices.' When we'd listed all the negative traits we'd discovered and written their opposites beneath them, we crossed out the *negative statements* and rewrote the positive versions on a fresh piece of paper. Then we each recorded our own voice, saying the positive traits we wanted to incorporate into our lives. And every morning for thirty days, when I woke I plugged in the ear phones of a small bedside tape player and played my recording to myself — the list of positive traits I wanted my inner wisdom to memorize so it could remind me not to control. It was a remarkable experience to hear my own voice saying things like, 'I respect the right of others to have their own opinions and live according to their own choices.'

"But even if one does this exercise alone, taking ten minutes to examine the behaviors — and committing to be as honest as possible — it sometimes happens that our usual defense mechanisms are by-passed. Some people, propelled by enough discomfort that they really want to change — or by a strong enough desire to be free and loving — can at least make a beginning toward recognizing and acknowledging some of their own denied behavior this way. Once the door to the unconscious mind has been opened and a repressed behavior or two is admitted, especially in the presence of others, it is difficult to go back to a state of total denial."

"Dr. M.," Carol said doubtfully, "did this exercise really help you change your negative habits? This one really sounds a little, well, hokey."

"Carol, I know what it sounds like. But remember, we're dealing with the power of intuitive knowing to change perceptions and behaviors. And the power and reinforcement of my own voice stating clearly for thirty days the changes I wanted so desperately to make were incredible in my case. I'm not suggesting that you do any of the things I've described. I'm just answering your questions about what has been effective for me."

"Doesn't dealing with these sorts of things with another person take a lot of trust?" Carol wondered.

"Absolutely. When one person is leading another through these discovery exercises, the process only works when the one doing the exercise trusts the person leading. And I do not recommend doing this exercise in a group until the group members have developed an atmosphere of trust on the dream-achieving journey. In counseling, I generally don't use this exercise until the counselee has evidenced a strong sense of trust in me, sometimes as a result of my sharing with them, and their discovering their dreams, or our having spent some time together counseling about other things.

"Actually, that's why I believe this idea of discovering personal defects and self-defeating behaviors will ordinarily be attempted only by people who are about to lose something they are not prepared to live without, like a marriage or other important relationship or job, or by dreamers on the adventure, who will become willing to get help from therapists or enter this discovery process when they realize that some personal, self-defeating behaviors may be blocking them from deeply desired fulfillment and happiness.

"Of course," Dr. Magie explained, "not every negative trait or behavior you see in others is part of your negative shadow side. I must say that in some cases, I just don't like what certain people do. My point here is that *many* times a behavior we detest and notice in others again and again in different contexts is likely to be a part of us that we have denied and denounced to avoid the shame of the same denied characteristic being discovered in ourselves.

Carol and John were silent. Their friend had given them much to think about and much of himself as well.

Carol looked at her watch. "How about a break, some free time? Will 12:30 be okay for lunch?"

The men nodded, and John grunted as he stood up, "Did I say the ten-minute process for awakening dreams was *simple?*"

Dr. Magie laughed, "No John, you said it was *simplistic.* Strange as it may seem, when people begin to awaken long dormant specific dreams and commit to achieve them some of their character *defects* and *defenses* wake up, along with their abilities and life energies and childhood wounds. I don't know why this is, but I've come to believe deeply that although the ten-minute dream process itself is simple, for a dreamer who takes it seriously and commits to achieve his or her life dreams, the discovery of character defects may be the beginning of a significant personality transformation. For me, making the necessary changes in my life required finding a way to access what was for me a new kind of guidance in the midst of a very busy schedule."

"Therapy?" John asked.

Dr. M. suddenly felt very tired as he replied, "No John, a kind of inner dialog. But could we take that nap break before continuing?"

EXERCISE TEN
Discovering Buried Personal Defects

1. For one whole day, write a description of every behavior in others whom you meet or interact with or observe that irritates you. Describe specifically what was done and said.

2. Take ten minutes to list all of the irritating behaviors and attitudes of others in your present or past. Describe briefly the part that irritated or angered you.

3. Combine the lists gathered in 1 and 2, leaving two spaces between each described behavior.

4. When you've combined the two lists, sign the list at the bottom, owning your willingness to see these behaviors as projected aspects of your shadow side. Share with your partner or group how you feel about having signed this list. In a group, describe whether you can see at this point that you are guilty of any of these behaviors. If you describe how your similar behavior works then, listen as each person responds and describes the way she or he does a behavior that expresses a defect on their list.

5. After you are alone again, try to recall and note any times you have been accused of one of the defects or behaviors on your list. Later you may want to ask for feedback and verification from your partner or your group. Before beginning to ask for this kind of feedback, you may want to have a discussion in the group about asking others for this kind of feedback. It's usually better not to give feedback about personal defects unless someone specifically asks for it.

6. Below each negative behavior, write a positive statement in the first person, singular (e.g., Negative: he always points out faults and belittles people's behavior. Positive: I look for the good aspects of people's performance and affirm them verbally.)

7. After writing the positive behavior below each negative description on your list, cross out the negative items.

8. If you want to, continue to look for additional things that irritate you in others to add to your list. Get feedback, if you want it. At the next meeting with your partner or group on the goal-accomplishing venture, report how and what else you are doing with regard to discovering and changing denied behaviors.

9. Get a tape recorder and read onto a tape the positive list of behaviors or attitudes.

10. First thing every morning, listen to the tape of recorded positive behaviors, either at home or in your car.

11. Continue to listen to the list every morning for thirty days, while looking for opportunities to practice the positive behaviors.

35

Learning an Inner Dialogue

~~~~~~~~~~~~~~~~~~~

While they were all napping, a late morning rainstorm began, the fall rain blowing across the back yard in sheets, drumming on the slate roof and sweeping occasionally across the plate glass of the scenic breakfast room window. Despite the rain, John was in a better mood at lunch. He said, "Dr. M, I'm in an ambivalent place. I'm definitely interested in developing the skills to cope with the stresses of a growing business, and expanding my inner world.

"But to be honest, one of my most tenacious problems is that I sometimes become stressed and anxious when I'm committed to reaching a large, specific goal. When I get tired, I tend to sabotage myself by focusing on everything that could go wrong. I lose perspective, obsess over what I'm doing at work, and before I know it, I'm out of touch with my positive life goals and the people closest to me." He nodded at Carol, "When this begins I wake up every morning almost frantic, my mind filled with commitments and unanswered communications swirling around in an emotional tornado. How do you maintain your motivation and stay so centered? You always seem so serene."

Their wise mentor chuckled, "John, I'm not always serene, of course. I've discovered that neither sharing with my wife nor interacting with my men's group offers adequate ways for me always to work from a calm center. But I have found other means to help me stay less agitated than I was."

"Like what?" John and Carol asked in unison.

Dr. M. stared into the fire. "Studying the major spiritual movements of the world showed me that most of the founders believed in some sort of regular prayer or meditation time to order their lives. They used this very private time to create an inner space in which they could let the anxious activities of their interactions with work and other people settle out of their consciousness so they could relax and be renewed. These spiritual leaders focused on something inside that was stable for them, far removed and quite different from the actual threats and challenges they faced. As they focused on the object of their meditation, a sense of peace or serenity settled into them. After meditation, they could move back into action and remain centered more easily in the midst of the commitments, relationships, duties or the maintenance activities of their lives. Unlike us, many of them evidently were able to avoid being overwhelmed or derailed as much by stress and complexity all around them. The development of a meditation time was an important element in their spiritual and psychological health. In fact, many of them felt that spiritual growth actually required the time off from work, almost as if the growth took place when one rested."

"That's interesting. What would an example be of growth taking place when one is resting?" John asked.

Dr. Magie considered John's question. "The prime example that comes to mind is the Sabbath of the Jews and other ancient peoples — the requirement to take one day off from all work each week. And thousands of people still take one day off from work every week."

"I don't see how they could do that in our kind of business," John chuckled. "How do you see meditation or rest as related to growth?"

Dr. Magie continued, "You lift weights as part of your physical conditioning program, don't you, John?"

John nodded.

"Knowledgeable body builders who lift weights to develop their muscles don't work the same muscles every day, because working a muscle by lifting weight tears down the muscle, so the muscle actually heals and grows on the days off, when it is resting. Perhaps mediation and observing the Sabbath operate in a similar way to promote healthy spiritual and emotional growth."

"But, as you know, I'm not a religious person."

"All kinds of people have benefited from centering their lives through prayer and meditation — whether or not they would be considered religious or spiritual people.

"In short, what I'm saying is that the experiences of outstanding thinkers and spiritual leaders throughout history indicate that a mature person needs to spend some time alone without a working agenda. Although there are many ways to spend such time, the most common basic attitude of those who meditate, for example, is one of listening awareness in silence. The renewed hope and direction that come from this practice seem to seep through the ordinarily impenetrable curtains of our unconscious minds, and calm our stress and fear during the meditation — often without our having to address or solve the particular issues that created the stress and fear. Paradoxically, when I can open myself to this level of experience, I have a sense of receiving help and support from a Reality beyond my consciousness. Then my mind is often clearer and better able to address the actual problems in my outer life."

He glanced at John and noted that his scowl had become a look of interest as he listened. "I can't speak for all people who meditate this way, of course," Dr. Magie said, "but for me, as a Christian, that 'Reality beyond' is the God of the Bible."

Carol sneaked a look at John, who now stared intensely at Dr. Magie.

"But," Dr. Magie continued, "even Christians disagree on what should happen in meditation. Some contemporary Christian teachers recommend clearing the mind by telling it in silence to be still and moving toward being totally open to God. On the other hand, in the New Testament, Jesus seemed to be listening for strength and specific guidance regarding his course of action in the world of relationships with people."[11]

John said, "That's intriguing, but what I want to know is what do *you* do when you practice mediation that works for you on a practical level?"

Dr. M. began thoughtfully, "When I began, sitting still and listening in silence did not come easily for me. For a long time — and even now — my mind tends sometimes to have an uncontrollable will of its own. It jumps around and shows me pictures of potential goals, regrets about the past, scenes of lust, grandiose schemes to become famous, potential vacation spots, or scenes of abject failure in the future. Achieving the inner stillness and focus required to benefit from listening is difficult for me and apparently for most people, even very dedicated ones.

"But I, and many of those who stick with this focused attempt at inner listening long enough to relax into it, experience a growing sense of serenity and other positive benefits regarding emotional and physiological stress levels. I met your Dr. Herbert Benson at Harvard Medical School. He's done a lot of work on certain results of meditation, pointing to what he calls 'the relaxation response.'[12] And for me, the paradox is this: the more I am able to go inside and surrender control of my attention from the tyranny of immediate problem solving, deadlines, and the need to succeed, the more clear-headed, calm and decisive I become. This calmness often carries over into the rest of my day as I attempt to accomplish my life's goals. And I'm more relaxed about outcomes as I go back and deal with the specific issues in achieving my goals and in relating to people who are important to me."

Carol softly cleared her throat. "So how do you deal with your wandering mind? I tried meditation in a relaxation class I took a few years ago but couldn't get the hang of it and gave it up." She glanced again at John, who had leaned forward, forearms resting on the table, gazing at his palms, side-by-side in front of him.

Dr. Magie didn't seem to be bothered by John's apparent detachment. He turned to Carol. "People have used different material or sensory objects to help them focus their minds and keep them from jumping around too much. For example, some people sit before a candle and focus on the flame. They gently bring their wayward attention back again and again until their minds are free from their worries or material concerns, until they are present and listening. Some people sing, or hum. Some repeat a chosen word or phrase or a series of words with pauses in between like 'be silent,' 'be still,' 'empty,' say nothing,' 'ask for nothing.' Still others read a passage from the Bible or some other inspirational literature to focus their minds and dislodge or replace stressful images of their outward lives.

"There are all kinds of different approaches to meditation, but many men and women I know — at least in Western traditions — who meditate as part of their ongoing lives, as I do, have faith in a personal God, to whom they have surrendered their lives, as the One for whom they are listening. Therefore, they see meditation as a way simply to be aware of God at a deeper, more intimate level, consciously accepting God's love and listening as a part of determining God's will for their lives. As I indicated last night, besides being a librarian/guide for me, the inner wisdom as both the inner experiential contact point with God and the translator of God's will about life."

John, to his surprise, found that although he was still disturbed, the possibility of better contacting and hearing his inner wisdom fascinated him. In spite of the sensitive way his older friend lived and the fact that he obviously wasn't trying to push John into anything, John's gut told him, "Be careful, this kind of meditation could lead to a loss of control over your life!"

"Go on, Dr. M.," John said, glancing into Carol's eyes across the table. "Is there some simple way you pray and meditate that fits what you've been teaching us about going for our dreams?" Carol looked back at John, as they both waited to hear Dr. Magie's reply.

The doctor's eyebrows rose as he watched the silent conversation between John and Carol. "My experience is colored by my own particular history and beliefs, but when I realized, many years ago, that stress and fear dominated my life, I began to look for someone who could be a spiritual guide for me. Several individuals I met told me they spent time communicating or talking with God every day, and I tried to do that, but I still didn't have a sense of being able actually to contact God or hear what God might want to say to me in the silence.

"Later when I met Paul Tournier, the physician from Geneva I've told you so much about, he shared with me that he and his wife, Nellie, spent a short time together in the morning, both listening for God and writing what came to them. Then they would share what they heard with each other.

"I was convinced that this couple had learned how to listen to God, but I myself still found it difficult. My mind seemed able to give me only shameful messages about how I should be working and not wasting this time just sitting around doing nothing. Finally, I gave up, just as you did, Carol." The doctor smiled. "I communicated with God only sporadically, mostly by giving him verbal instructions about how my part of the world should run, and how he should help that to happen.

"During one of my previous trips to the U.S., I was lucky enough to get to know and trust a wise therapist and Christian spiritual director. She also told me that she listened to God for ten minutes each day and wrote down everything that came to her mind during that time. So after hearing this method from three people I trusted, I began to try to listen for just ten minutes each day with a lined notebook open before me, writing everything that came to me during that time."

"Did writing things make the job of listening easier?" asked John.

"Well, yes and no. At first, all I got were messages about what I ought to be doing in my day, like 'get your car repaired,' or 'go to the bank this morning,' or 'call your son.' ! I resisted such obviously non-spiritual instructions and ignored them, because I thought I was supposed to hear something important or profound. At other times I rehearsed resentments. But my spiritual director told me not to fight what came to me, just write it *all* down. She said that these mundane matters might not be important, but whether or not they were, writing them down would clear them out of my mind. Also, the unacceptable thoughts might point me to areas in which I needed counseling or about which I could be praying.

"After a while I began to notice that I also heard things like, 'Tell your wife you're sorry for being sarcastic and hurting her last night.' And I discovered that by listening and writing what came to me, I became much more focused on what to do each day. Un-spiritual as it sounds, for the first five minutes in fact, most of what I heard consisted of things that I needed to do that day.

"As I continued to record these emerging thoughts onto a page, I became aware that many thoughts were new kinds of messages from my inner wisdom, things that were loving or that could help clean up the disarray of my days.

"This continued to happen throughout the first few months I meditated, until one day I realized that during my meditation time I was quickly planning my day in five minutes, compiling a list of everything I needed to do that day. So after the ten-minute period was over, I would take a few more minutes to reorder the list from the first five minutes in terms of my priorities and put the specific hours at which I planned to do each thing. Before long I realized that my days were virtually all planned in those first minutes of listening. Just a minute; I'll show you what I mean."

Dr. Magie stood up and stretched and then went into his bedroom. John moved behind Carol's chair and began to rub her shoulders, but they were both lost in thought. In a moment, Dr. M. returned with his attaché case, and pulled out his journal. He leafed through the pages and then said, "Here is one day's list I made and prioritized after returning from a trip the previous day. I had no patients to see that day."

7:30–8:00 a.m.	Listen for God and pray
8:00–8:30	Clear off desk, file or put in pending
8:30–noon	Work on current book
noon–1:00 p.m.	Lunch
1:00–1:20	Nap
1:30–2:00	Gather and stack correspondence
2:00–4:00	Answer calls, e-mail, dictate or write answers to letters
4:00–4:30	Order birthday present for son; return calls
4:30–5:30	Take a walk
5:30	Check calendar for tomorrow and then spend evening at home with family

"Granted, for me this was a very simple day, but the things on the list were basically what I did. I felt relaxed and confident that if I needed to do anything else, I would have written it on my calendar earlier or would hear about it by telephone, mail, or e-mail during the day.

"My inner wisdom knows what I need to do, and since my surrender to God, I feel that my inner wisdom is being gradually reprogramed to help me live more like I believe God would have me live. The amazing thing to me is that now, except for new challenges or input from the e-mail, mail, or telephone, I hardly ever have to add much to my list during the day. This process trained my inner wisdom to know or recover what I need to do about my own personal life and work. Meditation has trained me to listen for that kind of instruction. Sometimes if I don't get to certain tasks the day I list them, I add the undone items to my list for the next day.

"Of course, sometimes it takes only three minutes to compile this list, and other times it's six or seven. I had to learn to be flexible about these times. The purpose, as in all ten-minute processes, is to write as quickly as possible as I listen, in order to distract the censor and counteract the residual, self-defeating and compulsive habits of thought from my hidden motivator that wanted to analyze and sabotage the process of listening for God's guidance."

Carol broke in impatiently, "You've described the first five minutes very well. But then what do you do for the rest of the time?"

"The amount of time is arbitrary. After I listen for things to do that day, I keep listening and writing whatever comes to me for the full ten minutes. This was a problem at first. After I had my day outlined, I had an urge to jump up and get to it.

"But as my mentor advised me to, I just sat and continued to listen, although I didn't hear much else. One morning, however, I heard something I had never heard from any inner voice: 'Charles Magie, you are a fine person, and I love you very much.' I didn't know if these words came from God or my inner wisdom, but I do know that the message that 'I am valuable' came from the deepest part of me through those words, the first specific inner message of love and self-esteem I could recall. And I wept.

"From that point onward, I continued to hear some very positive statements periodically about my own character or abilities from my inner wisdom. Before this listening and writing habit, I had almost always received negative inner messages telling me things like, 'Magie, you did not do well,' 'You are not really very intelligent,' or, 'You're late!' When positive messages started coming, I first felt embarrassed, but then very grateful. Tears came to my eyes often. As I've told you, I've always had trouble believing good things about myself."

For the first time, John and Carol noticed a shy, hesitant look come over their friend. They glanced at each other and waited.

Dr. M. did not notice their exchange of glances as he used his napkin to wipe his eyes. He cleared his throat and continued. "I usually don't share these experiences with anyone, but I told you I'd explain things fully. I now sometimes hear things like: 'You are a precious child.' 'You're actually getting your life in order and accomplishing your dreams.' 'You're a good communicator.' 'You have a good mind.'

"And along with these messages, I'm shown things about myself I can't see consciously but that I realize I needed to improve. For example: 'You're a good person, but you're not trusting me with your future, as indicated by your working far too many hours.' 'You're taking on too many commitments.' 'You haven't spent time with your wife lately, just playing.' 'You're not getting enough exercise, or rest.' "

"Often I receive random things to do, such as a specific act of kindness I wanted to do but had forgotten, maybe visit a sick friend, or apologize to another, or make amends about a thoughtless or sarcastic comment that I made."

"But wait a minute," Carol interrupted. "How do you know if these things are coming from God or just from your own inner wisdom?"

"That's a good question, and the truth is I don't know for sure. But I decided it didn't matter to me, really, since if there is a God, then it would be most natural for God to use the vehicle of my own mind and inner wisdom to communicate with me.

"And if there is no God, I still get important guidance from my inner wisdom, including tasks that in my best moments I want to accomplish. So in answer to your question, after some experience trying to do the things I hear and write down, I began to recognize more easily whether or not things that come to me during this listening time are important things for me to do. As this began to happen, I realized I was beginning to trust God more and to know by experience how intuitive information could come from God. In ordinary human growth and development, if I spend a lot of time with a mature woman or man, someone I respect and want to emulate, I will spontaneously begin to pick up that person's perceptions, attitudes and skills. For example, I noticed that Paul Tournier listened to people's questions, and if he did not understand the question, he repeated what he thought the questioner said and asked 'Did I get that right?' Before long I found myself doing the same thing when I wasn't sure about what was being asked. I believe the same process of assimilation and adapting from a person one respects and admires applies to an intimate relationship with God. When my inner wisdom offers me a solution to a relational problem, the solutions will more and more over time come from the biblical descriptions of Jesus' perspective."

"What's an example of that? Carol asked.

"The first person who comes to mind is St. Francis of Assisi. After he surrendered his life and began living in the presence of God, his love of the poor and marginalized people had a haunting family resemblance to Jesus' ministry in the Bible to the lepers and other people outside the establishment of his day. I believe Francis picked these habits up from his prayer life, and reading about Jesus.[13]

"In my own life I've noticed that my inner wisdom began increasingly to urge me to forgive instead of retaliate — a remarkable change for me. Another kind of message began to come to me during the second part of listening and writing. I began to get 'suggestions' about some kind of creative act I could do. For example, once I heard and wrote down the title for a book, along with the suggestion, 'This is a book you should write.' The same message came for several days. Over the years, I have written several books I became aware of this way.

"I don't force myself to use what comes to me as a compulsory agenda, but if the thought that I am to do something keeps coming to me day after day in my meditation time, I eventually investigate the possibility of doing it."

He then turned to John. "Did you have any questions about this form of listening meditation?"

"As you realize, this whole subject of meditation is spooky to me," John replied. "Why do you think this listening meditation works, Dr. M.? And how do you know what to pay attention to and what is just wishful thinking?"

Dr. M. smiled and shrugged. "I really don't understand in the usual sense of that word why this meditation period has worked this way for me, but it certainly has. When suggestions have come to me this way, I've checked them out. Since nothing in my experience is perfect, I don't expect that everything I hear in my meditation is from God or my inner wisdom. I see my task as simply listening and writing what comes. Then I try to check it against what else I know about God, my goals, my inner wisdom, and the tested values my life. But as in all other things, I'm learning about God. I have to remind myself of my tendency toward self-centeredness and denial — that can skew any message from anyone."

"So," John summarized, "you hear positive affirmations of yourself, reminders of things to do, and you get creative ideas. Anything else come to you during this time?"

"Well, yes. Occasionally after the ten-minute listening I ask God, 'What questions would you like to ask me?' The first time I did this I heard, 'Why are you still working so hard and taking on so many things?' My spontaneous answer was, 'Because I say I trust you with my future, God, but in fact I only trust my own abilities and efforts. I'm afraid that if I don't take the entire burden of the future, I'll be alone and bankrupt.' Having already identified my central hidden motivator as an urge to compensate for my sense of inadequacy, I saw by my answer that I'd reverted back to lack of trust in God. That 'conversation' was sobering.

"Because I believe that God is the ultimate source of the other half of this inner dialogue translated for me by my inner wisdom, I take a period after this ten minutes of listening each day to thank God for what I've discovered about myself and life, and I've found a great deal of serenity in these simple ways of listening. Being open to God concerning what I should do, and responding to what comes to me works a lot better for me than the old habit I had of *advising* God about how he ought to run my part of the world, and being disappointed when he didn't do things my way.

"I must add that, as in any intimate communication, there are misunderstandings about what the other wants. However, in all intimate relationships, one is more likely to keep learning more about the other and about how to give and receive love by listening than by talking. This is also true for me about a relationship lived in surrender to God."

EXERCISE ELEVEN
A Ten-Minute Listening Meditation

The basic principle is to listen for ten minutes and write down anything that comes to you during that time. Many people's experience is that some of the things they "hear" are practical things to be done or even unacceptable thoughts. When practical things insinuate themselves, just write them down. The same goes for unacceptable thoughts. They may be pointing to areas needing correction or counsel. Other things you may "hear" are suggestions about achieving your goals, about the direction of your life or things to do to enhance or repair relationships with others, yourself or God. Some things that come to you may seem totally irrelevant. Write them all down; you can eliminate them later if you want to. Remember, you are retraining your mind to tune into a different source of wisdom, and it may take some time to tune in precisely to the new station.

Later, you may wish to transfer the list of things to do for the day to a calendar with time slots.

Some people begin using these guidelines and later try other ways of meditating. Just as each intimate relationship between persons develops in a unique way, evidently, so does each person's relationship with her or his inner wisdom — and with God.

36

Responding

John shifted in his chair and ran his hand through his hair. His eyes surveyed the ceiling, as if searching for a small insect there. "You know I'm skeptical about anything I can't see or touch. So I want you to know that I'm not buying everything you're saying about meditation and prayer, but I am listening because this means so much to you and you've obviously learned to live in a way that is personally fulfilling." He hesitated a moment and then smiled a little sheepishly. "Okay, I can't believe I'm asking this, but I'm curious now. Exactly what do you mean, 'talking with God.' Do you hear actual words or what?"

"John, I want you to know that it's all right with me if you don't buy any of this. You need to find your own way to live your life. But since this is the direction my own search for serenity — my overall dream — took me, and since you asked about my discoveries, I'll try to tell you how I experience talking with God.

"When I use the words 'hearing' and 'talking' to describe my inner dialogue with God or with my inner wisdom, I'm not trying to be scientifically accurate. Sometimes what I become aware of is conveyed by words, sometimes just mental impressions, ideas or symbols that immediately translate into words. So it's just easier to talk about 'hearing' when I am 'listening.' 'Talking' with God means that I'm responding with my words to the voice, words, thoughts or impressions that come to me in listening meditation. After years of practicing this type of mediation, most of the things I hear and attend to at this point seem wise and caring. So whatever the source is, the meaning comes to me after being translated by my inner wisdom, the same voice that helped me find and process my life dreams.

"As you know, prayer is what spiritual people call this dialogue with God. For me, prayer is simply reiterating and enlarging the scope and understanding of my surrender and opening myself intimately to God's way of living. As my sense of the reality of God as being Personal has grown, I have gradually changed into one who wants to give and receive his kind of love. Paul, the author of some of the letters in the New Testament told Timothy, a young man he was mentoring, 'The whole point of what we're urging is simply *love* — love uncontaminated by

227

self-interest and counterfeit faith, a life open to God.'[14] What I want to tell you two is that prayer for me is simply the language of an intimate, loving relationship between a grateful person and God.

"As I mentioned earlier, although I didn't know it, my first attempts at talking to God were about my unconscious need to control. They consisted primarily of advising God about how to run my world — my relationships and the things I thought should be done in my life. I used to spend my time complaining about the state of the whole world and other people, asking God to straighten them out — and how — so that they — and I — would be happier, more comfortable, more adequate. My prayers at that time reflected my hidden inner motivator: to avoid being revealed as not enough. Consequently, most of what I heard from God was garbled, confusing and not acceptable to me. My prayers were, after all, about getting my desires met, springing largely from my fear of being seen as inadequate. These requests for God to do what I thought God ought to do were the opposite of what I now understand praying to be. If true prayer is listening to learn how *God* can teach and guide *me* to be the authentic, loving person I now believe God wants me to be, then my prayers to try to control God's actions were keeping me from intimacy with him and people."[15]

"What's an example of sincere prayer being controlling and self-centered?" Carol asked.

Dr. M. smiled sadly, "Many years ago, I remember praying that my nephew would not marry a certain young woman, because I felt she wasn't good enough for the boy, so I told God all the reasons she would not be right for him, as if God needed this information from me. My nephew married that young woman, and as it turned out, she's a wonderful wife and a loving addition to our family. At that point I saw that I do not really know what is best for other people, and so, in my case, to instruct God is an attempt to get God to be my assistant, a self-centered personal agenda stemming from my pride and insecurity. That's why surrender to God was so crucial to me before meditation and prayer made sense. After surrendering and trying to learn God's will for me, I had a much better idea of what might be appropriate for me to pray about."

As Carol listened intently in quiet amazement from her place at the table, John stood and walked to the window, looking out into the rain at the misty outlines of the mountains in the distance. He shrugged his shoulders and rubbed the back of his neck. Finally, he turned, looked at Dr. Magie and took a deep breath. "Look, I don't know anything about God or prayer. I don't even know if I *want* to know about them. But I'm going to ask you this anyway, because I am intrigued about one thing. If you no longer give God his instructions about what you think he should do, how do you pray about your family? How do you pray about your goals and dreams?"

Dr. Magie nodded. "Good question. After discovering my entrenched tendency to control people and situations, I found the healthiest way for me to pray for members of my family was to use my creative imagination. Now I imagine that I'm holding each person or circumstance I'm concerned about — one at a time — in my cupped hands and lifting them up to God. I imagine God's hands are cupped like mine, and I place each person or situation in God's hands, not advising God at all or saying anything.

"As for my dreams and goals for the future, I put those, too, in God's hands in a similar way and imagine them being fulfilled and my being very happy. Along with this imaginative exercise I do add these words, 'Since I have such a long history of being self-centered, controlling and stubborn, God, I would appreciate hearing any counsel or adjustments you have to suggest concerning my life, my dreams and my prayers.'"

"I don't understand, and right now, I can't honestly pray as you do," John said quietly.

His older friend shook his head slightly and responded, "I don't really understand how this approach to meditation and prayer works either, John, but I've found that practicing it brings both order and surprises to my days. Since I began listening for God, I've noticed I listen more to the other people in my life, and pay more attention to subtle nudges from my inner wisdom throughout the day."

John sighed, "I can see how this way of meditating has helped you, I just don't believe it would work for me. Is there someplace I could read about this or even try it without surrendering to a God I'm not sure exists? I know you'd like for me to surrender, but I can't do that with integrity."

"The best thing I can suggest is that you try a prayer experiment for thirty days, whether or not you believe in God or your inner wisdom. Many people are amazed at what they discover in this way. You just take the hypothesis that God exists and pray as if you believe for thirty days — just as an experiment. As I keep saying, I don't know why this works, but I do know that using this process, including the prayer, for the past twenty years has finally given me a sense of being who I really am — a practical dreamer doing what is mine to do in life and learning to love other people. To have an internal two-way communication with God about this adventure — even with the static and periodic lapses — has brought serenity into my days and nights and a sense of security. It has made me much more grateful. Not to mention, from a practical standpoint, this regular, intimate opening myself to God has made me willing to try projects and goals I never would have risked trying before."

"But," John asked once again, "do you think a person has to believe in God to complete this dream-accomplishing process? My dreams seem to be going pretty well without that — at least so far."

Dr. Magie looked thoughtful. "No, I don't think one has to believe in God to achieve dreams," he acknowledged slowly. "Some people who commit to reach their dreams, even some who learn to meditate, may not believe in God at all. But you asked me what *my* experience has been, and God and meditating have been very important to me.

"I suppose that for me, the most practical discovery about this overall approach was becoming aware of how pervasive my need for control is, and how it manifests itself, especially my habit of taking on more than I can finish. I tend to go off in nine different directions, to try to do everything at once. Then I become overcommitted, frantic, and see myself as a failure if I don't finish everything on my ridiculously overbooked time schedule. By adopting this continual, daily period of listening for guidance and making a list of what is mine to do each day, I have discovered a calmer way and a place to create my daily schedule away from the noisy clamoring for my time and attention. It's as if that meditation space inside always maintains a temperature of quiet sanity, bringing my feverish mind back within a normal range."

"Hmm," John reflected, shaking his head and laughing, "I know the French word *magie* means magic in English. Are you sure you're not some sort of magician, Dr. M.? We've known you less than ten years, and in that time you've helped us find our dreams and change the whole direction of our lives to follow our dreams. Then you taught us how to discover and deal with our hidden personal assets and liabilities. Now you're telling us about God! — and coming from you, it all sounds natural — and almost sane!

"This ten-minute journey seemed very simple, yet it's putting me in touch with areas of my life I've never talked to anyone about." John chuckled, "And my inner voice is practically shouting at me to pay careful attention to what you're saying."

Carol asked, "Do you think there are a lot of people who might be interested in helping each other the way you're helping us?"

Dr. Magie thought about that. "I believe that in your country alone there are hundreds — perhaps thousands — of people who may be bored, frightened, frustrated or tired of the lack of adventure in their lives, who might be very interested in being part of a group that could help them discover and reach their dreams. And Carol, you just may be the person to show people how — to guide them into the intuitive world of dreams and freedom and loving spiritual wisdom."

John had become very still during Carol's conversation with Dr. Magie. He had the strange feeling that their wise mentor was detaching in a way as he prepared to leave the next day, to let them grow up on their own, and John was filled with a deep sadness. In the silence he finally announced, "Thank you, Charles Magie, for passing on to us a way to navigate the thicket of contemporary overstimulation to reach our dreams. Now I guess we'll just have to grow up and go for it, and see what happens."

He grinned, "Ten minutes at a time, of course." Dr. Magie smiled and nodded.

Carol wondered what would happen to them now as they were being gently nudged out of the nest. Would they fly, or crash and burn?

EXERCISE TWELVE
A Way of Silent Interaction with God

1. Find a place where you have the most privacy, in a room in which you feel safe and comfortable. Settle in your chair. Many people find this easier to do with eyes closed, to cut out distraction and gain privacy. Since this is an experiment, you can do it whether or not you believe in God just to see how it feels.

2. For five minutes, imagine that you are holding each member of your family (as if they were very small) in your cupped hands and lifting each one up. Imagine now that God is sitting facing you with hands cupped. Now imagine that you are placing each member of your family in God's cupped hands, and leaving them there, with no suggestions. Your intention is to put them in the place where they will be most loved, inspired, healed, and taught. Your releasing them this way into God's larger hands is a symbol of the fact that you realize your job is not to control them but to support and love them, as they find their own way.

3. When you have finished putting each member of your family in turn into God's hands, then you may want to put your own life, and your dreams, specifically in God's hands, too, in the same way.

4. Finally, you may want to express gratitude for the good things in your life, regardless of what is still painful and negative in your experience. (Even if there were no God, the expression of gratitude can be a very healing and integrating behavior.)

37

An Abdication — Or Two?

Carol was sitting in the kitchen alone. She had just finished reading the first chapter of the book of John in the *The Message* translation of the Bible that Dr. Magie had given her before he left. Relaxed and sipping her coffee, Carol had listened for ten minutes and was writing in her journal.

> *I'm very excited about life. I have a strong sense that John and I are entering a whole new chapter of our lives together. It's difficult to believe that almost ten years have passed since John first traveled to Glion and went through that first almost magical ten minute dreaming session with Dr. M.*
>
> *So much has happened. Martin Industries has exploded into the Denver commercial real estate scene, and has grown so rapidly John and I have been thinking that it may be time to move toward becoming a publicly traded company.*
>
> *Since graduating from Stanford and getting his master's degree, Wil has already made a significant contribution to the company's operating structure. But he and John are still clanking around in their "suits of armor."*
>
> *Celeste is a grown woman. It's hard to believe that she finished high school four years ago, and that tonight she is graduating from Colorado College.*

Carol stopped writing and made a note to call Wil and remind him that he is going to the graduation ceremony with John and Carol and taking Celeste out to dinner at the Metropolitan Club afterward. Also that Celeste was spending the night with the Martins tonight, and Wil had agreed to take her to catch her one o'clock flight to Geneva tomorrow.

Carol leaned back in her chair and looked at the glistening snow on the mountain peaks. She breathed a long sigh of contentment. Life was very good, Carol whispered, "Thank you, God." Then she frowned as she remembered that John was not in the same contented place she was. But at least she wasn't responsible for changing him — or Wil —

now. Glancing upward as she closed her journal notebook, Carol said with a grin, "And I'm sure glad I've passed the scepter back to you. I was really getting tired."

—*uun*—

"Hi, good looking," Carol said, coming down the stairs. She and John were having an early breakfast the morning after graduation. Celeste was sleeping late, planning to have lunch with Wil on the way to the airport.

Carol could see that John was nervous, she assumed it was about a meeting he had scheduled that afternoon with Wil. She'd noticed that something had changed between John and Wil since Dr. M. had left for Boston the week before, but she had no idea what it was. John was quieter — more thoughtful, less critical and edgy when Wil was around.

As Carol poured his coffee, John said, "I do not know how to relate to that boy."

"John, he's almost thirty years old. He's not a boy."

"I know that. And he's not only a man, but a brilliant businessman. I've been really off base in my approach to him all these years. And although you'd never guess it, I've hoped he'd decide to stay in the business with us. In fact I've tried to subtly manipulate him to stay. But I know he's got to make his own decision, and I'm planning to send him to do the dreaming process with Dr. M. in Boston to find out what *his* dreams for his life are. What do you think?"

Carol thought a moment and then said, "Sounds like a good plan. That way, whatever he decides to do, it will be his choice. But don't make a huge deal out of it, John. Wil is very smart. This problem is more like a mouse than a tiger. Don't bring out the twelve-gauge shotgun to kill it. And John, I know that Wil has probably forgiven you for the stuff that happened when he sabotaged his football career...."

"Wait a minute, Carol! In the first place, he's got some things to say 'I'm sorry' about too! And besides, how would you know if he's forgiven me? Forgiveness is not one of *your* highest aptitudes. You just left the Claudette Fontaine incident hanging on the headboard of our bed for five years!"

"John, I didn't want to go back into that with you, but since you brought it up, I decided after Dr. M. helped us — helped me to face the source of my jealousy, and helped me surrender my life to God, I decided that I'd imagine the worst, that you *did* sleep with Claudette Fontaine that night in Glion, and that I would forgive you. And I did...."

Just then they heard a gasp and looked toward the stairs. Celeste was standing at the foot of the stairs there in her jeans and sweatshirt. They hadn't heard her come down, and she didn't know what to do because they were arguing, and she was already down the stairs.

Now Celeste said, "I'm so sorry, I didn't know you were having... having a private conversation, but..."

John started to say, "That's all right..." when Celeste interrupted.

"But I've got to say something."

John interrupted, a little irritated, "I told you it was all right. You couldn't have known we were arguing." John got up and walked back to the kitchen to get a fresh cup of coffee.

Celeste's eyes brimmed with tears.

Carol asked gently, "What is it, Celeste?"

"Well, Mrs. Martin, I just realized when I overheard... there has been a terrible misunderstanding about Madame Fontaine all these years. I was working the night shift the night Mr. Martin and Madame Fontaine had dinner together. I was down the hall from Madame Fontaine's room when I heard a noise in the stairway. Madame Fontaine... he was carrying her, because she was unconscious. I watched him carry her to the doorway of her room. He tried to reach for her purse to get the key, when he saw me walking toward them." Celeste stopped to get her breath.

Carol was spellbound. "Go on Celeste, what happened?"

"Well, Mr. Martin asked me to see if Madame Fontaine had a key in the small purse she had clutched in her hands. But I just took my pass key and opened the door. Then I stepped back not knowing what to do... whether he wanted me to leave or not."

"Well?"

"He asked me to come in with him. Then he carried her into the bedroom of her suite and put her on the bed. He told me he was leaving and asked me to help her get ready for bed and lock her door when I left."

"What did he do then?"

"Well, he gave me a tip and left."

Carol's eyes were suddenly filled with tears. Celeste said, "What is the matter, Mrs. Martin. Are you all right?"

"Yes, Celeste, I'm fine."

John walked back into the breakfast room. "What's the matter with you two? You look like someone just died."

Carol smiled. "That's not too far off the mark." Then she turned to Celeste. "One more question, Celeste. Do you happen to remember seeing a small silver vase on the bedside table, before you left Madame Fontaine?"

"Oh yes, and I can see that I did a stupid thing. I could tell Madame Fontaine was probably not going to feel very well when she woke up, and I saw the vase and ran down stairs, got a beautiful red rose from the greenhouse outside, cut it, and put it in the vase — to make her feel better in the morning. But," looking sad, "I can see that may not have been a cool thing to do."

"Why did you do that, Celeste?" Carol asked.

Celeste thought for a few seconds and then, turning her palms up and shrugging slightly, she said, "Because I was a teenager, and a romantic . . . and I'm French!"

John saw what was going on and said, "Celeste I hope I gave you a big tip for helping Madame Fontaine."

Celeste assured him, "Yes, you did!"

When Celeste had grabbed a sweet roll and a cup of coffee, she excused herself and ran back up stairs with her breakfast to finish packing.

After Celeste was gone, Carol looked at John and said, "Please forgive me. I really blew, condemning you without a trial. Wil told me about alcoholic blackouts. It seems that he was in one when he stole my car."

"Oh, my God," John said. "And he didn't remember doing that either?"

Carol shook her head.

John said. "And I hit him when he told me he didn't remember stealing the car." John sat with his forearms on his thighs and stared at the floor.

Carol moved over and put her arm around John's shoulder, "I love you, John, very much, and I'm sorry I condemned you, and pulled away from you."

John put his hand on her knee and patted it. "Thank you, Carol. But I can't blame you. That was a dumb thing I did, getting blind drunk like that with a stranger in order to be a hero. I'm sorry that I wasn't even aware of what that would do to you. I hope you can forgive me, I . . . I don't know what I'd do without you." He got up and looked down at her.

Carol stood as John concluded, "I'm really grateful that you are the woman you are — and that you are the love of my life."

They stood very close looking into each other's eyes. She kissed him slowly, lovingly. They were home.

At 6:30 the next morning, John was sitting at the breakfast room table alone with a cup of coffee. He was making his first attempt at listening meditation. As he wrote down what came to him, he heard and noted several things about the business that needed to be done that day. Then, as he continued to listen, he heard from inside, "Confess to Wil about your abusive behavior in hitting him as a boy and isolating from him emotionally while you tried to control his life so he'd do and be what you wanted him to." Then "As a part of making amends to Wil, release him from any obligation to work at Martin Industries — and mean it."

John was stunned and skeptical at the same time. Was this just guilt, or an authentic message from his inner wisdom?

Carol walked in just then, "Good morning, Honey. How'd you sleep?"

"Often," John replied as he looked up at her smiling.

John closed his notebook, and was silent, still thinking about the 'message' he'd gotten concerning his son.

"Carol, I've known for years that there's something deeply wrong about my relationship with Wil — that's not just about his screwing up as a boy and my reaction. As I told Dr. M., every time Wil and I are alone together, it's like I intend to be a loving father one minute, but the next I morph into an angry Stephen King monster from another world — focused on controlling Wil's every move."

"Hey, Honey, don't beat yourself up. Wil's not perfect. He's young and rebellious and knows just which buttons to push to trigger your anger. . . . "

"No, Carol, Wil is a changed man since he came home from Stanford. He pays attention, is sensitive to other people, but is fiercely loyal to me when he thinks people are hurting the company. And he works his butt off — until I start in on him. It's not Wil."

"What then?"

Carol waited, and when John didn't say more, she asked, "What are you going to do?"

"It's too late to do anything to keep him in the company. He was so angry with me when we met yesterday he wouldn't speak to me. What do you think, Carol?"

Carol shook her head. Just then the telephone rang. As she picked it up and put her hand over the speaker, she shook her head and said lovingly, "I can't help you with this one, John. You and Wil are both grown now."

Then into the phone, "Hello, yes this is Carol Martin — what? Oh no! Was he asking for me? Thank you for calling, Elizabeth. Okay, thanks." Carol looked stunned.

"Who was that? What's the matter?"

Carol was on her feet turning toward the stairs. "Daddy's secretary, Elizabeth. He's had a stroke and is in critical condition at the hospital. I'm going right down."

"Do you want me to come with you?"

"No . . . I don't think so. Elizabeth didn't even know if he'd see me or not, but I'm going to go anyway. Please stay and see that Wil gets Celeste to the airport on time."

Carol walked up to the receptionist nurse in the noisy, crowded intensive care waiting room. "I just got a call that my father, Robert Latner, has been admitted to intensive care. I'd like to see him. My name is Carol Latner Martin."

The harried nurse half-smiled and scanned a printout of a list and then popped up a supporting file on her monitor, "Yes, he's here, but . . . he's not receiving visitors right now."

"I'll wait. When are the next visiting hours?"

The nurse looked uneasily at the monitor. "Well, that's not the problem exactly. He has requested that . . . you not be admitted."

Carol remembered clearly her father's e-mail to her when John went on his own, "Never contact me again." But she looked the nurse in the eye, "He may be dying and I'm his daughter!"

Just then, she heard a familiar voice from across the room behind her. "Carol, Carol, over here." It was her father's secretary, Elizabeth, making her way through the waiting families of all ages who talked in clusters in the central area of the large waiting area.

"Elizabeth, it's so good to see you!" Carol said as she gave the older woman a hug, and then pulled a tissue from her purse to catch her tears. "How's Dad doing?"

"As you know, your father is well defended against any kind of defeat — even death it seems. He's had a terrible stroke. Evidently it paralyzed his entire right side. They're still evaluating what's happened, but he's raising hell, shouting at them to get his clothes so he can go home — even though they can hardly understand him because he can only talk out of one side of his mouth." Elizabeth lost her composure and began to weep as she was talking. Carol held her.

"Oh, Elizabeth, I'm so sorry. What can they do?"

"They haven't said yet. Mrs. Latner is with him now. She and I are the only people he will see. You know how proud he is."

Carol nodded, "Well, please tell him that I love him, and that . . . I'm going to stay here until he's ready to see me. And that I don't care if he can talk to me or not."

Looking a little dubious, Elizabeth said, "Well, I'll try, but you know how he is."

Carol nodded again. She of all people did know how hardheaded Robert Latner could be. Elizabeth looked at her watch and started moving toward the metal double doors into the unit. "I've got to relieve Mrs. L."

Carol said, "You tell him I said for him not to worry about his face, it will actually be a better visit for me if he can't talk! And I'm going to wait until he'll see me anyway. You tell him that, Elizabeth."

Elizabeth raised her eyebrows, but nodded.

Carol called John on his cell phone and told him what had happened. Hearing his comforting words brought tears again. And she was so grateful for John's laughter when she told him she'd sent word to Robert that it would be a better visit if he couldn't talk.

John replied, "Well, that'll get you in — in less than twelve hours would be my bet. He'll want to cuss you out just to prove he can talk."

Carol spent the next two nights in the hospital. Sam Moses got her a room that doctors sometimes used for naps to have a few hours of sleep and a shower. John came down and spelled her when she left the waiting room in case Robert sent for her. Sam also checked Robert's medical records and reported that his condition was deteriorating fairly rapidly. Carol prayed almost constantly for Robert. Not knowing what to pray for him, she held him up in her cupped hand and placed him in God's hands in her imagination. But no word came to her from her father.

By 5:45 a.m. Monday morning, Carol was exhausted. Just then, she heard her name over the P.A. speaker: "Carol Latner please report to the nurses' station. Robert sent his private nurse to see if Carol was still waiting — and if so to bring her in. As she followed the nurse's directions and passed through the heavy metal doors, Carol shook her head and smiled in spite of herself. "Carol Latner" the call had said. As sick as he was, he couldn't resist getting in a lick at John, in case he was here, too.

Suddenly, Carol was frightened. The intensive care smell of alcohol, floor sweep and odor killers hit her. When she left the waiting room to go to his room, she was a grown woman. But could feel herself shrinking as she approached his door; and when she got there, she felt like a scared little girl reaching up for the door handle. She stopped, took a deep breath and knocked on the door."

A sound came from inside that sounded like, "Whoz at? I didn dorder anythim!" Then the nurse opened the door.

"You're his daughter?" Carol nodded.

She hardly recognized him. His skin was loose, like thin, faded suede, draped across his cheekbones. The only thing that was in any way the same was the tone of his gravely voice, although his tongue was thick and the words slurred coming out of the left side of his mouth only. His now gray eyes were not sharp with anger, but were muted by pain and something else — fear, Carol guessed.

"Hi, Dad. What are you doing taking time off from work? It's Monday?"

The good side of his face smiled, in spite of himself. Then he mumbled, very slowly, in voice that he no doubt intended to be harsh and frightening, "Daamm, ah razed uh schmart-azz! Ah stthought Ah tole yew nut tu kuntak mee!"

Carol smiled and said, "Yeah, but you were so vague about it that I thought I'd just take a chance on catching you in a weak moment." Then before he could reply, Carol stepped quickly to the bedside and the words flooded out of her, "Oh Daddy, I'm so sorry you are having to go through this. I just had to come and tell you that I love you, and how grateful I am for all you did for me, to help me get educated and start to grow up." Then she stopped and said, "And I want tell you how sorry I am that I was such a brat, and tried to hurt you when I was with mother. I hope you can forgive me someday."

Robert Latner closed his eyes and was silent — so long that Carol thought he might have died. But then he opened his eyes, and Carol saw a tear slide down the deep crease beside his hawk nose. He mumbled slowly, "S'okay, I wasn thu wor champon fathur!"

Carol leaned over and kissed her father on the forehead. Then he began to gasp, and his chest heaved. He was obviously having serious trouble breathing. The nurse pushed the emergency call button as she moved Carol aside, and nodded toward the door. And that was the last time Carol ever saw her father alive.

Carol called John and he insisted on picking her up. "Wil can pick your car up later today with someone from the office."

On the way home Carol told John what had happened. He looked surprised but he was quiet for several minutes. Why did you ask for his forgiveness? He's the one who abused you."

"I'm not sure why, John, but since Dr. M.'s visit everything looks very different to me — almost upside down. As I watched him dying, I realized that everything's not about me and insisting that I'm the only one who needs to be treated right. And that I hadn't been an easy daughter to raise. The surprise was that when I asked him to forgive me and tried to clean off my side of the street, I was . . . free — and I could tell he got something too."

"What?"

"I'm not sure, but I think I gave him his dignity back."

38

Just Below the Bottom Line

Two streets off the main drag near the Harvard University campus, Wil rang the doorbell of the narrow brownstone house — Dr. and Mrs. Magie's visiting faculty housing. His mind was replaying scenes of his grandfather's funeral two weeks before. A week later, at the attorney's office, Wil discovered he had inherited a substantial sum of money from his grandfather, enough that he had virtual financial freedom for several years.

Wil was particularly unhappy about his father's insistence that he come to Boston and let Dr. Magie take him through the ten-minute life dreaming process — as a condition of his continuing to work for Martin Industries. Since Wil didn't have to work for anyone now, he thought surely his choosing to stay at Martin would convince his dad that this was what he really wanted to do. He and John had argued for over an hour over lunch the day before Wil caught the plane to Boston. Finally, John put his palm out toward Will and changed his 'request' to an ultimatum.

Wil could still hear his father's surprisingly calm voice. "Wil, I want you to be a key person in this business, but recently I've realized that I have tried for years to lure you into working with us, and I want you to have an opportunity to discover for sure what your real dreams for your life are."

Laughing sarcastically, Wil said, "You tried to *lure* me? I must have missed something. You've done everything but give me a quarterly pay cut to discourage me from thinking you're interested in my working here."

His father nodded, but said, "I know it must look that way to you, but that was the way my father trained me. And my not showering you with affirmation was not intended to discourage you."

"Really? So now you're sending me to a psychiatrist to help me discover what *else* I can do with my life — instead of continuing to do what I demonstrated I wanted to do by applying for and accepting a job with Martin Industries — at a considerably lower salary, by the way — than my other offers. And you're saying now that giving me an opportunity to find a *real* dream is actually another *inducement* for me to stay and work with you?"

His father had nodded.

Just then the door opened, and a smiling Dr. Magie said, "Hello Wil, come in, come in, it's good to see you!"

That evening, at Dr. M.'s request, they had a visit to get acquainted. In the process of answering a few questions about his time at Stanford, Wil wound up telling Dr. M. his life story. After that Wil was very relaxed, and finally said, "Okay, what's next?"

Three hours later, Wil had listed his life dream and his vocational and personal dreams, prioritized them and put his number one vocational dream on a separate page: "Making a career in the commercial real estate business in Denver, Colorado, working for Martin Industries." Wil showed Dr. M. his lists and they discussed them at length. It was apparent to them both that Wil's number one dream was authentic.

As the two men sat looking across the dining room table with two yellow tablets and a couple of pencils between them, Wil said, "As I told you a few minutes ago, I love and respect Dad more than anyone in the world. Also, after studying the great business innovators in my work at Stanford, I think Dad is one of the most creative businessmen around. Not only has he obviously learned a lot from you about planning and organizing, but he has developed some unique but simple processes for working with a business team."

Dr. M. noticed that Wil was very animated when he spoke about what he was learning from his father. "Wil, talk to me about a creative approach John has developed to work with his business team."

Wil looked beyond Dr. Magie's shoulder for a few seconds and then replied. "Sometimes a group of executives gets bogged down. They can't seem to agree on anything. Before long it becomes apparent that the issue the group is stuck on and arguing about is not the real cause of the conflict, the real source of the group's differences."

"Can you give me a specific example?" Dr. Magie asked.

"I remember once when our Board of Directors was deadlocked. There was obviously a serious problem, but no one knew what was wrong.

"Capable, intelligent men and women made up the board, but they had gotten stuck for three months and couldn't get any creative work done. A lot of hostility and uncertainty emanated from two men who were both leaders in the group. When one made a suggestion, the other shot it down, and pointed out all the reasons the idea wouldn't work or was absurd. The other one killed suggestions from the first man with sarcasm or biting humor. Their hostility wound up destroying any creative process that might have gone on. Most of us had decided they came from such different business perspectives that we were witnessing an un-winnable philosophical war about how the business should be run.

"At the beginning of a particular board meeting, Dad, as chairman, addressed the board members in a way I'd never heard him do before. I can still remember. Dad said, 'Before we begin the meeting, I'd like to ask your help this morning for about ten minutes. I'm asking you to suspend your disbelief for a little while. I'd like us to take a few minutes for each of us to report about what's going on in the non-Martin Industries parts of our lives.' Dad began by sharing some personal pain he had because his favorite uncle recently had been diagnosed as having incurable cancer of the throat. Then he asked the vice-chairman of the board to speak next.

"Dad had talked to this man ahead of time asking him to consider talking about some personal issue. The VC talked about his mixed feelings concerning his oldest child who would soon graduate from high school. Then someone else reported having just come back from vacation with his family. He said, 'In two weeks, I'd had about all the 'fun' I could stand in a car with four other people.' The other group members laughed, nodding their heads. One woman reported, 'This week I was notified with no warning that I've been 'downsized,' fired, after twenty-five years with the Snowridge Bank.' As each person spoke personally, the atmosphere began to change. People seemed less tense and brittle, more able to share. They talked about all kinds of things, some of which were quite personal.

"At last it was Tom's turn, one of the two 'warring' leaders. He hesitated but finally said, 'For the last three board meetings, I've been eaten up with anger.' Then he looked over at Joe, his enemy on the board. 'About three months ago, there was a big write-up in the paper about AIDS victims and *you* said, 'I wish they'd take them all out and hang them. They deserve to be dead.' Tom paused and then continued: 'The week before you said that, my twenty-three-year-old daughter had been diagnosed with AIDS.' The room was totally silent.

"After a few seconds Dad said gently, 'Thank you very much for telling us that, Tom.' Just then Joe stood up, in tears. He whispered across the table, 'God, I'm sorry, Tom. I didn't know. I had no idea. What a dumb thing to say! I know I can never make it up to you, but I'm *really sorry*.' Then he sat down and, elbows on the table, buried his face in his hands.

"When the check-in was over, Dad said to the group, 'I really appreciate your being so honest during this sharing time. We're going to take a coffee break and come back in fifteen minutes. Then I'd like for us to get into the report on the proposed new project evaluation that's on the agenda for today.'

"During the break, I saw the Tom and Joe speaking in low voices to each other, and when we came back, the atmosphere was totally different. The group got a great deal of very creative work done that day, with no bickering or hostility, in a very short time. The war we had been witnessing for three months was not a philosophical 'business' war at all, but a personal one. The two men had been fighting a personal war on the wrong battlefield: the board meeting. Once the group discovered the hidden problem, the room lost its emotional charge.

"Dad told me he had learned from you, Dr. Magie, that our secrets can control us. Dad believed this was also often true of groups. As Tom confessed his secret anger and hurt, it lost its power over the group, and we discovered the real problem, all because Dad had created a very short time and space in which the group could suspend their disbelief and connect with each other on an intuitive personal level. The real problem surfaced spontaneously because of Dad's inner wisdom — in a very short time.

"After that meeting, Dad told me, 'This technique won't always work, but the principle is that sometimes you have to stop and discharge a group's snarled energies by listening to the personal situations of the members before a group can get back on track with its stated agenda. But,' he added, 'the exercise is sometimes good for community building even when there is no pressing problem issue. It allows group members to change the atmosphere from cognitive and competitive to an intuitive/creative ambiance.'"

Dr. M. nodded, making a note in his pocket notebook.

When Dr. M. didn't say anything further, Wil blurted out, "Dr. M., what's the real reason Dad sent me to see you? He says it's for my own good. What the hell does that mean?"

"Wil your father spent a decade working in a family business situation that almost broke his health and his heart, because he didn't know what else to do, and Carol's father's business had seemed like a good and logical opportunity. But it wasn't his dream. So because he loves you so much, he doesn't want you to get stuck in the same situation."

Wil said bitterly, "Well the truth is that we have discussed my coming to do this with you for years. Each time, he promised to take me to be with you, and each time, something more important came up. My question is 'If he loves me so much and wants me to find my true dream, why didn't he bring me to Switzerland to see you about this all the times he said he would." Wil shook his head sadly, "Dr. M., even though I really want to work with Dad, I may just have to find another place. Why should I think anything really significant has changed about Dad now that would make me trust that he really has my best interest at heart?"

Dr. M. looked at Wil while he expressed these feelings. Then he seemed to make a decision. He stepped to his writing desk and moved some papers aside, picking up an envelope that had been opened. Walking back to his chair, he looked at the silver pitcher on the buffet, tapping his chin with the corner of the envelope. Finally, he turned to his young friend.

As he handed the envelope to Wil, Dr. M. said, "Here's the letter your father wrote me when he told you he wanted you to come see me. He didn't ask me to let you see it, but I have a strong feeling I should show you what he wrote since it relates directly to what you just said."

Wil was totally alert as he carefully accepted the envelope. It seemed to be wired with an electric current. Sensing that the letter contained the secret to his relationship with his father, Wil started to take the letter out, but stopped and looked at Dr. M., who nodded. He read aloud, not wanting to be alone with his father's real feelings about him.

Dear Charles:

Wil is coming to Boston in a few days. I appreciate your willingness to see him. Not knowing how that time will go, I want to write this letter to tell you why I am sending him to meet you now — after years of saying I was going to and not doing it. It has to do with what you taught me about the necessity of discovering my secret unconscious motivator that has programmed my inner wisdom and dominated my life — if I ever wanted to find peace and personal fulfillment.

I knew that whatever my secret purpose was, it was involved in raising my pain level high enough ten years ago to ask you for help, the help that changed my whole life. And this last visit when you led us through the process to discover our unconscious controlling motivator you asked me to record what I thought about in a recurring fashion when my mind wasn't engrossed in work. I didn't want to tell you then what I came up with because it was a bunch of confusing thoughts about being a father to Wil, and I couldn't sort them out at the time.

But after you left I put my thoughts together, and it began to make sense that being a good father to Wil really was my most important motivator, because although we have argued over almost every sub-ject that ever came up, I love Wil more than anything. He's brilliant, a lot smarter than I am, and almost as bull-headed. And of course he wouldn't let me be a father to him, because as crazy as it sounds my secret motivator was to shape him (control him) into being what I thought he ought to be — so I'd be the 'loving father' I wanted to be.

Recently, after Wil and I had been going at it almost to the point of swinging at each other, I asked myself, "What would a good father look like?" The answer I got — no doubt straight from the files of my inner wisdom — was a picture of you, leaning over my chest on the examination table with that ice-cold stethoscope. Then came another picture of you, calmly listening to my sophomoric contradictions and discounting of what you hold most dear. I know now (since I've read all your books that have been translated) that you could have ground me up like hamburger, intellectually. Instead, you just listened to me as if I had good sense, until I got quiet enough to ask the real questions.

Your acceptance and lack of judgment changed something deep inside me. It opened the door to the world of dreams, and you gave me a personal invitation to step into that world with you and awaken them. I watched you like a hawk as you lived out a kind of wisdom and caring that I'd never even heard about.

For a long time, I thought your greatest gift as a father figure was to show me the ten-minute process and teach me how to use it as a machete to cut a path to my dreams. At last I had a sword to get through the impenetrable cactus-thicket of cognitive theories, fears of failure, lack of commitment, and informational overload of the "real world." I pulled that "ten-minute-brush-land-sword" out of the stone of my own depression, and with it succeeded far beyond my original dreams.

But Wil kept being the thorn in my side, and the demon of the 'failure to be able to control him' kept throwing me to the ground from the high altar of my success. And so I focused on trying not to control Wil. That was a real fiasco. All my techniques, exercises, and discipline only seemed to make things worse. And Wil and I just kept on fighting.

So, I had to come back to you several years ago. After a couple of visits, I wanted to roar at you and tell you to "quit nodding your head, and tell me plainly how to be a good father to Wil!" But you just... kept nodding to let me know that you understood, and that you believed I would find out what I needed to know about my relationship with Wil. I was furious!

That's when I backed off from you for several months. I was hurt. My questions were no longer primarily about stuff like how to build a company, make money, buy cabins, planes, vacations. That stuff is easy now. I wanted to know how to have a good relationship with my son like I had with you I knew that for me, somehow, underlying that father-son and relationship was the key to all that really mattered to me now — the meaning and purpose of everything else I'd learned — and my life dream: peace of mind.

My inner wisdom acted so much like you it made me sick. It listened, but then just shrugged — as I've seen you do so often — leaving me to figure this one out for myself. I was desperate. By this time, Wil and I were hardly speaking.

After you left Denver last month, I was at the end of my rope. As a last resort, I sat down with a pencil and paper. I put on the top line: "Everything It Will Take To Make Me A Good Father." I set the clock for ten minutes, and began to write. The top two items on that list were:

1. *Quit trying so hard. Your intensity is scaring Wil.*
2. *Think about how Dr. M. treats you, and do that.*

There were a number of other things, but those two were first on my reprioritized list. Then I wrote at the top of a clean sheet, "How has Dr. M. treated me?" The first few behaviors on that list (which for some reason I addressed to you) were:

1. *You always listened to find out who I was and what was really on my mind. That kind of focused listening made me feel like somebody of importance, maybe for the first time.*

2. *Later, when you knew me, warts and all, you didn't try to fix me, change me, or make me think like you. That convinced me that you loved me, just as I was and not for what you could change me into.*

3. *Instead of trying to "show me the way," you tried to help me awaken my dreams and find my own way, even though it was miles apart from yours.*

4. *When I'd worked hard and was set to move into the winner's circle, you did a very irrational thing: you backed off from active participation somehow, sort of handed me your set of keys and went up into the grand stand to watch me drive.*

Although there were some other great things I saw you do as a "good father," I want to go straight to the last behavior which led me to make the appointment for Wil to come see you.

You and I both know that I consider you to be the father my father never could be, and you once told me how much I remind you of your oldest son who was killed in World War II. I knew we had some kind of unspoken agreement concerning how we felt about each other. Well, in our recent meetings, when you wouldn't cave in and tell me what to do to get out of my pain, I got to the end of my rope. Then I saw you do something that I couldn't even comprehend at the time: You gave up your dreams of getting me, your 'son,' to do the right thing. You took your hands off and surrendered me, entrusted me to God.

Finally, I understand that surrendering your agenda for me was your greatest gift, freeing me to make the toughest decision of all — about Wil.

Old friend, the step I've taken this morning is by far the most difficult thing I've ever done, but it's already brought the peace of mind I only dreamed of as my overall life's goal years ago, in your study. Thank you.

I've finally surrendered, and . . . here comes my son!

Love,
John

EXERCISE THIRTEEN
Community Building

The following describes a process for people to check in before a meeting begins. It allows group members to change the atmosphere from cognitive and competitive to intuitive/creative ambience. (Leader will need a timer)

1. The leader of the group using this exercise states that the purpose of the time is to take a few seconds for each person present to check-in about what's going on in his or her life besides the business (or whatever the task is for which the group is responsible). Each person will have two minutes to share. When each two minute period is up the leader or timer will call time and the person sharing will complete their sentence and stop. It is often helpful if the leader points out that anyone can "pass" if they want to, by simply saying "I pass."

2. Before the meeting begins, the leader may find someone else in authority who would be willing to follow the leader and share second in the meeting. The leader may tell that person what he/she plans to share, to help set the level of vulnerability.

3. The leader checks in first, telling about some personal issue going on in his or her life in two minutes or less.

4. This second person speaks (in two minutes or less).

5. Other group members can then share. It may be help everyone to participate if the leader suggests a simple structure (e.g., that the sharing process after the second sharer, continue around the room in the direction it started — reiterating the freedom for anyone to pass by saying "I pass").

6. After the check-in time, the leader may want to ask if anyone has anything else they'd like to say in a few seconds. If not, move into the meeting's agenda.

Appendix

Exercises

~~~~~~~~~~~~

Notes

~~~~

1. "Finding a Business Plan That Works and Sticking with It," *Wall Street Journal,* October 9, 2001.

2. Tom J. Fatjo Jr. and Keith Miller *With No Fear of Failure: Recapturing Your Dreams through Creative Enterprise* (Waco, TX: Word Books, 1981).

3. Roy H. Williams, *Secret Formulas of the Wizard of Ads* (Austin, TX: Bard Press, 1999).

4. Paul Tournier, *The Meaning of Persons,* trans. Edwin Hudson (New York: Harper, 1957); *Guilt and Grace: A Psychology Study,* trans. Arthur Heathcote (New York: Harper, 1967); and *The Healing of Persons,* trans. Edwin Hudson (New York: Harper & Row, 1965).

5. Blaise Pascal, *Pascal's Pensées and the Provincial Letters* (New York: Random House, 1941).

6. C. S. Lewis, *Surprised by Joy* (New York: Harcourt, Brace, 1956).

7. Augustine, *Confessions* (New York: Penguin, 1961).

8. Martin Buber, *I and Thou* (New York: Charles Scribner's Sons, 1958), 110.

9. Carl G. Jung, *A Psychological Approach to the Dogma of the Trinity, Collected Works of C. G. Jung,* vol. 11, 2nd rev. ed. (New York: Pantheon Books, 1969), 199.

10. Frederick Buechner, *The Magnificent Defeat* (New York: Seabury Press, 1966), 42.

11. See Matthew 4:1–11 and Matthew 26:36–45.

12. Herbert Benson, *The Relaxation Response* (New York: William Morris, 1975).

13. *The Little Flowers of St. Francis: The Acts of Saint Francis and His Companions,* trans. E. M. Blacklock and A. C. Keys (London: Hodder and Stoughton, 1985).

14. Eugene H. Peterson, *The Message* (Colorado Springs: Nav Press, 2002), 1 Timothy 1:5, p. 2162.

15. These are passages in the New Testament that urge Christians to ask for what they want and need, but the overall message is that such prayers should be prayed in the same humility Christ had with the father — prayed in Jesus's perspective (his "name"). John 14:13, 14.

An Autobiographical Word
from the Author

All my life I have been searching to discover what is real. As a child, I was told that "*God* is real. At church, people talked about God and Jesus, but the *way* they talked seemed to me that they didn't really expect God to show up personally...although they said he would be "with us."

Just as I graduated from high school, my only brother was killed while serving in the Air Force. During my second year in college I broke my neck in a car accident and thought I would die. A year later year my father died. I buried my mother, who died of cancer in 1956. By the time I was twenty-eight, every member of my family had died.

During the 1960s I went through my own business and personal struggles and finally surrendered my life to God. I looked for a place to teach and share what I was learning, and Howard Butt Jr. invited me to become the first director of Laity Lodge. This new conference center in Texas was helping lay business and professional people explore the Christian faith in new ways. Laity Lodge became very successful, and I wrote a book there, trying to capture what we were experiencing. It was called *The Taste of New Wine,* and it sold worldwide and was translated into eleven languages. Then, after writing other bestselling books, traveling and speaking in the United States, Europe, and the Far East, getting graduate degrees in theology and psychological counseling along the way, my world crashed. The pressure of all the attention and material success (I'd prayed for) was too much for me to handle. I began to drink too much and had what we Americans call a full-blown midlife crisis. Terrible, destructive events occurred, which resulted in the end of my marriage of twenty-seven years.

Finally in 1985, I checked into a treatment center, where I found out all kinds of interesting — and devastating — truths about myself. Everything in me rebelled at seeing the unreality of my fine Christian personality. Eventually I entered my own personal desert experience, which was to last fifteen years. During that time I did do my own inner exploration and education. Eventually I met and married Andrea Wells, and now we are writing, speaking, and enjoying life on the edge of the adventure of faith.

J. Keith Miller holds a B.A. from Oklahoma University, an M.A. in Religion from the Earlham School of Religion, and an M.A. in Psychological Counseling from the University of Texas. He is the author or co-author of two dozen books including the international bestseller, *The Taste of New Wine.* He and his wife, Andrea, live in Texas.

A Word from the Editor

I have these two images in my mind. One is from about thirty-two years ago when I was a young student at Fuller Theological Seminary in Pasadena, California. Keith Miller and Bruce Larson — who were both leaders in a new national small group movement that was sweeping through the churches — paid a visit to our campus and in a private meeting spoke with the Faith Renewal Team, mentored and directed by the late Rev. Robert Munger. The FRT was composed of small groups that went out to churches on weekends to further the small group movement and also to model a new kind of honest community of faith. As a captain of one of those teams I was paying close attention to their words and I was enthralled by the clarity and candor of these two men who were trying to help the churches understand about honest struggles and candid conversation in churches, where honesty was the last thing one usually experienced. It was a meeting that eventually changed my deepest perceptions of how I might live more honestly on my journey of faith.

A second image is from several years later in a hotel room in northern California. Keith Miller was in town speaking and had invited me and my daughters, Erica and Vanessa, over to say hello. My daughter Vanessa was already writing and showing signs of talent. She and Keith had a conversation about poetry that stunned me. At eight years of age she had a conversation with Keith that was beyond me, about how one "captures" metaphors and language for poetry, and at the time I was a senior editor in the book publishing world. Again the words that Keith spoke were profoundly honest and inspirational. This man has been speaking like that for several decades to millions of people, and fortunately for me he was also writing like that. His books were now legendary in the publishing world, and they had sparked a whole new level of honesty when talking about personal faith.

Keith seemed to have an intuitive grasp of what the truth meant and how it could be communicated. He was willing to share his own struggles, which was completely unheard of during those times and even today it is hard for any of us to hear — and believe — that one can truly be a flawed person and still experience God's grace. But as anyone who knows Keith will tell you, he is relentless. The story never changes and he keeps telling it, but the wisdom and knowledge behind the story have matured, deepened, and grown even more inspirational. Even to-day, a few decades later, I am still calling Keith when I need an honest response to one of my own struggles.

In this book, all of that wisdom, knowledge, and intuitive insight about how humans struggle with life are graphically and vividly portrayed. It is a book that you can't put down because you are captivated by the characters (who turn out to be a version of yourself in some form) and their story of struggles and growth. Of course, it would be Keith Miller who puts a nonfiction book into a narrative style. You can always count on Keith to find a new way to put old wine into new wineskins. He has been doing it for more than forty years and will continue to do it.

ROY M. CARLISLE
Senior Editor